Teacher
Effectiveness
and Teacher
Education

Teacher Effectiveness and Teacher Education

The Search for a Scientific Basis

by N. L. Gage   Stanford University

Pacific Books, Publishers Palo Alto, California

International Standard Book Number 0-87015-190-8

Library of Congress Catalog Card Number 71-134225

Printed and bound in the United States of America

PACIFIC BOOKS, PUBLISHERS
P. O. Box 558
Palo Alto, California 94302

To Maggie

Acknowledgments

The chapters of this book are considerably revised versions of papers written by me over a period of years. I have added and reorganized ideas and have examined more recent literature to bring the argument up to date. None of these chapters has previously been published in its present form.

Chapter 2 is based on a paper presented to the Second Invitational Conference on Elementary Education, sponsored by the College of Education of the University of Alberta, at Banff on October 25, 1967. The paper was subsequently published in the Proceedings of the Conference and also in the *Phi Delta Kappan*, 1968, Vol. 49, pp. 399–403.

Chapter 3, based on a lecture presented on February 14, 1966, in the series arranged to commemorate the Diamond Jubilee Year of the School of Education at New York University, was prepared while I was a fellow at the Center for Advanced Study in the Behavioral Sciences. It was subsequently published in *Educational Sciences: An International Journal*, 1967, Vol. 1, pp. 151–161.

Chapter 4 is based on my chapter, "Theories of Teaching," in the Sixty-third Yearbook of the National Society for the Study of Education, *Theories of Learning and Instruction*, edited by E. R. Hilgard, 1964, Vol. 63, Part I, pp. 268–285.

Chapter 5 is based on the first half of my chapter, "Paradigms for Research on Teaching," in the *Handbook of Research on Teaching*, edited by N. L. Gage (Chicago: Rand McNally, 1963, pp. 94–141), and on part of a paper entitled "This Side of Paradigms: The State of Research on Teaching English," presented at the San Francisco Conference of the National Council of Teachers of English on November 27, 1963, and published in *Research Design and the Teaching of English: Proceedings of the San Francisco Conference, 1963* (Champaign, Ill.: National Council of Teachers of English, 1964, pp. 22–31).

Chapter 6 is also based on my chapter in the *Handbook of Research on Teaching* and on "Theoretical Formulations for Research on Teaching," a chapter by N. L. Gage and W. R. Unruh in the *Review of Educational Research*, 1967, Vol. 37, pp. 358–370.

Chapter 7 is based on a lecture presented to the University of Wisconsin's Research and Development Center for Cognitive Learning in November 1966 and subsequently published in *Research and Development for the Improvement of Education*, edited by H. J. Klausmeier and G. T. O'Hearn (Madison: Dembar Educational Services, 1968, pp. 119–125), and also in the *Phi Delta Kappan*, 1968, Vol. 49, pp. 601–606.

Chapter 8 is based on a paper entitled "Research on Cognitive Aspects of Teaching," presented at a seminar on teaching arranged by the Association for Supervision and Curriculum Development and the Center for the Study of Instruction of the National Education Association in Washington, D.C., in April 1965 and subsequently published in *The Way Teaching Is: A Report of the Seminar on Teaching* (Washington, D.C.: Association for Supervision and Curriculum Development and the National Education Association, 1966, pp. 29–44).

Chapter 9 is based on "Psychological Theory and Empirical Research for Teacher Education," an address to the annual meeting of the American Association of Colleges for Teacher Education in February 1964 and subsequently published in *Freedom with Responsibility in Teacher Education* (Washington, D.C.: American Association of Colleges for Teacher Education, 1964, Vol. 17, pp. 94–105).

Chapter 10 was originally presented to the Associated Organizations for Teacher Education in October 1963 and then, in extended form, at a Conference on Interprofessional Communication of the National Association of Social Workers in Chicago in April 1964. It was subsequently published in *Society and the Schools: Communication Challenge to Education and Social Work*, edited by R. H. Beck (New York: National Association of Social Workers, 1965, pp. 86–103).

Chapter 11 is based on a paper prepared for the Conference on the Appraisal of Teaching in Large Universities organized by W. J. McKeachie at the University of Michigan in October 1958. It was subsequently published in *The Appraisal of Teaching in Large Universities* (University of Michigan) and in the *Journal of Higher Education*, 1961, Vol. 32, pp. 17–22.

Chapter 12 is based on "A Method for 'Improving' Teacher Behavior," *Journal of Teacher Education*, 1963, Vol. 14, pp. 261–266. As will be noted, it refers to subsequent research along the same lines by my students and others.

Chapter 13 is based on a paper prepared for the International Conference on the Changing Roles of Teachers Required by Educational Innovations, sponsored by the National Association of Secondary School Principals, the Educational Research Council of America, the

National Catholic Education Association, and the Pädagogisches Zentrum (Berlin), in Berlin on October 16–19, 1967, and on a paper prepared for the Conference on "How Teachers Make a Difference" held on April 19, 1971, by the Bureau of Educational Personnel Development, U.S. Office of Education.

I am grateful to the publishers, journals, and organizations mentioned above for their support, encouragement, and permission to use the materials originally published by them.

My intellectual debt to colleagues and students over the years is complex and varied. Of much of that debt I fear that I am no longer conscious, others' ideas and emphases having become unrecognizably mixed into mine. To those fellow workers in research on teaching whose papers and conversations have thus been used without due credit, I extend my apologies and plead only that my failure to acknowledge is unintentional. To the sources of which I am aware, let me say that the citations of works in the list of references betoken my thanks as well as my acknowledgment.

My colleagues in the Stanford Center for Research and Development in Teaching have helped by providing a supportive and stimulating environment for the development of many of the ideas in this book. The supportiveness has given me heart to believe that the ideas were not altogether off the mark. The stimulation has made me think about matters that otherwise might never have crossed my mind. So I have to thank Professors Norman Boyan, Robert N. Bush, Frederick J. McDonald, and Richard E. Snow, and, among former students, Drs. James C. Fortune, Robert Pinney, Barak Rosenshine, Robert Shutes, and Waldemar Unruh. The manuscript was criticized by members of my Freshman Seminar on "Teaching as a Field of Theory, Research, and Practice," namely, Ella Anagick, Jane Bold, Margery Colten, Roger Hill, Elizabeth Lemus, David Nasca, Nanette Smith, and Carol Wainwright, by Mary Seifert, the Seminar's lecturer in English, and also by my research assistant, Chandrakala Dhar; to them I express much gratitude for many helpful suggestions.

Romayne Ponleithner of Pacific Books, Publishers, gave the manuscript a careful editing and contributed to my early approaches to the organization of the book. My secretary, Margaret E. Bander, skillfully retyped many heavily revised pages of manuscript. My greatest debt over all the years during which my ideas about research on teaching have developed is to my wife, Margaret Burrows Gage, to whom this book is dedicated.

Contents

Chapter 1   **Overview**

Educators are understandably fond of quoting H. G. Wells's statement that history is becoming more and more a race between education and catastrophe. This thought gives educators an importance which, in their more self-congratulatory moments, they gladly accept.

But the Wells dictum is, of course, an oversimplification. It makes education too much the cause of historical movement. It leaves unmentioned the economic, political, and social forces that determine, or at least interact with, what education can do to affect history. Population growth, nuclear power, poverty, prejudice, nationalism—and other "bombs" now ticking away and threatening catastrophe—cannot be defused by education alone. It will take all social institutions acting in concert to ward off the multiple disasters facing civilization.

Education as an institution cannot do the job by itself, it is true, but we shall never be rescued without its contribution. Parents in all nations need to be educated to want fewer children than their parents had. Electorates, scientists, and statesmen today need to be educated not to trigger arsenals that dwarf the aggregate destructive power previously available in all of history to the world's military forces. Producers and distributors of economic wealth—capitalist and communist alike—need to be educated toward economic practices that will eliminate poverty both in rich nations and in developing ones. And the citizens and leaders of all nations must be educated to establish peace with justice between racial, cultural, and national groups on a planet being made ever smaller by communications satellites, supersonic transportation, and the pictures from cameras on the moon. Education has important work to do in insuring human survival in the years ahead.

For many centuries, education has usually been conducted in schools by persons occupying the position of teacher. This is not to say that human beings have not learned many important things outside of schools and without the help of someone designated as the teacher. Recent decades have seen the role of the teacher challenged within the school by new instructional techniques, such as programmed instruction, sometimes aided by computers. As we shall see, this challenge means that the process of teaching must be re-examined. Teachers of one kind or another will continue to be needed. But their work must be changed so as to improve their contribution to the educational process.

One part of the massive enterprise called teacher education is the preparation of teachers before they start teaching in a school system. Such "pre-service" teacher education is universally regarded as needing supplementation by further effort, called "in-service" teacher education, after teachers have gone to work in the classroom. Both kinds of teacher education are aimed at equipping teachers with knowledge, understanding, and ways of behaving that are useful in promoting their students' achievement of educational objectives. So teacher education is important almost to the degree that education itself is important.

What knowledge, understanding, and ways of behaving should teachers possess? During most of the history of education, the answer has been based on raw experience, tradition, common sense, and authority. Philosophers and theologians have applied their modes of truth-seeking to the problems of education, including the question of how teachers should behave. Then, with the emergence of the behavioral sciences in the twentieth century, attempts were made to apply scientific method to the problems of school learning, teacher behavior, and teacher education. Within the behavioral sciences, there developed a sub-discipline—one that may be called "research on teaching."

"Research" is defined as scientific activity aimed at increasing our power to understand, predict, and control events of a given kind. All three of these goals involve relationships between variables. We understand an event by relating it logically to others. We predict an event by relating it empirically to antecedents in time. We control an event by manipulating the independent variables to which it is functionally related. Hence, research must seek out the relationships—logical, temporal, and functional—between variables.

"Teaching" in turn may be defined as events, such as teacher behavior, intended to affect the learning of a student. The teacher behavior, an interpersonal influence, may be frozen in the form of a book or a film, or a set of programmed instructional materials. Typically, teacher behavior is the voice and motion of a human being.

Given these definitions of "research" and "teaching," we can define "research on teaching" as the study of relationships between variables, at least one of which refers to a characteristic or behavior of a teacher. If the relationship is one between teacher behaviors or characteristics, on the one hand, and effects on students, on the other, then we have "research on teacher effects," in which the teacher behavior is an independent variable. If the teacher behavior or characteristic serves as a dependent variable in relation to some variable in the program of selecting and training teachers (the teacher education program), then we have "research on teacher education." Both kinds of research taken together make up the field of research on teaching. Figure 1–1 shows these relationships. The variables of teacher behavior and characteristics are at the center of concern. They serve as independent variables in relation to effects on student learning and as dependent variables in relation to teacher education.

Variables other than those referring to behaviors or characteristics of teachers are, of course, admissible and desirable in research on teaching. Our definition merely states that behaviors or characteristics of teachers must be involved, not that other kinds of variables may not be involved.

This book is concerned with research on teaching defined in this way. It deals with a variety of approaches and issues in the conduct of such research. Its claim to attention is based on the importance of such research. If the contribution of education to human welfare is to be adequate to the demands of the last third of the twentieth century, then teaching must be improved. That improvement will be hastened and enhanced to the extent that the scientific study of teaching—research on teaching—succeeds in producing significant knowledge.

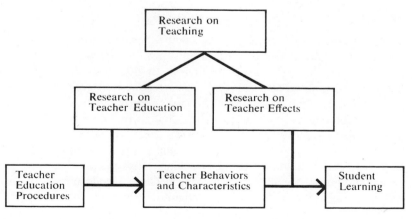

Fig. 1–1. The field of research on teaching, shown as consisting of research on teacher education (relationships between teacher education procedures as independent variables, and teacher behaviors and characteristics, as dependent variables) and research on teacher effects (relationships between teacher behaviors and characteristics, as independent variables, and student learning, as dependent variables).

In dealing with approaches and issues, we take up matters on which research workers are not in complete agreement. Yet these matters are among the most important confronting persons concerned with research on teaching. Such persons may be students, teachers, potential or active research workers, teachers of teachers, administrators of schools or school systems, or citizens. Positions on these issues determine whether research on teaching will be done at all, what kind will be done, to what ends, how the research will be used, and how fruitful it will be for theory and practice. In some ways, the issues dealt with here are more important than the substantive and methodological technicalities that typically absorb the attention of research workers. Decisions on these broad issues often determine how useful research will be. Some decisions can render research valueless regardless of its finesse in such matters as sampling, measurement, and statistical analysis. Other decisions can make research useful even though it falls far short of perfection in various methodological and substantive respects.

The following chapters are offered on the assumption that anyone planning to conduct or use research on teaching must be concerned with at least some of these issues. If the present formulations do not always hit the mark, they may suggest others that will come closer to suggesting the right questions and answers.

RESEARCH ON TEACHER EFFECTS

Can Science Contribute to the Art of Teaching?

First we consider the question of whether science can contribute to the art of teaching. Any answer based on the record of research accomplishment thus far cannot be unhesitatingly affirmative. And, in the view of some writers, there is reason to question even the possibility of improving that record. The issue here is whether the whole idea of research on teaching promises enough practical payoff to be worth pursuing. Yet there are reasons for questioning the pessimism. More careful analyses of past research and improved future research may yield more sanguine conclusions. Some illustrative examinations of the literature—dealing with teacher behaviors and characteristics labeled "warmth," "indirectness," "cognitive organization," and "enthusiasm"—are offered.

Psychological Conceptions of Teaching

Psychological conceptions of teaching have not, until recently, been prominent within educational psychology. It seems desirable to place increased emphasis on teaching, but that does not mean that teaching can become dominant, with learning processes being adapted to it. Rather, the two processes, teaching and learning, should be regarded as coordinate and interactive, neither one completely controlling the other. Since different kinds of learning exist, teaching may be regarded as the exertion of influence in correspondingly different ways, such as conditioning, modeling, and cognitive restructuring. These three approaches to teaching are sometimes applied to the same kind of learning; this point is illustrated by approaches to the task of fostering creativity. The three approaches also provide rationales for some of the teacher characteristics that have been studied empirically, such as warmth and cognitive validity. When taken seriously, cognitive validity suggests great demands on teachers. These demands, in combination with those of individual differences among students, raise questions about the role of human teachers as against programmed instruction.

Theories of Teaching

One path often urged as a way out of the wilderness in any field of research is that of paying more attention to its theoretical foundations. In research on teaching, this means greater attention to theories of teaching—theories to which psychologists, at least, paid little attention until recently. Are such theories possible? How should they be related to the much better established theories of learning? In other fields of research, attempts to formulate theory have proceeded through analyzing phenomena into less complex, "purer," more controllable, and more carefully definable units. To develop theory of teaching will require just such analyses of teaching, and illustrative efforts toward such analysis are offered here. Then some attempts should be made to use these analyses to formulate different kinds of teaching and learning. The approach is closely linked to major families of learning theory, namely, conditioning, modeling, and cognitive theories. In this approach, teaching becomes the process of providing for the learner what a given learning theory regards as essential. For the conditioning theorist, the teacher must provide cues for a given response and reinforcement of that response. For the modeling theorist, the teacher must provide a model to be observed and imitated. For the cognitive theorist, the teacher must provide a cognitive structure or the stimuli that will produce one.

The Uses of Paradigms and Theories

Theories in any field of science may prove inadequate, in the sense of failing to yield understanding, prediction, or control of phenomena in that field. When a theory does prove inadequate, research workers tend to re-examine their paradigms—the models and schemata by which they define the basic problems and methods of the field.

If paradigms in research on teaching are to be re-examined, first their nature and uses must be set forth. It is argued that paradigms should be made explicit even though the research process is not always orderly. The definition of theory as "explanation at a different level of phenomena" may lead to an anti-theoretical position. But this position does not apply to theory defined as systematic and parsimonious formulation of the relationships between the concepts or variables of a field.

Substantive Paradigms

From paradigms in general, we go on to substantive paradigms for research on teaching. In the early decades of such research, the dominant paradigm was that of measuring some criterion of teacher effectiveness, measuring characteristics of teachers considered to be possible correlates of that criterion, and then determining the actual correlation between the characteristics and the criterion. Choices among criteria of effectiveness can be made in terms of their "ultimacy" and the career level to which they apply.

The criterion-of-effectiveness paradigm can be extended by introducing "process," or behavioral, variables between the teacher characteristics and the criteria. Such variables deal with actual behaviors of teachers and students in the classroom as determined by counts of observed or recorded classroom phenomena. Other comprehensive models specify major, broad categories of variables relevant to research on teaching. The criteria may be analyzed into more specific, less complex variables, or "micro-criteria," that may enter into more lawful relationships with other variables than have been found for the more complex criteria used in the past.

The analysis of classroom events or teaching processes has become a major part of the field of research on teaching. Teaching can be regarded as information-processing or as an interaction process. The latter approach has been taken in a variety of paradigms. The common element in these process paradigms can also be found in the components of a model of teaching by machine.

An Analytic Approach

The development of paradigms should lead to analysis of the teaching process into various component activities, as independent variables, and kinds of criteria, such as types of achievement, as dependent variables. Such an analytic approach may be contrasted with the global-criterion approach that led to gross ratings of ill-defined teacher characteristics without clear referents in classroom teacher behavior.

The analytic approach has been manifested in the formulation of lists of "technical skills" of teaching. Which technical skills should be defined, in what way, are still largely moot issues. But the analytic approach has led to the development of microteaching, a highly controllable arrangement for the modification of teacher behavior.

In research on teacher effects, one microcriterion has been effectiveness in explaining. A series of studies of such effectiveness is described to illustrate research on a technical skill. Effectiveness was defined as the mean score of the teacher's students on an achievement test, this score being adjusted for student ability and sometimes also for the relevance of the teacher's "content" to the test's content. The studies have dealt with (a) the generality of such effectiveness over lessons and students, (b) the modality, or medium of transmission—audio, video, transcript, or combinations of these—of cues to such effectiveness, (c) behavioral predictors of effectiveness based on analyses of transcripts and videotape records of teacher performance, and (d) the use of computers for counting the words and phrases reflecting such variables as "vagueness," and for correlating the frequencies of such words with the teacher's effectiveness in explaining.

Cognitive Aspects of Teaching

Research on cognitive aspects of teaching can be distinguished from that which deals with the social and emotional aspects. Until recently, cognitive aspects were relatively neglected.

Most research on cognitive aspects has taken what has been called a "passive" approach. That is, classroom processes have been studied as they occur under "natural" conditions of classroom life. This passive, or descriptive, approach has been challenged by advocates of an active, improvement-oriented approach that seeks entirely new models of instruction. Typically, the new model offered by these advocates has been one based on teaching by machine or on programmed instruction.

Some analyses of the requirements of teaching for cognitive objectives indicate that it calls for great complexity in the arrangement of ideas. Most human teachers may be unable to manage such complexity in classroom discourse. Also, instruction should be individualized according to the needs, abilities, and other characteristics of the individual student. The needs for complexity and individualization point away from conventional classroom arrangements and toward programmed instruction. The role of the human teacher, and research on that role, must be re-examined in the light of the potentialities of programmed instruction.

RESEARCH ON TEACHER EDUCATION

The Promise of Research on Teacher Education

This chapter begins with a discussion of the way in which Conant's volume, *The Education of American Teachers*, deals with research on teacher education. Conant's attitude toward research was reflected in his treatment of educational psychology, which he considered to deal for the most part in rather obvious ideas. So the issue of obviousness in educational psychology is examined.

Then, the status and prospects of research on teacher education are explored in terms of two sets of distinctions. One set differentiates among the *substantive knowledge* yielded by such research, the *methodology* of such research, and the *logistical arrangement* for conducting it. The second differentiates among what is currently *available and being used,* what is *available and going unused,* and what is *unavailable and needed*. Combining these two sets of distinctions yields nine categories of ideas about current research on teacher education. If such research is to be improved, well-trained research talent—and much more than we have now—is crucially needed.

Educational Psychology in Teacher Education

The discussion then returns to educational psychology, which is an almost universal component of the education of American teachers. The nature of that course, its purposes, and the rationale underlying the major categories of its content are described. The special needs of education in the great cities demand psychological research especially concerned with students and teachers in those cities. Examples of such research are offered.

The Evaluation of Teaching

Another major issue in teacher education, especially for teachers already in service, is the evaluation of teaching. Such evaluation can be attempted to serve administrative purposes, to help teachers to improve themselves, and to obtain data for research purposes. The first of these purposes bears on in-service teacher education, as conducted or implied by school administrators and supervisors when they evaluate teachers for the purpose of determining promotions in rank or pay. The second bears on teacher education as it may be conducted by the teacher himself when he uses evaluation in improving his teaching.

Various issues arise in using the practical procedures—students' ratings, measures of student achievement, and observation in the classroom—that have been adopted for these purposes.

The research uses of the evaluation of teaching would be improved by process descriptions, like those provided by an influential study of medical practice. That study suggests that teaching practices can be evaluated on the basis of reasonable inferences from what is known about logic, school subjects, interpersonal relationships, and the like. Such a basis may be more valid and realistic than insisting that every item of teacher behavior exhibit an empirical relationship to student achievement of some educational objective. Not every item of good medical practice has been shown to be correlated with measures of the patient's health. So it should not be necessary to defend every item of desirable teaching practice in such a way. The desirability of many items of both medical practice and teacher behavior can be defended by reasonable inference from knowledge in the underlying disciplines, such as physiology and anatomy in medicine, or educational and social psychology in teaching.

Feedback of Ratings to and from Teachers

Ratings of teachers by their students have been defended and used as a basis for teacher self-improvement. This kind of "teacher education" rests on the assumption that the teacher's awareness of how his students evaluate his behavior will affect the teacher's behavior. To test that assumption, experimental groups of teachers have been given reports on ratings of their behavior by their students, while such information has been withheld from control groups. Results of a number of such experiments encourage further use of students' ratings in this way. Several possible invalidating factors have been shown not to influence the amount of change in teacher behavior that occurs.

The teacher's principal or department head also affects the teacher's environment and performance. So experiments have been conducted on the effects of feedback from teachers to principals or department heads. Here, also, the results have been encouraging. Although many researchable issues remain, the feedback of ratings from subordinates seems to offer a highly practical and workable approach to the in-service education of teachers and other educators.

Toward the New Roles of Teachers

Finally, how will the role of teachers be changed in response to educational innovations such as individualized instruction, programmed instruction, television and film instruction, team teaching, flexible scheduling, and non-graded schools? Research assists in revision of the teacher's role by deriving and evaluating the ways in which teacher behavior is changed. The new roles of teachers can be based on the size of the instructional group: (a) the individual student working alone, (b) the small group of students engaged in a discussion, (c) the conventional classroom group of 25-35 students, and (d) the large-group audience of the lecture, television presentation, or motion picture. Teachers' roles should differ in these teaching situations in ways that have not yet been clearly derived and evaluated.

Once new roles are developed, the problem arises of getting teachers to change their behaviors. One approach to bringing about such change is that of giving the teacher some "product"—an instrument, procedural checklist, manual, device, program, guide, game, and so on. Using the product may bring about a desirable change in teacher behavior, where traditional teacher education programs have failed to do so. Such products should avoid the inflexibility of the programming approach to teaching and the disorder of conventional classroom teaching. They will give teachers tools, such as technical skills and algorithms, that will free them for creative adaptation. A manual for training teachers to explain more effectively illustrates this approach.

In conclusion, there is reason to hold high expectations of the search for a scientific basis for teacher education and the improvement of teacher effectiveness.

Part I
Research on Teacher Effectiveness

Chapter 2   Can Science Contribute to the Art of Teaching?

Can science contribute to the art of teaching? To successful teacher behavior? It would be nice if the answer could be a resounding "Yes," based on a long parade of conclusive evidence and examples of richly useful findings. Unfortunately, that happy paper cannot yet be written in any honest way. Instead, the question must receive a rather more complex response.

First, I shall define the term "successful teacher behavior" and delimit the setting of the kind of teaching to be considered. Second, I shall outline reasons for pessimism as to whether research on teaching has any real likelihood of yielding scientific findings that can be used to improve teaching. Then I shall sketch the nature of the findings that would alleviate the pessimism.

DEFINITION AND DELIMITATION

My definition of "successful teacher behavior" is one based on research on teaching. The findings of such research may or may not accord with common sense. They may or may not accord with the virtues of personality and character, or desirable behaviors, described in writings on ethics, the Boy Scout Handbook, or a Dale Carnegie course. Also, a research-based characterization of successful teacher behavior may not be extremely original, or completely non-obvious. Neither must such a description of behavior be highly systematic, since research findings at any given moment do not necessarily form a coherent scheme. As for validity, it is not inconceivable that in the long run, some non-scientific insight or artistic hunch may turn out to be superior to what can now be cited on the basis of research evidence. The truths propounded in the past by novelists, essayists, or skilled supervisors of teachers may eventually prove more valid than the results of research now available.

Despite these possible limitations, I shall consider here only what the research literature has to offer. This literature takes the form of reports on empirical studies of one kind or another. In these studies, various kinds of teacher behavior have been related to other variables on which some sort of educational valuation can be placed. So, by the present definition, "successful" teacher behaviors or characteristics are those that have been found through empirical research to be related to something desirable about teachers. The "something desirable" may be improved achievement by students of any of the various cognitive, affective, or psychomotor objectives of education. Or, the "something desirable" may be a favorable evaluation of the teacher by students, a supervisor, a principal, or someone else whose judgment is important.

The empirical relationships between the teacher behaviors and the desirable somethings may be found in two different ways. First, the relationships may be demonstrated in true experiments; if so, they may be considered to be genuine causal or functional relationships. Or they may be found only through correlational studies; if so, the inference that the teacher behavior causes the something desirable may be hazardous. Although it may be urged that conceptual, logical, or historical methods can also establish what is "successful teacher behavior," I am going to exclude them from my present definition of scientific method. That is, I shall assume that scientific knowledge as to what constitutes successful teacher behavior must be based on inference from an experiment or a correlational study that the behavior is related to something desirable.

Now let us specify the kind of setting in which the teacher behavior to be considered takes place. Various innovations now being considered by educators may more frequently in the future make the setting of teaching something other than the conventional classroom. The setting may change in accordance with the needs of the students and the kinds of learning in which they are engaged. For some kinds of learning, students may be taught in large-group settings, such as motion picture theaters and lecture halls. For other kinds, the setting may be the small-group seminar, or a booth for programmed instruction, "individually prescribed instruction," or independent study. In the future, these settings will, it is said, supplement and perhaps supplant today's conventional classroom.

But these different kinds of settings still lie in the future, for the most part. And my definition of successful teaching requires empirical research demonstrating a relationship between the behaviors of teachers and other desirable things. Most of that research, by far, has been done in classrooms. So this discussion will be restricted to the behavior of teachers in the conventional classroom.

REASONS FOR PESSIMISM

Let us now consider reasons for pessimism on the question, Can science contribute to the art of teaching? To begin, it should be noted that making positive statements about the results of research on successful teacher behavior is not fashionable among educational research workers. Many reviewers of research on teaching have concluded that it has yielded little of value.

This disparaging style in appraising research results has had a great vogue. In 1953, a Committee on the Criteria of Teacher Effectiveness rendered the verdict that "the present condition of research on teacher effectiveness holds little promise of yielding results commensurate with the needs of American education" (American Educational Research Association, 1953, p. 657). In 1958, Orville Brim (1958, p. 32) concluded from his examination of reviews of the literature that there were no consistent relations between teacher characteristics and effectiveness in teaching. In 1963, in the *Handbook of Research on Teaching,* the authors of the chapter on teaching methods reported an impression that "teaching methods do not seem to make much difference" and that "there is hardly any evidence to favor one method over another" (Wallen & Travers, 1963, p. 484). The authors of the chapter on teacher personality and characteristics concluded that ". . . very little is known for certain . . . about the relation between teacher personality and teacher effectiveness" (Getzels & Jackson, 1963, p. 574). And the authors of the chapter on social interaction in the classroom concluded that "until very recently, the approach to the analysis of teacher-pupil and pupil-pupil interaction . . . has tended to be unrewarding and sterile" (Withall & Lewis, 1963, p. 708). It would not be hard to find other summary statements to the effect that empirical research on teaching has not yielded much enlightenment about successful teaching.

After a thorough review, Dubin and Taveggia (1968) concluded that college teaching methods make no difference in student achievement as measured by final examinations on course content. Their review was unique in that they examined the data, rather than merely the conclusions, of nearly 100 studies made over a 40-year period. Of 88 independent comparisons of the lecture and discussion methods, reported in 36 experimental studies, 51 per cent favored the lecture method and 49 per cent favored the discussion method! Then they standardized the differences between 56 pairs of average scores, on the final examination, of students taught by these two methods; the standardization made the differences comparable. The average of the differences between standardized averages turned out to be .09, not significantly different from zero. Similar results were obtained from independent comparisons of the following kinds of instruction:

Lecture vs. lecture-discussion (7 studies)

Discussion vs. lecture-discussion (3 studies)

Supervised independent study vs. face-to-face instruction (25 studies)

Supervised independent study vs. lecture (14 studies)

Supervised independent study vs. discussion (3 studies)

Supervised independent study vs. lecture-discussion (9 studies)

Unsupervised independent study vs. face-to-face instruction (6 studies)

Some writers hold that all research on school variables, not merely research on teacher behavior, has yielded negative results for the most part. The view that educational research yields negative findings has even been assimilated into a whole theory of the origins and process of schooling. Stephens (1967), after looking at the research reports and summaries, concluded that practically nothing seems to make any difference in the effectiveness of instruction. He considered this "flood of negative results" to be understandable in the light of his theory of spontaneous schooling. This theory postulates spontaneous, automatic forces in the background of the student—his maturational tendencies, various out-of-school agencies such as the home and the general community, and the reputation of the school as a place concerned about academic matters. The theory also refers to various spontaneous tendencies on the part of humans in the role of the teacher—tendencies to manipulate and communicate. These two kinds of force, the background forces and the automatic teaching forces, account for most of the learning that takes place. Furthermore, these spontaneous and powerful forces operate early in the growth process, when influences on learning have greater effects. Hence, the changes introduced by research variables, administrative factors, and pedagogical refinements of one kind or another are inadequate to produce any major difference.

Stephens documented his position with references to summaries of studies of a host of educational variables, procedures, practices, and orientations—namely, school attendance, instructional television, independent study and correspondence courses, size of class, individual consultation and tutoring, counseling, concentration on specific students, the student's involvement, the amount of time spent in study, distraction by jobs and extracurricular activities, size of school, the qualities of teachers that can be rated by principals and supervisors, non-graded schools, team teaching, ability grouping, progressivism vs. traditionalism, discussion vs. lecture, group-centered vs. teacher-centered approaches, the use of frequent quizzes, and programmed instruction. Studies of all these have failed to show that they make a consistent and significant difference.

Stephens considered briefly the possibility that the negative results were due to methodological errors, such as concentrating on one narrow segment of achievement, using insensitive tests, employing poor controls, exerting overcontrol that holds constant too much and thus restricts the differences, and using too stringent a criterion of statistical significance. But all in all, he concluded that negative results are only to be expected, because "in the typical comparison of two administrative devices [such as teaching methods] we have two groups that are comparable in the forces responsible for (say) 95 percent of the growth to be had and which differ only in the force that, at best, can affect only a small fraction of the growth" (Stephens, 1967, p. 84). At any rate, according to many writers, of whom Stephens is perhaps the most systematic, the major generalization to be drawn from research is that variations in teaching and educational practice do not make any consistent, significant, or practical difference.

Apparent support for this view of the effects of educational variables on scholastic achievement can be found in the massive report on *Equality of Educational Opportunity* (Coleman, et al., 1966). According to that report, when the social background and attitudes of individual students and their schoolmates are held constant, achievement is only slightly related to school characteristics, such as per-pupil expenditures, books in the library, and a number of other facilities and curricular measures. Conversely, the report found that family background accounted for a relatively high proportion of the variance in student achievement. Stephens seems to be vindicated by these findings.

QUESTIONING THE PESSIMISM

So far we have considered reasons for pessimism about the promise of empirical research on teaching. Now let us raise some questions about these lugubrious views.

In the first place, these dismal generalizations may not do complete justice to the research domains for which they have been made. Here and there, in research on teaching methods, on teacher personality and characteristics, and on social interaction in the classroom, it may be possible to come up with more sanguine judgments about the meaning of the research findings.

We need more searching reviews of what research on teaching has to offer. Such reviews would piece together the evidence from a variety of approaches to a given problem and determine whether it supports constructive suggestions concerning the practice of teaching. The new Educational Resources Information Centers, with their improved facilities for tracking down and collating research, ought to make possible

"state-of-the-art" papers based on more meticulous sifting of the literature. If so, future conclusions about research on teaching may be less
melancholy. Later in this chapter, some preliminary examples of such
sifting will be offered.

What about the report on *Equality of Educational Opportunity*?
Here also there are reasons to question the pessimism. According to
Bowles and Levin (1968a), the research design of that study "was
overwhelmingly biased in a direction that would dampen the importance of school characteristics." For example, expenditure-per-pupil
was measured in terms of the average expenditure within an entire
school district rather than within the given school in which the pupils
were located. Hence, the expenditure-per-pupil was overstated for
schools attended by lower-class students and understated for schools
attended by students of higher social status.

Further, as Bowles and Levin pointed out, the study used faulty
statistical models in estimating the importance of school factors in ac-
counting for achievement. The importance of a variable was estimated
in terms of how much the proportion of variance in achievement explained was increased by adding that variable to the predictors.

But, as Bowles and Levin indicated, if two predictor variables are
correlated, then the additional proportion of variance in achievement
that each will explain is "dependent on the order in which each is entered into the regression equation. . . . the shared portion of variance
in achievement which could be accounted for by either X_1 or X_2 will
always be attributed to that variable which is entered into the regression first. Accordingly, the explanatory value of the first variable will
be overstated, and that of the second variable understated" (Bowles &
Levin, 1968a). So, when the family background characteristics are
entered into the regression first, and school resources are entered
second, the amount of variance accounted for by the school resource
variables is "consistently derogated."

Despite these biases, the report found that measures of teacher
quality were significantly related to achievement, probably because
teacher characteristics were measured individually and averaged for
each school. Indeed, the report stated that teacher characteristics accounted for a ". . . higher proportion of variation in student achievement than did all other aspects of the school combined, excluding the
student body characteristics" (Coleman, et al., 1966, p. 316). These
teacher characteristics were family educational level, years' experience,
localism (living in the area most of their lives), teachers' own educational level, score on a vocabulary test, preference for middle-class students, and proportion of teachers in the school who were white. And

such factors make a bigger difference, according to the report, for Negro than for white students, perhaps because their out-of-school environment contributes less of the spontaneous educative forces to which Stephens referred.

Accordingly, the characteristics of teachers who work with culturally disadvantaged pupils become all the more important. In subsequent re-analyses of some of the data of the report, Bowles and Levin (1968b) found that teacher characteristics were very significantly related to the verbal achievement of twelfth-grade Negro students, even when social background factors were held constant. When school and teacher characteristics were entered first, their ability to account for student achievement was found to be considerably greater.

But this general approach, as employed in studies like *Equality of Educational Opportunity*, has severe limitations as a basis for determining the degree to which teachers can make a difference in student achievement. Subsequent re-analyses of the data from the *Equality* study and similar studies, made by the most sophisticated techniques available, have yielded only equivocal answers. The regression equations that result from such analyses cannot be regarded as informing us about *causal* relationships between student achievement and teacher characteristics. Thus, although the teacher's verbal ability receives a large weight in such equations, we cannot proceed to improve student achievement by hiring teachers with greater verbal ability. "If we went about increasing the verbal ability of teachers, the increase that might result in student achievement would be far less than what would be calculated by using the equation that relates it to achievement. The reason is that a specific increase in verbal ability would probably not be accompanied by a corresponding increase in all the other attributes that verbal ability is serving as a proxy for" (Mood, 1970, p. 3).

Further, it is almost impossible in data of this kind to separate the influence of school and teacher factors from that of community and family factors. No available technique can "determine how much of the higher achievement should be attributed to the home and how much to the teachers" (Mood, 1970, p. 4), because the home and teacher factors are themselves correlated. "When one tries to control on one set in order to assess the effect of another set he finds that he has overcontrolled and the sought effect is very small" (Mood, 1970, p. 4). In short, ". . . *the present rudimentary state of our quantitative models does not permit us to disentangle the effects of home, school, and peers on students' achievement*" (Mood, 1970, p. 6, italics in original).

One way to improve these models is to obtain better measures of a larger number of the teacher attributes that are significant to the ability of teachers to improve learning. Such measures will come closer to estimating the full effect of teachers, independently of home and school factors (Mood, 1970, pp. 10–12). Furthermore, these measures should be aimed at process variables, "those human actions which transform the raw materials of input into opportunities for learning" (Gagné, 1970, p. 170), i.e., teacher activities, rather than teacher characteristics such as amount of education, experience, or verbal ability. Fortunately, a substantial amount of research has been conducted on such process variables. These are the studies of teacher behavior in the classroom to which, in part, we now turn and to which we shall return in later chapters.

SOME POSITIVE STATEMENTS

Having emphasized the difficulties of making positive research-based statements about successful teaching behaviors, I wish nonetheless to attempt such statements. My purpose is merely to illustrate the nature of the conclusions that might be drawn from more adequate examination of better research. My procedure will be to present a series of operational definitions of teacher behaviors that seem, more or less, to belong on the same dimension. These definitions will be drawn from various research procedures and measuring instruments. Then I shall cite some of the evidence on which it is possible to base the inference that these behaviors or characteristics are desirable.

Warmth

One example of this dimension can be seen in the responses of teachers to the Minnesota Teacher Attitude Inventory (MTAI) (Cook, Leeds, & Callis, 1951). Here, the teacher responds on a five-point agree-disagree scale to such statements as "Most children are obedient," "Minor disciplinary situations should sometimes be turned into jokes," "Most pupils lack productive imagination," and "Most pupils are resourceful when left on their own."

As a second example, consider teachers' responses to the California F scale (McGee, 1955), which has been found to correlate substantially ($r = .7$) with the MTAI (Gage, Leavitt, & Stone, 1957; Sheldon, Coale, & Copple, 1959). Among the F scale's items are "Obedience and respect for authority are the most important virtues children should learn," "People can be divided into two distinct classes: the weak and the strong," and "Most of our social problems would be solved if we could somehow get rid of the immoral, crooked, and feeble-minded people."

A final example can be drawn from the work of Ryans (1960), who developed a Teacher Characteristics Schedule that included such items as the following: "Pupils can behave themselves without constant supervision," "Most pupils are considerate of the teacher's wishes," and "Most teachers are willing to assume their share of the unpleasant tasks associated with teaching."

Now what is the basis for the proposition that certain patterns of responses to attitude statements of this kind are "desirable"? The answer is that these kinds of attitudes and behaviors tend to be correlated positively with favorable assessments of the teachers by students and trained observers, and with students' scores on achievement tests. The Minnesota Teacher Attitude Inventory has fairly consistently been found to correlate positively with favorable mean ratings of the teachers by their pupils (Yee, 1967). The items of Ryans' inventory correlated positively with observers' ratings of elementary school teachers on all three of his teacher behavior patterns—warm, understanding, friendly vs. aloof, egocentric, and restricted; responsible, businesslike, systematic vs. evading, unplanned, and slipshod; and stimulating, imaginative vs. dull, routine (Ryans, 1960). McGee (1955) found that teachers' scores on the California F Scale correlated .6 with previous ratings of the teachers by trained observers on dimensions like aloof vs. approachable, unresponsive vs. responsive, dominative vs. integrative, and harsh vs. kindly. Cogan (1958) found that descriptions of teachers by their students on similar items correlated positively with the amount of required and also voluntary school work done by the students.

In short, a substantial body of evidence supports two conclusions: (a) Teachers differ reliably from one another on a series of measuring instruments that seem to have a great deal in common. (b) These reliable individual differences among teachers are fairly consistently related to various desirable things about teachers.

What term can be applied to the desirable end of this dimension of behaviors and attitudes? Teachers at this desirable end tend to behave approvingly, acceptantly, and supportively; they tend to speak well of their own students, students in general, and people in general. They tend to like and trust rather than fear other people of all kinds. How they get that way is not our concern at the moment. The point is that it is not impossible to find extremely plausible similarities among the teacher behaviors measured and found desirable by a number of independent investigators working with different methods, instruments, and concepts. Although any single term is inadequate, it seems safe to use the term "warmth." Warmth, operationally defined as indicated above, seems—on the basis of varied research evidence—to be quite defensible as a desirable characteristic of teacher behavior.

Indirectness

To identify a second dimension of teacher behavior, we begin with two of Flanders' categories. His Category 3 is "Accepts or uses ideas of student: clarifying, building, or developing ideas suggested by a student," and Category 4 is "Ask questions: asking a question about content or procedure with the intent that a student answer." In the classrooms of teachers that behave in these ways relatively often, one also finds more instances of Category 8: "Student talk-response: talk by students in response to teacher. Teacher initiates the contact or solicits student statement," and Category 9: "Student talk-initiation: talk by students which they initiate. If 'calling on' student is only to indicate who may talk next, observer must decide whether student wanted to talk. If he did, use this category."

A second example of this dimension of teacher behavior may be seen in the research on what is called "learning by discovery." This research deals with the question, "How much and what kind of guidance should the teacher provide? . . . the degree of guidance by the teacher varies from time to time along a continuum, with almost complete direction of what the pupil must do at one extreme to practically no direction at the other" (Shulman & Keislar, 1966, pp. 182, 183). This dimension consists of the degree to which the teacher permits pupils to discover underlying concepts and generalizations for themselves, giving them less rather than more direct guidance. The teacher at the higher level of this dimension realizes that it is not always desirable merely to tell the pupil what you want him to know and understand. Rather, it is sometimes better to ask questions, encourage the pupil to become active, seek for himself, use his own ideas, and engage in some trial and error. This kind of teaching represents a willingness to forbear giving the pupil everything he needs to know; it does not mean abandoning the pupil entirely to his own devices.

Now what is the evidence that this dimension of teacher behavior— exemplified in Flanders' categories, and teaching-by-discovery—has a significant relationship to something educationally desirable? Flanders and Simon (1969) concluded from their examination of a dozen studies that *"the percentage of teacher statements that make use of ideas and opinions previously expressed by pupils is directly related to average class scores on attitude scales of teacher attractiveness, liking the class, etc., as well as to average achievement scores adjusted for initial ability"* (p. 1426, italics in original). Ausubel (1963, p. 171) reviewed the experiments on learning by discovery and concluded that the furnishing of completely explicit rules is relatively less effective than some degree of arranging for pupils to discover rules for themselves.

It seems safe to say that some use of the guided discovery method, and "indirectness," in teaching is desirable. Teachers not sensitized to its desirability typically exhibit too little indirectness. As Flanders (1960, p. 114) put it, "our theory suggests an indirect approach; most teachers use a direct approach."

Cognitive Organization

The third dimension of teacher behavior is more difficult to define operationally. And its connection with desirable outcomes is, despite great plausibility, not as well established empirically. This is the kind of behavior that reflects the teacher's intellectual grasp, or "cognitive organization," of what he is trying to teach.

In one investigation, teachers were tested as to whether they understood the processes and concepts of arithmetic, such as the reason for moving each sub-product one digit to the left when the multiplier has more than one digit (Orleans, 1952). Other studies have dealt with the degree to which the teacher's verbal behavior reflects an understanding of the logical properties of a good definition, explanation, or conditional inference (Meux & Smith, 1961). Others have studied the degree to which the teacher, or his instructional material, provides a set of subject-matter "organizers" that embody "relevant ideational scaffolding," discriminate new material from previously learned material, and integrate it "at a level of abstraction, generality, and inclusiveness which is much higher than that of the learning material itself" (Ausubel, 1963, p. 214). Similar ideas have been put in such terms as "cognitive structure" (Bruner, 1966), "learning structure" (Gagné, 1965), and "logic tree" (Hickey & Newton, 1964).

Although the general conception of this aspect of teaching behavior can be identified, operational definitions are hard to come by. Perhaps the best operational definitions of such variables must be inferred from the procedures of those who develop programmed instructional materials. These procedures call for behavioral definitions of objectives and detailed "learning structures" (Gagné, 1965) that analyze the steps involved in achieving a "terminal behavior" into hierarchies of subtasks. Gagné (1965) illustrated such learning structures in mathematics and science; Glaser and Reynolds (1964) worked out a detailed example in the form of the sequence of sub-behaviors involved in programmed instructional materials for teaching children to tell time from a clock.

In some ways, the lessons derived from this kind of technical work on teaching and learning have implications for curriculum development rather than for teaching as such. But the curriculum is inevitably shaped through the teacher's behavior in the classroom as well as by the materials that his pupils read. The implications of such instructional research for the behavior of the live teacher in the classroom seem clear: if curricular material should exhibit a valid cognitive organization, so should the behavior of the teacher.

Enthusiasm

Our last example of a sifting of the literature to identify a desirable kind of teacher behavior is one recently provided by Rosenshine (1970). He reviewed the evidence from a variety of sources on the degree to which the teacher's "enthusiasm" was desirable. Some of the studies reviewed were experiments in which "enthusiasm" was manipulated. In other, correlational, studies, enthusiasm as it occurred "naturally" was rated, counted, or measured with an inventory. In some of the studies, the dependent variable was measured achievement; in others, evaluative ratings of the teacher by his students or other independent observers. The varied evidence seemed remarkably consistent in supporting the desirability of teacher enthusiasm. Positive differences between means and positive correlation coefficients appeared far more often than did those indicating a negative relationship between teacher enthusiasm and something desirable about the teacher.

Two examples of experiments will illustrate these findings. Coats and Smidchens (1966) had two 10-minute lessons presented by two teachers in a static, or unenthusiastic fashion (read from a manuscript, with no gestures, eye contact, or inflections), and also in a dynamic, or enthusiastic fashion (delivered from memory, with much inflection, eye contact, gesturing, and animation). Tests immediately after the lesson indicated much greater learning from the dynamic lecture. Similarly, Mastin (1963) had 20 teachers lecture on two different topics a week apart—presenting one topic in an "indifferent" manner and the other "enthusiastically." In 19 of the 20 classes, the student's mean achievement was higher for the lesson taught enthusiastically.

These four variables—warmth, indirectness, cognitive organization, and enthusiasm—merely illustrate the kinds of contributions that research on teaching, in its present early stages, can support. In themselves, these findings are far from startling. Any clever student, teacher, or novelist could have told us decades ago about these characteristics of good teaching. But what is important about these tentative conclusions is their basis in empirical research. The ease with which others have told us such truths in the past is matched by their untrustworthiness. Glib insights based on uncontrolled experience can lead us astray. Research on teaching—the effort to apply scientific method to the description and improvement of teaching—is much more laborious and usually makes much less interesting reading than the essay of the shrewd, compassionate, and imaginative observer. The same tortoise-hare comparison would have applied in past centuries to research on psychiatry and the writings of phrenologists, to research on chemistry and the writings of alchemists, and so on. In the long run, as humanity has learned, it is safer in matters of this kind to rely on the scientific method. Applying that method to the phenomena and problems of teaching is our concern.

Chapter 3   Psychological Conceptions of Teaching

For anyone aware of the tides now running in American education, these are exciting times. Today, as never before, the educational world is hungry for ideas. The federal government has appropriated billions to improve education. We are not only being driven by the urgent problems that beset education, but we are also being attracted by unprecedented support for the tryout of fresh conceptions.

THE NEW VALUATION OF EDUCATIONAL IDEAS

Federal support of educational research has achieved substantial levels. The trend reached a new crest with the establishment of an altogether novel kind of institution in American education—the regional laboratory. Added onto the already functioning programs of research and development centers and cooperative research projects, and joined to a ready-made market for their products in the form of the supplementary educational centers, the laboratories are launching multifaceted attacks on the whole array of educational problems, both national and regional.

The nation's support for educational research, development, demonstration, and dissemination has begun to approach the level that students of our needs and potentials have long been asking for, have hardly dared to hope for, and are now leaping to take advantage of. For years, educational research workers have been asking for more tools in the form of dollars, trained men, and organizations. We now bid fair to have such tools in adequate supply.

THE NEED FOR NEW CONCEPTIONS OF TEACHING

This situation heightens the importance of another kind of tool—the conceptions of teaching that will inevitably lie close to the heart of all this research and development effort. These conceptions determine what gets done just as much as do the trained men, the buildings, the computers, the research designs, and the methods of development and dissemination. Our conceptions of teaching give direction to our choices of the kinds of variables that we study, measure, and manipulate.

For the behavior of teachers is one of the major avenues through which a society can influence what its children learn. Apart from the curriculum materials, the physical facilities, and the administration of the schools, it is through teachers that a society implements its interest in having students learn certain things.

Concern with Teaching in Educational Psychology

Although this kind of stress on teaching may seem banal to anyone outside educational psychology, within that field it has not been adequately honored. The educational psychologist has not been giving prospective teachers enough of the kind of training they need. As noted in more detail in Chapter 10, most of the first course in educational psychology has been concerned with the characteristics of learning and the learner, with the learner's adjustment, with the learner's growth and development, and with measurement and evaluation of the learner. It has not offered enough help on methods of teaching or teacher behavior. And yet, since it is largely through the process of teaching that our theories and principles of learning can be put to use, it is conceptions, theories, and methods of teaching that educational psychologists should develop. This neglect of theories of teaching is discussed again in Chapter 4.

This is not to say that a prior concern with learning is misplaced. It is to say rather that we should not stop with learning, but should go on from there to develop what such knowledge means for teaching.

Let us consider briefly a somewhat more extreme position than the one I am advocating. This is the position that teaching should be regarded as an autonomous, self-determined process coordinate with learning. This point of view erects the study of teaching as a discipline in its own right, independent of the study of learning, just as learning can be studied independently of teaching.

The trouble with this idea—the idea of making research on teaching an autonomous discipline—is that our schools, after all, have learning as their objective, with teaching only a means to that end. We cannot let teaching go on in whatever way seems to be convenient or necessary and then require learners to adapt to the kind of teaching they are provided with. Instead, if teaching procedures and learning processes are not well suited to each other, then it is teaching that will have to change so that it brings about the kind of learning that the school is intended to produce.

But even as we reject this notion of making teaching an autonomous discipline, we must perceive that, if teaching is not to be studied by itself, neither must learning. The two processes must be studied together, as a teaching-learning process. That is, a valid conception of teaching must be tied closely to a conception of learning. How human beings learn should provide much of the basis for our derivations of how teachers should teach. In the past, treatments of human learning have not often been followed through to the point of making such derivations. The analysis of the learning process has too often been the end of the matter, and not enough effort has been made to spell out what the learning process implies for the method of teaching. It is implications such as these that I wish to consider.

TYPES OF LEARNING TASK AND PROCESS

One basic proposition is that learning may not go on in the same way for all behaviors learned. Some things may be learned by one process, and some by another. The notion of a single general theory of learning that can account for all the kinds of learning that human beings can manifest seems to have great viability. We still hear contiguity theorists, reinforcement theorists, identification theorists, and cognitive theorists claiming that each of them has the formulation that is adequate to account for all the learning that takes place in all species.

But the idea of a general theory of learning has certainly had its critics. Lewin (1942) asked, "Have we any right to classify the learning to high-jump, to get along without alcohol, and to be friendly with other people under the same term, and to expect identical laws to hold for any of these processes?" Lewin distinguished at least four types of changes within what is called learning: changes in cognitive structure; motivation; group belongingness or ideology; and voluntary control of the body musculature. Tolman (1949) suggested that "our familiar theoretical disputes about learning may *perhaps* . . . be resolved, if we can agree that there are really a number of different kinds of learning. . . . The theory and laws appropriate to one kind may well be different from those appropriate to other kinds." Tolman tentatively offered six types of learning, which he called cathexes, equivalence beliefs, field expectancies, field-cognition modes, drive discriminations, and motor patterns; for each of these he saw the possibility of a different theory of learning.

In the volume edited by Melton (1964), we find six categories that were "chosen because they seem to represent the categories most commonly employed by investigators in thinking about and doing research on human learning, and have become for this reason part of the tradition of descriptive language of the science of human learning." The categories were conditioning, rote learning, probability learning, skill learning, concept learning, and problem solving. But even these were regarded by Melton as having little usefulness in the scientific analysis of learning; he regarded as more useful the rather large and steadily increasing set of "subcategories of these primitive major categories" whose dissimilarities in terms of process and phenomena were "much more striking than the similarities."

A further attempt at the delineation of types of learning was offered by Gagné (1965); he proposed eight kinds in the following order of increasing complexity: signal learning, stimulus-response learning, chaining, verbal-association learning, multiple discrimination learning, concept learning, principle learning, and problem solving. The basic distinction between one of these forms of learning and another, according to Gagné, lies in its prerequisites, or what the individual must previously have learned. He considers each of his types of learning to depend on certain outcomes from types earlier in his hierarchy.

TEACHING AS THE EXERTION OF BEHAVIORAL INFLUENCE

Now I should like to offer one view of teaching, and examine some conceptions of teaching, and their implications for research and practice.

First, I propose that we conceive of teaching as the exertion of behavioral influence. Everyone agrees that learning should be defined as a change in capabilities or ways of behaving that may be attributed to experience. The experience must, however, be behavioral in character rather than physiological or mechanical. That is, we rule out changes in behavior due to drugs, fatigue, disease, or sensory adaptation, and we also rule out the effects of being mechanically pushed or pulled by something. Behavioral influence is hard to define, but it refers to stimuli that affect organisms via sensation and perception and influence behavior in some more or less lasting way. Without going into these matters, let us merely characterize learning as a fairly stable change in behavior due to behavioral rather than other kinds of forces.

The influences that produce learning are described by theories of learning. Such theories fall into three broad categories: conditioning theories, imitation theories, and cognitive theories. These conceptions of the learning process have value for the organization of ideas about teaching. That is, since conceptions of learning deal with the kinds of influence that bring about learning, teachers can exert three corresponding kinds of influence. They can (1) condition the learner; (2) provide a model for imitation by the learner; and (3) change the cognitive structure of the learner's environment.

Conditioning Influence

Teaching by conditioning consists in arranging stimuli so as to bring forth desired responses and then providing a reinforcement as quickly as possible. We want a child to volunteer more often in class. When he eventually volunteers, we call on him and praise him as quickly as possible, so that this desired response will be more likely to occur the next time he is in this situation. For certain kinds of behavior, the idea of teaching by conditioning makes eminently good sense. It may well be that affectively toned behaviors, much involved with fears and hopes, and not much bound up with any logic, lend themselves well to being viewed as behaviors to be taught by conditioning.

Conditioning theory is concerned with the way in which relationships between stimuli and responses are learned. In so-called classical conditioning theory, new stimuli acquire the power to elicit already available responses by being made to occur just prior to other stimuli which already have the power to elicit these responses on the basis of innate reflexes or previous learning. This is the kind of conditioning that Pavlov's dogs exhibited when, by presenting a bell ring just prior to introduction of food powder into the dog's mouth, the experimenter made the bell became a conditioned stimulus for the response of salivation.

According to Skinner, this kind of classical, or respondent, conditioning is far less important in everyday life than another kind of conditioning, which he calls operant conditioning. Operant conditioning does not concern itself with the elicitation of responses by stimuli because most of the responses with which we are concerned are not elicited by any stimuli that can be readily identified. Rather, most of these responses are described by Skinner as being "emitted," rather than elicited. That is, it is seldom any single stimulus that invariably precedes a given response. The response may come under the control of stimuli, but the control is not that of elicitation. In classical conditioning, the reinforcing stimulus is paired with a stimulus. In operant conditioning, however, the reinforcing stimulus is paired with, or follows upon, a response. It is operant conditioning, that is, the change in frequency of responses on the basis of their being made contingent in various ways upon reinforcements, that forms the basis for the kind of theory of learning that Skinner has advanced.

It is safe to say that Skinnerian operant conditioning nowadays provides the basis for the most influential applications of psychological learning theory to research and development in education. It is, of course, the basis upon which the programmed instruction movement has developed. In many writings, Skinner has developed extremely complex and subtle ways of using the operant conditioning approach to elucidate not merely simple animal behaviors such as lever-pressing by rats or pecking by pigeons, but also many more complex kinds of behavior on the part of both animals and human beings.

Many of the applications to human behavior are still programmatic and extrapolational. But the widespread adoption of programmed instruction indicates the ways in which the Skinnerian approach can be applied to complex cognitive learning by human beings. Skinner's writings also contain many applications of the model to the explanation of behavior of people in groups and in various social institutions— government and law, religion, psychotherapy, economic life, and education. With more or less ingenuity and creativity, human behavior can be controlled by manipulating the reinforcement contingencies of the environment in which the behavior is emitted. That is, the frequency of behavior can be increased by making a positive reinforcer occur as soon as possible after the behavior has occurred. It can be decreased by withholding a positive reinforcer after the occurrence of the behavior.

Some kinds of school learning are easy to understand in terms of this model. That is, it is easy to see how the operant conditioning model can be applied to the instruction of children in the multiplication table and in spelling, in the knowledge of isolated facts in geography, social studies, and science.

But what about the more complex cognitive outcomes of education, such as concept formation, the understanding of principles, and the ability to solve problems? And what about the various affective and social outcomes of education, such as appreciation of art or favorable attitudes toward one's self and others? These kinds of behavior and learning are also amenable to analysis and control by means of the operant conditioning formulation, according to Skinner, especially when they are made overt, rather than covert.

Problem-solving, for example, consists of the learner's changing a situation so that a desired response can occur. Such changes in the situation can take many forms—clarifying stimuli, changing them, rearranging them to facilitate comparison or grouping or organization, and so on. Teachers can help students acquire problem-solving behavior by teaching them the various techniques for changing situations that will permit the desired responses to occur. For example, the student can be taught to translate a verbal statement of a problem into a set of mathematical symbols and then to rearrange these in standard ways until a solution appears. Thus, thinking is reduced to behaving in various ways, and the operant conditioning paradigm is found by Skinner to be applicable both to problem-solving itself and to teaching others how to solve problems. Even so-called second-order problem-solving, or solving the problem of how to solve problems, which has been called the acquisition of heuristic techniques, can be reduced, according to Skinner's analysis, to a set of emitted behaviors controlled by reinforcement contingencies. Even so-called "productive thinking," of the kind invoked by the Gestalt psychologist Max Wertheimer when he described how students discover how to find the area of a parallelogram, is reducible by Skinner to operant behavior. The kind of "insight" that Wertheimer cited, or the student's seeing the solution, can be regarded as an instance of the emission of an operant response controlled more or less by the nature of the conditions, and previous learnings, which make the solution response occur.

Modeling Influence

The value of the operant conditioning approach in the learning and teaching of complex behaviors has been questioned by some writers, like Bandura (1969). In learning and teaching how to drive a car, for example, one would need to go through a long and altogether non-feasible sequence of steps if one were to follow the operant conditioning approach. First, the learner would be reinforced for incipient responses of approaching the car, then he would be similarly shaped into making the proper responses for opening the car door, sitting in the driver's seat, turning the ignition key, and so on. If one had to learn to drive a car by the same procedures as those whereby pigeons must learn to execute fancy steps, that is, by having various approximations of the desired terminal behavior reinforced as they occur, most of us would never, according to Bandura, learn to drive.

Instead, Bandura regards social-learning, i.e., identification and imitation models, as more valuable for the description and analysis of this kind of learning and teaching. That is, the learner observes the way in which a powerful or prestigious or exemplary model carries out the desired behavior, and then he does the same things himself. It is observational learning rather than operant conditioning that Bandura invokes as a more appropriate characterization of this kind of learning.

Teaching by modeling consists in the teacher's behaving in ways that he wants the learner to acquire through imitation. Bandura and Walters (1963) identified three kinds of effects of the learner's exposure to a model:

1. a modeling effect, whereby the learner acquires new kinds of response patterns,

2. an inhibitory or disinhibitory effect, whereby the learner decreases or increases the frequency, latency, or intensity of previously acquired responses, and

3. an eliciting effect, whereby the learner receives from the model merely a cue for releasing a response that is neither new nor inhibited.

The modeling effect occurs when a teacher shows a pupil how to hold a pencil or write a capital *Q,* and thus inculcates a new behavior. The inhibiting or disinhibiting effect occurs when he lets the pupil know, through modeling, that it is or is not permissible to look at pictures of nudes in an art book, and thus inhibits or disinhibits an old response. The eliciting effect occurs when, through modeling, he teaches a pupil to rise when a lady enters the room and thus provides a cue eliciting a response neither new nor inhibited.

It should be noted that these examples of things learned by imitation are behaviors that have no intrinsic logic or rationale. The situations or stimuli calling forth these behaviors have no structure that makes the desired response logically necessary or "true." Learning through imitation seems to be especially appropriate for tasks that have little cognitive structure.

Bandura does regard reinforcement theories of instrumental conditioning, such as Skinner's, as able to account satisfactorily for the *control* of *previously* learned matching responses. But he does not regard them as able to account for the way in which new response patterns are *acquired* through observation and imitation. Particularly when the learner does not overtly perform what he observes while he is acquiring the new behavior, and where reinforcers are not administered either to him or to his model, and where the first appearance of the imitative response occurs only days or months after it was observed, he finds it difficult to see how operant conditioning formulations can account for observational learning.

Apart from the question of the way in which imitative responses are acquired, how can operant conditioning account for the way in which they are emitted or *performed* on certain occasions after they have been acquired? In general, imitative responses are made when the person is able to discriminate the situation as one in which behavior of a given kind will be reinforced. "When we see people looking into a shop window, we are likely to look, too—not because there is an instinct of imitation, but because windows into which other people are looking are likely to reinforce such behavior. So well developed is the imitative repertoire of the average person that its origins are forgotten, and it is easily accepted as an inherent part of his behavior" (Skinner, 1953, p. 120). Thus, imitation in the sense of emitting previously acquired responses that resemble those of a model is simply operant behavior being emitted because of the presence of a discriminative stimulus that, it has previously been learned, is the signal that a given kind of behavior is likely to be reinforced.

When it comes to explaining the *acquisition* of new behavior, however, Bandura and others refer to the acquisition of perceptual or other symbolic responses. These responses resemble the sequences of modeling stimuli while they are occurring. Then they are "stored" as internal representational processes. And these processes, in turn, mediate subsequent reproduction of the behavior—days or years later. Thus, the images of the observed behavior get stored as representations of the observed stimulus events. But they also get coded symbolically, as in the form of words. Then, when the proper occasion arises, these words can serve as cues for reproducing the modeling or imitative behavior.

At any rate, whether learning through imitation and observation of prestigious others can be reduced to a kind of operant conditioning, or whether it must stand to some degree by itself, the kind of learning to which it refers must be considered sufficiently important to warrant separate consideration. In real life in the school and elsewhere, it is convenient to formulate much of the learning that goes on as observational learning that proceeds by imitation and identification. In this kind of learning, the characteristics of the model are extremely important. In general, the model must have prestige, he must be seen as a source of rewarding power, and he must be able to serve as a source of cues that a given kind of behavior will be reinforced.

Cognitive Influence

Teaching by changing cognitive structure consists in arranging facts, concepts, and principles in such relationships that the desired kinds of learning will result. If we want a student to understand a strange phenomenon, we can influence him to understand it by showing him how it is merely an instance of a general principle. So we teach someone to understand why mercury rises in a thermometer, when the temperature goes up, by referring to the more general principle that heat causes metals to expand. We influence someone to understand why water doesn't fall out of a can when we swing the can around vertically, by showing that this phenomenon is an instance of centrifugal force. In doing so, we can exert perceptual and cognitive influences such as those of figure and ground; similarity and contrast; grouping; emphasis; analogy; context; logic. Properly used, these influences will make the student see the cues to a concept, a principle, or the solution to a problem. These influences operate to bring about the change in cognitive structure that many kinds of learning consist in.

The distinguishing mark of learnings that can be produced by the use of cognitive forces is that they possess a cognitive structure. The tighter the logical or perceptual ties that hold a body of ideas or behaviors together, the better we teach in this way. It makes little sense to employ conditioning or modeling forces to teach the multiplication table, for example, when the cognitive forces in those tables are so strong.

Cognitive theories of learning and the corresponding conceptions of teaching deal with the way in which meanings are learned and communicated. In Ausubel's view (1968), the principle of subsumption is crucial to these learning and teaching processes. That is, new ideas and information can be meaningfully learned only insofar as they can be subsumed under more inclusive and appropriately relevant concepts. Subsumption refers to the way in which an individual's own organization of subject matter is hierarchical, with the most inclusive concepts at the top and progressively less inclusive and more differentiated ones falling below. Gagné (1965) referred to similar ideas as "learning structures." Highly generic concepts and propositions thus provide a stable anchorage for related material. The subject matter can have both a logical and a psychological structure, the latter being an idiosyncratic elaboration of the former. In short, in terms of cognitive approaches to learning and teaching, the hierarchical organization of the subject matter is of extreme importance, and the learner's pre-existing cognitive structure for this subject matter is the most important of his characteristics in determining the degree to which he is ready to learn, to retain, and to transfer what he learns. A body of knowledge, well organized in a clear and stable form, is thus the most important outcome of classroom learning and also the most important determiner of the acquisition of meaningful new knowledge.

It is not inconceivable that the cognitive structure conception of learning and teaching can be reduced in various ways to the operant conditioning process. In these terms, such cognitive learning would become a kind of acquisition of verbal behavior and the acquisition of classes of verbal responses. One advantage of such a reduction of cognitive theory to the operant conditioning formulation would be scientific parsimony. Also, it would permit cognitive theorists to profit from the many ingenious analyses and operational definitions that have been developed by operant conditioning theorists. Such a unification of approaches to learning and teaching has not yet, however, been carried out sufficiently well to make it useful for educational work. Thus far, most of the attempts by conditioning theorists to take into account the kinds of considerations concerning organization and structure that cognitive theorists emphasize have been, for the most part, unconscious and unwitting. For example, Taber, Glaser, and Schaefer (1965), in discussing procedures for developing programmed instruction materials, based on an operant conditioning paradigm, found it necessary to refer to such concepts as the dependence of one rule upon another, rational sequence, meaningfulness, context, similarity, and common property.

In short, the present stage of development of conditioning and cognitive theory probably makes it desirable to use both approaches in practical school work. For some purposes, the curriculum planner and teacher educator should pay close heed to the importance of reinforcement, to schedules of reinforcement, to the use of appropriate models, to the minimizing of aversive stimulation, and many other factors emphasized by Skinner and his disciples. For other purposes, or at other stages in the development of practical programs and procedures, it is important for educators to pay heed to the importance of cognitive structure, logical and psychological organization, meaningfulness, context, relevance, and the sequence of ideas. Although scientific consistency and elegance may be sacrificed by practicing this kind of eclecticism, the gains for practical purposes make it worthwhile. Educators are less likely to overlook important considerations if they take into account the concerns, variables, and formulations of both the operant conditioning theorists and the cognitive theorists.

Examples of All Three Approaches: Fostering Creativity

Sometimes it is not easy to distinguish the kinds of influences that ought to be employed to bring about a given kind of learning. My examples have thus far been as pure as I could make them, to show as convincingly as possible the ways in which different kinds of teaching-influence make better sense for different kinds of things to be learned.

But what about such an outcome as creativity? This is a relatively new concern in education, and conceptions of it are not as well formulated as those that call for convergent thinking. Perhaps this is why it is possible to find the teaching of creativity characterized by one writer as a matter of conditioning, by another as modeling, and by a third as cognitive restructuring. Rosemary Allen (1965) furnished the following quotations on methods of training for originality or creativity:

First, a believer in modeling theory (Mouly, 1960) speaks as follows:

"It is, of course, necessary that the teacher himself be original, flexible, and enthusiastic and that, in his teaching, he emphasize experimentation and discovery rather than routine."

Another writer (Brown, 1965) takes a similar position:

"If the students perceived the instructor as a model worthy of identification or imitation, a superordinated person . . . who held creative behavior as an important value—it could be learned, creative behavior was good—then they, too, could relax and become confident participants in the creative process. . . . "

Another writer (Henry, 1957), however, seems to be invoking conditioning theory:

"Creativity . . . is a way of life that involves constant error; hence it is interesting to study how a human being learns error as a way of life. Since reward is, even in human beings, a fundamental way of establishing learning, a reasonable hypothesis is that anyone who follows error as a way of life, must have had his errors reinforced by rewards, until error *as a response* was firmly established, while at the same time his correct responses were few in number or not as strongly reinforced as the incorrect."

Finally, a cognitive theorist (MacLeod, 1962) writes as follows:

"When we think creatively, we shake ourselves loose from our old assumptions, we see old instruments as capable of new functions— the rigid structure of the field has been broken down so as to permit new configurations. From this point of view, it is obvious that wherever restructuring takes place there is the possibility of creative thinking."

Allen (1965) concluded from these statements that "all three of the theories of teaching could be utilized in the training of creative individuals." Each of the different theories, or kinds of teaching-influence, seems to apply better to a different aspect of the teaching task. The teacher's over-all role is complex and has many facets. Some aspects of the teacher's role can be understood best in terms of one kind of teaching influence, and some, in terms of another.

TEACHER CHARACTERISTICS AND THE CONCEPT
OF TEACHING INFLUENCE

The view of teaching as the exertion of a conditioning, modeling, or cognitive influence throws light on some of the variables that have impressed research workers with their validity as characteristics of effective teachers. To illustrate this kind of clarification I should like to deal with two characteristics of teachers—warmth and cognitive organization—considered in Chapter 2. Each of these is, of course, merely a label for something quite complex. For each I shall give a rationale as to how the characteristic follows from one or another of the conceptions of teaching.

Warmth

Warmth refers to the degree to which the teacher tends to be approving; to provide emotional support; to express sympathetic attitudes; to accept students' feelings; and so on. Warmth may be understood in relation to conditioning theory as the teacher's over-all tendency to emit positive reinforcements. Hence, students who have warm teachers are less inhibited about making responses, because whatever they do is more likely to be met with positively reinforcing behavior on the part of the teacher.

In another sense, however, the value of teacher warmth may be understood in terms of modeling and identification theory. Heider's theory of cognitive balance predicts that we will tend to like someone whom we recognize as liking us (Heider, 1958). Warm teachers are perceived by students as liking them, and the students tend to reciprocate the affection. Heiderian theory also predicts that students who regard a teacher favorably will tend to adopt that teacher's attitudes and orientations toward the objects and ideas in the environment. So we have a rationale for the importance of warmth in terms of modeling theory. Heiderian theory also predicts that students who perceive a teacher as liking them and liking their fellow students will tend themselves to like their fellow students; this is exactly what Sears found, namely, that "teachers who like pupils tend to have pupils who like each other" (Sears & Hilgard, 1964).

Cognitive Organization

By cognitive organization I mean the degree to which the teacher possesses, and reflects in his behavior, a valid, systematic cognitive structure of the concepts and principles of the discipline he is trying to teach. We would ordinarily put here the teacher's "knowledge of his subject," except that the latter term does not signify well enough the organization and sequence of ideas, concrete and abstract, with which we are concerned.

New ideas about cognitive validity and subject-matter structure have been developed by students of programmed instruction and technical training. Gagné and his co-workers (1965) provided illustrations of how a task performance set up as a goal can be analyzed into pre-requisite subtasks, ordered in successive steps that are true both to the logic of the subject and to the way in which it can be learned. Such planned sequence of instruction militates against skipping essential steps in the development of understanding of a problem, a principle, or concept. This kind of meticulous analysis of what, cognitively speaking, amounts to walking before one runs—and to crawling before one walks—in any given content has often been performed intuitively and artistically by skillful teachers. We now have principles to guide this kind of subject-matter analysis and sequencing into learning structures.

The importance of cognitive organization is that the teacher must understand what he is to teach. B. O. Smith (1964) called our attention to the miserable logic that can too often be found in classroom discussions of the definition of a concept, for example, imperialism, or of the explanation of an event or a state of affairs, such as the Boxer Rebellion. These research workers are proceeding on the hypothesis—consistent with a conception of teaching as the exertion of cognitive influence—that "the quality of teaching will improve if the performance of the logical operations involved is improved."

The same kind of conception of teaching seemed to imbue the work of Hilda Taba (1964), who worked to formulate teaching strategies aimed at developing the ability of students to form concepts, make inferences, induce generalization, and explain phenomena. Her exploration and analysis led her to imply some rather severe demands on the teacher. She stated, for example, that:

> Prolonged assimilation of facts without a corresponding reshaping of the conceptual schemes with which to organize them is bound to retard the maturation of thought. On the other hand, a premature leap into a more complex or a higher level of thought is likely to immobilize mental activity and cause reversion to . . . a lower level of thought. . . . An appropriate transition from one [level of thought] to the other demands a proper match between the current level and that which is required. Determining the proper match is one of the most difficult tasks in teaching. . . .

Thus, Taba's teacher is required to make quick and subtle judgments about the cognitive processes of her students, about when the discussion has gotten to the point that an attempt at generalization is called for. But that is not the teacher's only burden; she also has the problem of individual differences. Even if she possesses the teaching strategies for implementing the principles of sequence, some of her students need more concrete instances than do others before they are ready for the leap to formal or abstract thought. Indeed, as Taba says: "It is not beyond possibility that by far the most important individual differences may be found in the amount of concrete thinking an individual needs before formal thought can emerge."

The Demands of Cognitive Organization and Individual Differences. So our concern with cognitive processes and the cognitive organization of the teacher can lead us into what looks like an impasse. The task of teaching begins to seem too hard, if not impossible. Other students of teaching have raised this question but on different grounds. B. F. Skinner reasoned that the student's enormous need for reinforcement contingencies cannot be met by the classroom teacher. A different reason for similar pessimism stems from the need for cognitive organization in teaching, a need of the kind to which the analyses of research workers like Smith and Taba inexorably lead us, and from a confrontation with the facts about individual differences.

Suppose good teaching demands impossibly complex, subtle, and rapid cognitive feats on the part of the teacher. And suppose the individual differences among students in both stable and momentary cognitive readinesses inevitably force the teacher to miss many of his targets. What can be done? According to this analysis, what we need, for some important kinds of teaching, is some kind of individualized, self-paced, prearranged yet flexible sequences of give-and-take between teacher and student. This kind of give-and-take is well known to all of us and occurs in most classrooms, as Bellack and others (1966) reported in their detailed study of language in the classroom (see page 129).

That is, most of the time teachers ask questions and students answer them, and then the teachers evaluate the answers; sometimes the teacher may also tell the students what to think about, or provide background information. But the trouble is that the teacher's side of the conversation cannot be as cognitively organized as Smith and Taba (and I) would like it to be. And, in any case, even when the teacher is saying the right thing for some of his students, he may very well be saying the wrong thing for the rest of them.

Programmed Instruction.   As may be evident, this line of argument leads toward programmed instruction. The "individualized, self-paced, prearranged yet flexible sequences of give-and-take between teacher and pupil" to which I referred are exactly what programmed instruction tries to provide. It is little wonder that many thoughtful students of teaching are moving toward programmed instruction as a solution to *part* of the problem of teaching. For example, Gagné (1965) took his stand, near the end of his book on the conditions of learning, as follows:

"The major possibilities of predesigning instructional content to allow for individual differences have been exhibited, not in the class-room or in the textbook, but in *programmed instruction.*" Similarly, Broudy (1962) held that:

. . . there is less ground than is commonly assumed, to believe that there are kinds of instruction that only a live teacher can provide . . . any ma-terial that can be symbolized, that has some kind of logical and syntactical structure, can be adapted for machine instruction. . . . As to strategies of motivation, presentation, eliciting of a trial response, correction of trial responses, practice of correct responses, inducement of insight into rela-tional patterns and evaluation of any and all responses, there is little doubt that properly programmed machines will not let us down, for this is their strong point. . . .

So we see that analyses of teaching as the manipulation of cognitive influences lead to programmed instruction just as conditioning theories do. How will the issue be resolved between programmed and live in-struction for many kinds of cognitive learning? In some quarters, it is held that the programmed instruction bubble has already burst, and that schoolmen are now feeling somewhat embarrassed over their brief surrender to the fad. In other quarters, it is held that programmed in-struction is steadily gaining; that better theory and practice are being developed; that further technological advances through computeriza-tion are being made; that programmed instruction will give teachers relief from certain grave problems of live teaching.

However programmed instruction goes, and we shall return to it, there is little question that the role, the task, the behavior, and the education of the human teacher are going to be carefully studied in the years ahead. The national interest in such study has been expressed through firm support for research and development in teaching and learning. Scientific interest in teaching has brought learning theorists and researchers into the school. Theory and research on teaching may hold the attention of psychologists in the decades ahead as much as learning theory and research have held it in the past. Conceptions of teaching of the kind we have considered should then give way to the rigorous and educationally relevant principles that will deserve to be called theories of teaching.

Chapter 4   Theories of Teaching

Until the 1960's, the limited usefulness of learning theory in education was frequently acknowledged. Near the close of his *Theories of Learning,* Hilgard (1956) stated, " . . . It is not surprising, therefore, that the person seeking advice from the learning theorist often comes away disappointed." Educational psychology textbooks usually included treatments of learning that drew in general terms upon learning theories. But these treatments had only slight resemblance to the elaborations of the theories as portrayed in Hilgard's book. Spence (1959), a leading learning theorist, noted that experimental psychologists "have been under no illusions as to the applicability at the present time of our theoretical formulations to the practical problems of education" (p. 85). Estes (1960), writing on "Learning" in the third edition of the *Encyclopedia of Educational Research,* judged that "no convergence is imminent between the educator's and the laboratory scientist's approaches to learning," and he was able to report little progress "toward bridging the gap between laboratory psychology and the study of school learning."

Statements about the relevance of learning theory to teaching became more sanguine during the 1960's. Thus a later edition of *Theories of Learning* listed 20 "principles" potentially useful in practice (Hilgard & Bower, 1966, pp. 562–574). Similarly, in the article on learning in the fourth edition of the *Encyclopedia,* Glaser (1969) held that "There is abundant evidence that the psychology of learning is entering a stage in which it can make increasing contact with techniques of instruction . . . " (p. 726). But in both of these discussions it was noted that much further development was needed to make this knowledge applicable to teaching.

A distinction can be made between theories of learning and theories of teaching. While theories of learning deal with the ways in which an organism learns, theories of teaching deal with the ways in which a person influences an organism to learn. Although theories of learning are necessary to the understanding, prediction, and control of the learning process, they cannot suffice in education. The goal of education—to engender learning in the most desirable and efficient ways possible—would seem to require an additional science and technology of teaching. To satisfy the practical demands of education, theories of learning must be translated into theories of teaching.

In this chapter, I attempt to support this thesis by considering (a) the need for theories of teaching, (b) the need for analysis and specification of teaching in developing such theories, (c) some illustrative analyses and specifications of teaching, and (d) the kinds of research that might yield improved empirical bases for theories of teaching.

THE NEED FOR THEORIES OF TEACHING

That theories of teaching are needed in addition to theories of learning may seem in the main to require no argument. Yet, the development of theories of teaching has been neglected. In comparison with learning, teaching goes almost unmentioned in the theoretical writings of psychologists. Many signs of this disregard can be observed. For example, *Psychological Abstracts* contains large sections on laboratory learning and school learning but only a small section on teaching, and that within the section on "Educational Personnel." The *Annual Review of Psychology* usually includes a chapter on learning but seldom more than a few paragraphs on teaching. Many volumes have been devoted to theories of learning, but only one or two books deal with theories of teaching. Textbooks of educational psychology give much more space to discussions of learning and the learner than to methods of teaching and the teacher. *A Comprehensive Dictionary of Psychological and Psychoanalytical Terms* (English & English, 1958) has three pages, containing 50 entries, concerned with learning but devotes only these lines to "Teaching": "The art of assisting another to learn. It includes the providing of information [instruction] and of appropriate situations, conditions, or activities designed to facilitate learning."

The reasons for the neglect of theories of teaching are in themselves of interest. Examining these reasons may help determine whether such theories can indeed be formulated and whether they are desirable. The attempt to develop theories of teaching implies the development of a science of teaching. Yet, some writers reject the notion of a science of teaching. Highet (1955) entitled his book *The Art of Teaching,*

. . . because I believe that teaching is an art, not a science. It seems to me very dangerous to apply the aims and methods of science to human beings as individuals, although a statistical principle can often be used to explain their behavior in large groups and a scientific diagnosis of their physical structure is always valuable. . . . Of course it is necessary for any teacher to be orderly in planning his work and precise in his dealing with facts. But that does not make his teaching "scientific." Teaching involves emotions, which cannot be systematically appraised and employed, and human values, which are quite outside the grasp of science. "Scientific" teaching, even of scientific subjects, will be inadequate as long as both teachers and pupils are human beings. Teaching is not like inducing a chemical reaction: It is much more like painting a picture or making a piece of music, or on a lower level like planting a garden or writing a friendly letter.

But we should not equate the attempt to develop a theory about an activity with the attempt to eliminate its phenomenal, idiosyncratic, and artistic aspects. Painting and composing, and even friendly letter-writing and casual conversation, have inherent order and lawfulness that can be subjected to theoretical analysis. The painter, despite the artistry in his work, often can be shown by students of his art to be behaving according to a theory—of color, perspective, balance, or abstraction. The artist whose lawfulness is revealed does not become an automaton; ample scope remains for his subtlety and individuality. His processes and products need not remain immune to attempts at rational understanding on the part of critics and scholars.

So it is with teaching. Although teaching requires artistry, it can be subjected to scientific scrutiny. The power to explain, predict, and control that may result from such scrutiny will not dehumanize teaching. Just as engineers can still exercise ingenuity within the theory of thermodynamics, teachers will still have room for artistic variation on the theory that scientific study of teaching may establish. And for the work of those who train, hire, and supervise teachers, theory and empirical knowledge of teaching will provide scientific grounding.

Even if it had no practical value, a scientific understanding of teaching should still be sought. Like interstellar space and evolution, learning has been studied for its own sake. So teaching can be studied as a phenomenon of interest in its own right. Theories of teaching are desirable for their practical value if any is forthcoming, of course, but they are desirable in any case.

Relation of Theories of Teaching to Theories of Learning

The need for theories of teaching stems also from the insufficiency *in principle* of theories of learning. Theories of learning deal with what the learner does. But changes in education must depend in large part upon what the teacher does. That is, changes in how learners go about their business of learning occur in response to the behavior of their teachers or others in the educational establishment. Much of our knowledge about learning can be put into practice only by teachers.

And the ways in which these teachers would put this knowledge into effect constitute part of the subject of theories of teaching. Practical applications have not been gleaned from theories of learning largely because theories of teaching have not been developed. *The implications of learning theory need to be translated into implications for the behavior of teachers.* Teachers will then act on these implications in such ways as to improve learning. Theories of teaching and the empirical study of teaching may enable us to make better use of our knowledge about learning.

Is theory of learning and behavior so all-encompassing as to preclude any valid concern with theory of teaching? Hilgard (1956, p. 2) pointed out that Hull "scarcely distinguishes between a theory of learning and a theory of behavior, so important is learning in his conception of behavior. . . . Hence the systematic aspects of learning theory have come to be important to all psychologists interested in more general theories." Because teaching is a form of behavior, adequate theories of learning, or general theories of behavior, would, in this view, encompass teaching as well. But this view applies only to teaching considered as the "dependent variable," the thing to be explained. In this sense, the behavior of teachers will indeed be understood by the same theories that apply to the behavior and learning of students. The kind of theory of teaching being considered places the behavior of teachers in the position of "independent variables" as a function of which the learning of students is to be explained. That is, theories of teaching should be concerned with explaining, predicting, and controlling the ways in which teacher behavior affects the learning of students. In this perspective there is ample room for theories of teaching. Such theories would deal with a whole realm of phenomena neglected by theories of learning.

The notion that teaching itself can be autonomous (see Chapter 3, page 41), that is, a self-determined process co-ordinate with learning must be rejected, however. With learning as the dependent variable, theories of teaching become only a subclass of theories of learning: a subclass in which the independent variables consist of the behavior and characteristics of teachers. Such a conception of theories of teaching seems altogether admissible within the present argument. Theories of teaching would still need to be developed as a substantial discipline. even if they are not co-ordinate with theories of learning.

In recent years, several writers have considered the nature of a theory of teaching. On the question of whether theory of teaching must depend on theory of learning, Scandura (1966) took the position that many learning principles may be of only incidental importance to a theory of teaching. Some teaching concepts and laws, he said, have no direct counterparts in learning theory, e.g., technologies like task analysis and sequencing. Teaching theory operates at a molar level, i.e., with relatively large and unanalyzed units of behavior. And reductionism, i.e., reducing molar teacher behaviors to molecular learning principles, or principles dealing with relatively small units of behavior, is not likely to be fruitful. Ausubel (1968) held that the present "irrelevance" (we should say "inadequacy") of learning theory is not inevitable; it holds only for learning theory to date and not for "a truly realistic and scientifically viable theory of classroom learning" (p. 210). Ausubel similarly took exception to B. O. Smith's position (1960) that learning and teaching are different and that a theory of learning cannot tell one how to teach. Rather, "learning is still the only feasible measure of teaching merit . . . valid principles of teaching are necessarily based on relevant principles of learning, but are not simple and direct applications of these principles. . . . I would classify basic principles of teaching as special derivatives of school learning theory" (pp. 212, 213).

Bruner (1966a) saw a theory of instruction as differing from descriptive theories of learning by being prescriptive and normative; that is, such theory is "concerned with how what one wishes to teach can best be learned, with improving rather than describing learning" (p. 40). The theory should specify the experiences that predispose the individual toward learning, the ways in which a body of knowledge should be structured, the most effective sequences in which to present the materials, and the nature and pacing of rewards and punishments. The problem of "predispositions" refers to the activation, maintenance, and direction of the learner's exploration of alternatives. The structure and form of knowledge refer to the ways in which the mode of representation, economy, and power of the structure of any domain of knowledge affect the ability of the learner to master it. In discussing "sequence and its uses," Bruner proposed that the optimal sequence will proceed from "enactive" (e.g., movement) through "iconic" (e.g., pictorial) to "symbolic" (e.g., verbal) representations. As to the form and pacing of reinforcement, he held that knowledge of results is useful at the right time and place.

In a "Discussion of Bruner's 'Theorems' " (Bruner, 1966b, pp. 245–252), participants in a Working Conference on Research on Children's Learning agreed that, whether or not learning theory can handle the problem of instruction, it is not doing so now. On the question of whether separate theories of instruction are needed for different subject matters and grade levels, it was urged that it is possible to concentrate on "general parameters, on transdisciplinary principles which could be concretely applied in different disciplines" (p. 246). Further, it was held that a theory of instruction must rest not only on a theory of learning but also on a theory of development.

Problems concerning the nature of theory that must be faced prior to any valid development of a theory of instruction were examined by Travers (1966). He objected to the position, implied by Bruner's term *prescriptive,* that such a theory must focus on "optimum conditions."

Optimum conditions of various kinds derive from theories but are not the essence of scientific theories. . . . I would conceive of a theory of instruction as consisting of a set of propositions stating relationships between, on the one hand, measures of both the conditions to which the learner is exposed and the variables representing characteristics of the learner (p. 50).

Travers held that a major obstacle to such theory development is that the technical language needed for such a task has not yet evolved. A theory of instruction should be empirically based, and the data must be closely related to the phenomena of the classroom. Further, the dependent variables, rather than being specified in terms of behavior, should be specified in terms of tasks or problem situations or task solutions. Thus, a useful taxonomy of objectives would involve a taxonomy of tasks. The task characteristic should be directly observable rather than inferred. The tasks should be arranged into a system of scales such that, for a given outcome, all lower tasks can be successfully completed and all higher tasks cannot.

The major independent variables, in Travers' view, can be classified as relating to students, student tasks, teachers, and teacher tasks. Student task variables include those that teachers can manipulate to optimize learning; examples are reading difficulty level, sequencing variables, perceptual complexity, and concreteness versus abstractness. As for research on teacher behavior variables, the difficulty is that hypothetical patterns can be concocted but not acted out by actual teachers.

The Demands of Teacher Education

Explicit concern with the theory of teaching should benefit teacher education. In training teachers, we often seem to rely on mere inference from theory of learning to the practice of teaching. Yet, what we know about learning is inadequate to tell us what we should do about teaching. This inadequacy is clearly evident in our educational psychology courses and textbooks. The irrepressible question of students in educational psychology courses is, "How should I teach?" While they may infer a partial answer from a consideration of how pupils learn, they cannot get all of it in this way. Much of what teachers must know about teaching does not directly follow from a knowledge of the learning process. Their knowledge must be acquired explicitly rather than by inference. Farmers need to know more than how plants grow. Mechanics need to know more than how a machine works. Physicians need to know more than how the body functions. Teachers need to know more than how a student learns.

Teachers must know how to manipulate the independent variables, especially their own behaviors, that determine learning. Such knowledge cannot be derived automatically from knowledge about the learning process. To explain and control the teaching act requires a science and technology of teaching in its own right. The student of educational psychology who complains that he has learned much about learning and learners, but not about teaching, is asking for the fruits of scientific inquiry, including theories of teaching.

THE NEED FOR ANALYSIS AND SPECIFICATION

How should work toward such theory proceed? What seems to be needed is the analysis and specification of teaching. As a concept, "teaching" is a misleadingly generic term; it covers too much. It falsely suggests a single, unitary phenomenon that may fruitfully be made the subject of theory development.

Learning theory has long been hung up on a similar fallacy. Because the single term "learning" has been applied to an enormous range of phenomena, psychologists have been misled into believing that a single theory can be developed to explain all these phenomena. Animal learning in puzzle boxes and Skinner boxes, human learning of nonsense syllables and eyelid responses in the laboratory, and the learning of school subjects in classrooms have all been termed "learning." Because all these activities have been given the same name, psychologists have attempted to account for all of them by a single, unified, general theory.

Yet, as is well known, no such unification of learning theory has materialized. Research and theorizing on learning have had three main foci—animal learning, human learning in the laboratory, and human learning in the classroom. (In recent years, a fourth focus has developed: programmed learning. In time this new development may strengthen the connection between the laboratory and the school.) The various kinds of learning have not yet been embraced completely and successfully by any single learning theory. The single term, "learning," does not guarantee that a single, universally applicable theory of learning can be developed.

Some analogies to other processes may clarify this point. Medicine does not search for a single theory of illness or healing. Physicians long ago discovered that people can get sick in several basically different ways, such as being infected with germs or viruses, having organic malfunctions, suffering traumatic impacts of energy, or experiencing environmental deprivations. And, rather than a general theory of healing, physicians use several basically different approaches, such as giving medicines, using surgery, improving environments, or changing diets.

Another example is "getting rich," which is, like learning, concerned with the acquisition of something. Getting rich also takes place in many different ways—inheriting, gambling, stealing, making profits, or earning wages—and no one has tried to develop a general, unified theory of how to get rich. The concept of "getting rich" simply has no scientific value; it covers too many different processes. As a unitary concept, school learning may also have no scientific value, because it covers too many distinct phenomena and processes.

The same then might be said of teaching. The term "teaching" should not be taken to imply that teaching is a basic process to which a general theory may apply. For "teaching" embraces far too many kinds of process, of behavior, of activity, to be the proper subject of a single theory. We must not be misled by the one word "teaching" into searching for one theory to explain it.

WAYS OF ANALYZING THE CONCEPT OF TEACHING

If this argument is valid, the concept of teaching must be analyzed to reveal processes or elements that might constitute the proper subject of theories. What kinds of analysis can be made? Several can be suggested.

First, teaching can be analyzed according to *types of teacher activities*. Teachers engage in explaining activities, questioning activities, mental hygiene activities, demonstrating activities, guidance activities, order-maintaining activities, housekeeping activities, record-keeping activities, assignment-making activities, curriculum-planning activities, testing and evaluation activities, and many other kinds of activities. Sorenson and Husek (1963), in their attempt to analyze the teacher's role, specified six dimensions: information-giver, disciplinarian, adviser, counselor, motivator, and referrer. If everything a teacher does *qua* teacher is teaching, then teaching consists of many kinds of activity. It is unreasonable to expect a single theory to encompass all of these.

Second, teaching can be analyzed according to the *types of educa-*

tional objectives at which it is aimed; examples of major types are affective (emotional), psychomotor (motor skill), and cognitive (intellectual) objectives. Teaching processes can then be classified according to the domain of objectives to which they seem primarily relevant. When the teacher uses words to define, describe, or explain a concept, such as "extrapolation," his behavior may be primarily relevant to the cognitive domain. When he offers warmth and encouragement, we may consider him to be acting in ways primarily relevant to the affective domain. When he demonstrates the correct way to write a capital *F*, his behavior may be primarily relevant to psychomotor objectives. At any given moment, more than one of these domains of objectives may be affected. It may sometimes be difficult to distinguish the teacher's influence on cognitive change from his influence on affective change in students. So, when the teacher fails to explain something clearly, the student may become not only confused (cognitively) but discouraged (affectively) as well. Nonetheless, analyses of this kind may have strategic value. We should not assume that a single theory of teaching will apply to all kinds of objectives.

A third way to analyze teaching stems from the notion that teaching can be viewed as the obverse, or "mirror image," of learning and therefore has components corresponding to those of the learning process. If the learning process can be analyzed into basic elements or components—let us use Miller and Dollard's (1941) "drive," "cue," "response," and "reward" as examples—then teaching can be analyzed similarly. Corresponding components of teaching might be "motivating," "perception-directing," "response-eliciting," and "reinforcement-providing." For some elements of this analysis of learning, there are well-established separate domains of theory, such as theories of motivation and theories of perception. Similarly, theories of motivating, perception-directing, response-eliciting, and rewarding, corresponding to such elements of the teaching process, may develop. In any event, it is questionable whether a single theory of teaching should be sought to encompass all these components of the teaching process.

A fourth way to analyze teaching, already set forth in Chapter 3, derives from *families of learning theory*: conditioning theory, modeling theory, and cognitive theory. Some writers (e.g., Mowrer, 1960) conceive learning, in all its forms, to be a matter of conditioning with punishment or rewards consisting of primary or secondary reinforcements associated with independent or response-dependent stimulation. Such a conditioning theory of learning may imply a corresponding kind of theory of teaching. Other writers (e.g., Bandura, 1962) emphasize that learning consists, at least in major part, of the learner's observation of a model, whom the learner imitates. In this case, a second kind of theory of teaching is implied. A third kind of writer (e.g., Luchins, 1961) holds that learning consists of the cognitive restructuring of problematical situations. Here, a third kind of theory of teaching is suggested.

It is conceivable that the second and third of these major conceptions of learning can be reduced to the first, with some gain in parsimony and in tools of analysis and control. In some ways, the three kinds of theory seem at present to be compatible, in the sense that they do not lead to different predictions of the same data. Rather, they seem to have been developed to account for different data—for the learning of different kinds of things in different situations. If so, all three approaches to the development of theory of teaching should be of some value. Eventually, one family of theory, such as conditioning, may prove to be able to embrace all the powerful factors in learning—not merely reinforcement but also the model and the organization of content.

APPLICATIONS OF THE ANALYSES

What would a theory of teaching be concerned with, if it were to become specific? To consider some illustrative answers, let us make various selections from among the various analyses. The reader may find Table 4–1 helpful in following the argument.

TABLE 4–1. THREE EXAMPLES OF COMBINATIONS OF ACTIVITIES, OBJECTIVES, LEARNING COMPONENTS, AND CONCEPTIONS OF LEARNING

TEACHING ACTIVITY	OBJECTIVE FOR LEARNER	LEARNING PROCESS COMPONENT	APPLICABLE CONCEPTION OF LEARNING
1. Explaining	Cognitive: Ability to Extrapolate Trends	Perception of Cues	Cognitive Restructuring
2. Mental Hygiene	Affective: Security, or Willing to Respond in the Classroom	Motivation	Conditioning, or Reinforcement, of Responding
3. Demonstration	Psychomotor: Ability to Write a Capital "F"	Response	Identification with, or Imitation of, a Model

Explaining

From the teacher's activities, let us select the one called "explaining," leaving aside for the moment the mental hygiene, demonstrating, and other activities. Of the types of objectives, let us focus on the cognitive domain, and, even more specifically, on the student's ability to extrapolate trends beyond the given data. Of the components of the learning process, let us choose the perceptual, or the teacher's corresponding function of directing the student's perceptions to the salient part of his environment, which, in the present instance, consists of the kinds of trends in data that we want him to learn to extrapolate. Finally, of the families of learning theory in accordance with which we wish to derive a theory of teaching, let us choose the cognitive restructuring approach.

Having made these choices, we have reduced the problem to a much narrower concern than all of teaching. Omitted are such matters as motivating students, evaluating achievement, promoting mental health, increasing information, improving motor skills, developing students' effectiveness as group members, and so on. We are focusing on one relatively specific, although still immensely broad, aspect of all teaching: the teacher's role in engendering ability to exercise a particular intellectual skill (extrapolation) in the various academic disciplines. Motivation, mental health, social relationships, and the like, are important in the acquisition of such a skill. But for the present purpose, we regard them as subservient to the moment of truth in any classroom, when the teacher has the attention of his well-motivated, secure, and otherwise fully ready students, and faces the task of producing in them an intellectual skill with which he is concerned. What should he do? What *must* he do, if his behavior is to have the desired effect? How can the behavior of one person, a teacher, have an effect on another's acquisition of the ability to extrapolate?

We chose the cognitive restructuring as against the conditioning or the imitation conceptions of learning and, hence, of teaching. The cognitive restructuring conception is that the learner arrives at knowledge and understanding by perceiving the situation (the problem) before him and then rearranging it, through central cognitive processes, in ways that yield meaning of a rational, logically consistent kind. The teacher can engender this restructuring by pointing, either physically or verbally, and by manipulating the parts of the cognitive configuration so as to make the structure he wants learned stand out as a kind of figure against the ground of irrelevancies and distractions. The teacher manipulates the cognitive field in accordance with laws of cognition—analogous to the laws of perception governing the constancies, groupings, and whole-qualities in visual and auditory stimuli. Then the student apprehends the cognitive structure to be learned. He can no more avoid learning in this instance than he can avoid seeing the phi-phenomenon (the appearance of motion when two lights are flashed in brief succession) under proper conditions, or the Big Dipper when someone points it out to him by calling attention to it and giving him a set for a certain perception of this particular pattern of stars.

This conception of teaching follows the metaphor of the manipulator of stimuli who *compels* perceivers to see the stimuli in certain ways. Following certain principles of, say, similarity and proximity, we can compel a person to see a configuration of dots as falling into rows rather than columns. Similarly, following certain principles of cognitive structure, the teacher can "compel" his students to understand the principles of extrapolation.

Can we justify not using the conditioning and identification conceptions for this kind of teaching? The conditioning approach seems to fall short simply because such teaching does not proceed by successive approximation of responses to the objective, as is implied by the term "shaping behavior." The teacher does not get the student to move gradually toward correct extrapolating behavior by feeding him stimuli that gradually take on the form of the problem to be understood, eliciting responses that gradually approximate what is correct, and providing reinforcement appropriately along the way. Rather, the teacher can often produce the desired behavior all at once by judiciously restructuring the student's cognitive field.

As for the identification approach in this instance, it would hold that the teacher gets his results by being prestigious or positively regarded. This approach to understanding the teaching of a logically consistent set of ideas implies that prestigious models can succeed in teaching even logically inconsistent or invalid ideas. But it is unlikely that the model can get a learner to imitate behavior that the learner can plainly perceive to be logically or cognitively inconsistent. Asch's conformity-producing group-pressure situations seem to produce mere compliance rather than learning, since much of the yielding disappears in private retests (see Krech, Crutchfield, & Ballachey, 1962). Much of what we teach has an iron logic of its own; mathematics is a prime example. *To the degree that the content is logically structured,* the learner will be influenced by the structure rather than by his human model.

There happens to be a movement that is concerned with exactly the aspect of teaching being discussed. This is the effort to develop principles of programming instructional materials. For various reasons, at least some of which seem to be merely incidental and irrelevant, these efforts are currently being made on the basis of a conditioning, or reinforcement, paradigm of the learning process. Yet, at the heart of the programmed instruction movement, where principles of programming are being developed, there lies not a reinforcement psychology but a cognitive psychology. Consider the following statement from a discussion of the Ruleg (rule-example) system of programming:

> The third step is to arrange the ru [rule] index cards in an approximate order for program presentation. . . . Ordering may be according to a continuum of complexity. . . , chronology. . . , spatiality. . . , or dependence on other ru's. Interdependent relationships among rules should be carefully considered, because the understanding of one rule may depend upon the mastery of some other rules (Taber, Glaser, & Schaefer, 1965, p. 67).

Later, in describing another way of systematizing the programmer's task, the same authors discuss outlining the material to be taught and state that the major headings should be "ordered in some *rational* sequence" (Taber, Glaser, & Schaefer, 1965, p. 69, my italics).

It is not only in the broad structuring of the subject that cognitive properties of instruction are invoked. Within the frames, or small units, of a program, the programmers are also advised to give heed to laws of cognition. Thus, we are told that, in all good frames, "the response is evoked in a *meaningful* context which is often new to the student" (Taber, Glaser, & Schaefer, 1965, p. 88, my italics). In discussing prompts, or stimuli in a frame intended to make it more effective in evoking the desired response, the authors say they provide "context" (p. 90). Presumably, a prompt depends for its effectiveness on such perception-relevant or cognition-relevant properties as its similarity to, proximity to, contrast, or continuity with the other stimuli in the frame and the response to be evoked by the frame. Formal prompts work because of their mere visual or auditory similarity, while thematic prompts depend on their similarity in meaning to the desired response. Without saying so, the authors refer to perceptual and cognitive properties of stimuli throughout their discussion of the many different kinds of prompts that they describe and illustrate.

Finally, it would be easy to identify references to ideas about perception and cognition in the programmer's treatments of sequences of frames and general program characteristics. Such ideas as that of the "generalization sequence," aimed at broadening the range of stimuli to which a given response will be made, are described as including statements describing the "common properties" of the stimulus class involved. The notion of common property is a perceptual or logical one, and principles of perception and cognition enter into the determination and communication of a common property in a class of stimuli.

So there seems to be a saturation of the programmed instruction movement with cognitive psychology. For some aspects of teaching, reinforcement models seem pertinent indeed. For other aspects of teaching, however, and particularly for understanding and improving the work of live teachers in promoting comprehension within the academic disciplines, we need to focus on the cognitive aspects of teacher behavior, just as the students of programming principles have focused, however unwittingly, on the cognitive aspects of their programs. As will be noted in more detail in Chapter 8, this kind of concern has until recently been notable for its absence in research on teaching. Such research has often been concerned with who talks to whom and how much in the classroom. Or it has dealt with the teacher's warmth, permissiveness, or authoritarianism. Or it has dealt with the amount of organization and systematization that a teacher displayed in his preparation for and conduct of classroom work. Only rarely have we been concerned with the actual intellectual content, the cognitive organization, and the logical validity of what teachers say to their pupils and of what the pupils say to their teacher and to one another. When we examine a textbook, of course, these aspects of its content and organization come to the fore. We pay close attention to the logic of its arguments and the aptness and compelling power of the data and examples that the authors adduce. As is further argued in Chapter 8, we ought to look in the same way at what teachers do in the classroom.

Mental Hygiene

Let us now try another fairly likely combination of the components resulting from our analyses. From the teacher's activities, let us select his mental hygiene function. From the types of educational objectives, let us select one from the affective domain, such as the student's emotional security in the classroom situation. Of the components of the learning process, consider the motivational one, or the teacher's corresponding function of arousing in the student a desire to learn what the teacher wants him to learn. And finally, of the families of learning theory, we choose conditioning.

In this particular selection of specifications, we pay particular attention to the teacher's acts of rewarding the student's provisional tries. Dispensing praise and warmth, almost without regard to what the student does so long as it remains within classroom requirements, the teacher positively reinforces the student's efforts to comply with the teacher's demands for effort and activity. Basking in a shower of laudatory remarks and approving glances, the student gradually becomes more responsive. He shows evidence of improved security.

We select the conditioning approach here because what has to be learned has no particular cognitive structure. No set of logically organized ideas is to be grasped by the student. The goal of getting the student to feel secure enough to respond in the classroom cannot readily be achieved through any process of rational explanation or intellectual argument. Also the goal in this instance is not to get the student to behave the way the teacher does. The emotional security and activity that the student should exhibit in the classroom cannot be achieved through imitating the teacher's security and activity. Indeed, the teacher's confidence and high activity may be precisely what overwhelms the student and causes him to withdraw into nonparticipation. For this particular combination of (a) mental hygiene activity, (b) affective objective, and (c) motivational component of the learning process, it is not the student's identification with the teacher that will bring about the security we want. It is rather the teacher's consistent reinforcement, following the conditioning approach to the teaching process, that will gradually "shape" the student's behavior into a form reflecting emotional security.

Demonstration

A third selection from our analyses of teaching will illustrate still a different theory of teaching. Here we select the teacher's demonstrating activities, aimed at psychomotor objectives, with special concern for the response component of the learning process. Consider the teacher demonstrating the proper way to write the capital letter F. Here it seems appropriate to emphasize the modeling imitation conception of the teaching process. The teacher goes to the blackboard and writes the letter F with the motions that he wants his students to use. The teacher's prestige makes his way of performing this task unquestionably correct in the eyes of his students. His students watch him do it and then do it themselves. Depending on the maturity of their psychomotor skills, their success may be complete or partial. But given sufficient maturity, the students will write the letter F with the motions that the teacher wants them to use. They makes responses matching those of the teacher. Their imitation involves combining responses into relatively complex new patterns solely by observing the performance of another person.

Again, what is to be learned has no necessary logic. Many different ways of writing the letter F could be defended on rational grounds.

So the teacher does not carry out his task by explaining the reasons for a particular solution of the problem of how to write the letter. He does not derive his solution by building on earlier conclusions or premises. He has no ideational structure for his students to incorporate into their own thinking. The notion of teaching by cognitive restructuring does not seem to apply to this particular form of teaching.

The conditioning approach here would entail a highly inefficient kind of gradual approximation to the desired behavior. To proceed through a painstaking process of response differentiation and extinction, gradually reinforcing desired bits of writing behavior and extinguishing the undesired ones, would be a wearisome and ineffective undertaking. It seems better to characterize the teaching process in this instance as a matter of inducing imitation of what is demonstrated by a prestigious model with whom the student identifies.

Sometimes, the choice of teaching and learning theories is much more arguable. Thus in Chapter 3 we indicated how the three conceptions of learning, and their corresponding approaches to teaching, have been applied to the objective of making students more creative.

The foregoing may nevertheless not represent the most fruitful ways of analyzing the concept of teaching. Other analyses, yielding different components, are possible. Other combinations of resulting components may be more interesting to persons developing theories of teaching. But some such analyses and choices must be made before the properly specified concern of a theory can be isolated. Otherwise, attempts to develop theories of teaching will founder on excessive generality. To avoid such analyses and choices is to assume that the single word *teaching* denotes a single process amenable to a single, general theory. Although learning the Morse code, learning political attitudes, and learning mathematics are all called "learning," they do not necessarily involve the same kind of process. Although the teaching of all these things is called by the one name of teaching, it does not follow that a single theory of teaching can account for how the teacher does his work.

Chapter 5   The Uses of Paradigms and Theories

Whatever may have been its status in an earlier period, the term *theoretical* has an attractive connotation now. If it once suggested the opposite of "practical," it now is recognized as referring to the fundamental basis of practice. If "theorizing" once implied an escape from empirical research, it is now considered necessary to the planning and interpretation of such research. It is no longer necessary to proclaim, at least as a precept, the thesis that theoretical concerns are centrally significant in any branch of science or technology.

In the physical sciences, every schoolboy knows about the explosive potential of the theoretician's scribblings. In the social sciences, theories were once expected to be overarching world views and master prescriptions, like socialism and the single tax. Now theories are developed for much more modest topics, like learning, leadership, and cooperation, and one need not don a charismatic mantle in order to attempt to theorize.

Despite its present acceptance, the idea of "theory" still keeps many students at a distance. Theorizing is something that they hesitate to attempt. Other aspects of research, like collecting and analyzing data, seem familiar and comfortable in comparison with the task of developing or using theory. As one author put it:

> There is no more arcane term in general use among humanists and social scientists than the term "theory." To the graduate student it carries with it a modest prestige suggesting that a person who is a theorist is brighter, deals with "deeper" and more complex material, and has insights which others who identify themselves differently do not have (Lane, 1961, p. 26).

Yet, of course, all men, including graduate students, are theorists. They differ not in whether they use theory, but in the degree to which they are aware of the theory they use. The choice before the man in the street and the research worker alike is not whether to theorize but whether to articulate his theory, to make it explicit, to get it out in the open where he can examine it. Implicit theories—of personality, of learning, and indeed of teaching—are used by all of us in our everyday affairs. Often such theories take the form of folk sayings, proverbs, slogans, the unquestioned wisdom of the race. The scientist, on the other hand, explicates his theory and goes through procedures that help him test it.

The present chapter will not examine theory from the point of view of philosophy of science. We shall rather display some of the forms that theoretical work has taken in research on teaching. In the first section, we consider the nature of paradigms as working tools in behavioral research. In the second section, we examine the ways in which theorizing fits into the work of behavioral scientists, i.e., how theories serve as both ends and means in such research. In the next chapter, paradigms for research on teaching will be described and their implications examined.

PARADIGMS: THEIR NATURE AND USES

Paradigms are models, patterns, or schemata. Paradigms are not theories; they are rather ways of thinking or patterns for research that, when carried out, can lead to the development of theory.

Paradigms derive their usefulness from their generality. By definition, they apply to all specific instances of a whole class of events or processes. When one has chosen a paradigm for his research, he has made crucial decisions concerning the kinds of variables and relationships between variables that he will investigate. Paradigms for research imply a kind of commitment, however preliminary or tentative, to a research program. The investigator, having chosen his paradigm, may use only a part of it for any given research project, but the paradigm of his research remains in the background, providing the framework, or sense of the whole, in which his project is embedded.

Paradigms may represent variables and their relationships in some graphic or outline form. Events or phenomena that have various temporal, spatial, causal, or logical relationships are portrayed in these relationships by boxes, connecting lines, and positions on vertical and horizontal dimensions. The classical portrayal of Pavlovian conditioning, shown in Fig. 5–1, illustrates this aspect of a paradigm. The left-hand part of Fig. 5–1 shows an unconditioned stimulus, S_u, eliciting an unconditioned response, R_u. The center part shows S_u being regularly preceded by a conditioned stimulus, S_c. Eventually, as shown in the right-hand part, S_c alone elicits R_c.

Fig. 5–2 shows the paradigm for operant conditioning. Here the unconditioned stimulus for the response R is unknown and is indicated by the small s. For some reason, R occurs. If R is followed by a reinforcing stimulus, S, it becomes more probable and its rate increases.

Here, the generality of the paradigms implies that the process will occur regardless of the particular kinds of stimuli and responses in-

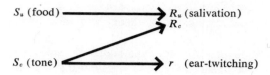

Fig. 5–1. Paradigm of Pavlovian conditioning. The two unconditioned reflexes shown are (a) food-salivation, (b) tone ear-twitching. The conditioned reflex, the tone-salivation, develops after repeated occurrences of the tone just prior to, or simultaneously with the food.

Fig. 5–2. Paradigm for operant conditioning. The response R is emitted (i.e., its unconditioned stimulus cannot be specified) and is followed by a reinforcing stimulus, which increases the probability, rate, or strength of R.

volved. The stimuli may be bells, food, lights, words, electric shocks, the sight of people, an approving "uh-huh" expression, or whatever; the responses may be salivation, bar pressing, use of the word "I," favorable self-references, or whatever. The paradigms are intended to be general and apply to all of the possibilities. They serve research by suggesting that various specific instances of stimuli and responses be tried. Also, various temporal relations between S_u and S_c can be explored; thus, the question can be raised whether S_c must always precede S_u, and whether the interval between S_u and S_c affects the conditioning process.

Explicit and Implicit Paradigms and Their Effects

Paradigms, like theories, can be either explicit or implicit. Some have been set forth in full panoply, with diagrams and elaborations of their connections with completed or projected research. Other paradigms are implicit in what authors have done or proposed by way of research. In either case, we seek to use the paradigm as an intellectual tool for examining crucial aspects of research on teaching.

Choice of a paradigm, whether deliberate or unthinking, determines much about the research that will be done. The style, design, and approach of a research undertaking—indeed, the likelihood that it will bear fruit—are conditioned in large part by the paradigm with which the investigator begins. Whether he will perform an experiment, in the sense of actually manipulating one or more variables, or a correlational study, in the sense of studying relationships between variables measured as they occur in nature, may be determined by his paradigm.

Whether he will seek relationships between variables that have some promise, on logical and empirical grounds, of being related, may be determined by his paradigm. A good paradigm may lead him to search for relationships between variables that have a good likelihood of being related. So one investigation (Rocchio & Kearney, 1956) examined the correlation between the teacher's authoritarianism on a verbal, printed test, and the teacher's tendency to nonpromote students, because a paradigm (implicit in this case) portrayed a connection between these variables; the results supported the hypothesis and the paradigm was strengthened.

Paradigms and Scientific Revolutions

Although the concept of paradigm has been around for a long time in discussions of science, it has recently received fresh attention from historians and philosophers of science. In particular, Kuhn (1962) has made much of the importance of paradigms. By one of his definitions, a paradigm consists of the "universally recognized scientific achievements that for a time provide model problems and solutions to a community of practitioners" of science (p. x). Paradigms include "ways of seeing the world" (p. 4), "conceptual boxes" (p. 5), "a set of commitments" (p. 6), which determine the problems available for scientific scrutiny and provide "an intertwined body of theoretical and methodological belief" (p. 17). In science, successful new paradigms make old ones disappear and compel the allegiance of all reputable scientists. New paradigms lead to new journals, new societies, and new curricula for the training of scientists. Having a good paradigm makes it unnecessary for scientists to examine first principles and to justify themselves continually. It is symptomatic of the state of research on teaching that we should re-examine our first principles.

What makes a paradigm successful, and how can we tell when we need a new one? A good paradigm solves crucial problems, eliminates anomalies, and improves the match between the facts and the paradigm's predictions. Normal science, which is what Kuhn calls the activity of scientists working with successful paradigms, consists mostly of "mopping-up operations" (p. 23), and it is what engages most scientists throughout their careers. This mopping-up consists of determining facts with greater precision in a larger variety of situations, verifying new predictions from the paradigm theory, and resolving ambiguities through articulation of theory. The paradigm provides criteria for choosing scientific problems. Embracing conceptual, theoretical, instrumental, and methodological commitments "in a strong network," a paradigm sets the task for a whole generation or more of scientific workers in the field to which it applies. Eventually, however, new findings, anomalies, and disappointments of paradigm-induced expectations create a crisis in the science, and a new paradigm appears. Such an event, according to Kuhn, constitutes a scientific revolution. (It should be noted, parenthetically, that Norval Hanson [Phi Delta Kappa, 1964, pp. 180–181] considered this conception circular. Kuhn seems to define paradigms as sets of ideas whose overthrow occasions scientific revolutions and to define the latter as events in science that follow upon new paradigms.)

For his examples, Kuhn drew entirely upon the history of the natural sciences. He gave much detail on the course of the scientific revolutions that yielded such new paradigms as Copernican theory, Lavoisier's theory of oxidation, Newton's laws, Darwin's theory of evolution, Einstein's theory of relativity, and Marie Curie's theory of radioactivity.

Can paradigms in Kuhn's sense be found in the behavioral sciences, of which research on teaching is a branch? In psychology, the whole field of factor analysis exemplifies a paradigm, originated by Charles Spearman and developed by such men as Thurstone, Kelley, Thomson, and Hotelling. Conditioning theory, as originated by Pavlov and Thorndike, and extended by Hull and Skinner, constitutes a paradigm. And, of course, so does the kind of theory associated with the name of Freud.

These diverse movements in psychology have much in common with one another and with the paradigms of the physical and biological sciences. Each has set the pattern for conceptual, theoretical, and methodological developments that have kept generations of scientists busy in the mopping-up operation that, in Kuhn's view, constitutes the work of normal science. Factor analysis is still very much alive today as a way of structuring and dimensionalizing not just mental abilities, with which it got started, but also attitudes, individuals, occasions, and other things. It has generated new journals, courses, and societies of research workers who share this paradigm and shape their careers according to it. The same thing can be said of operant conditioning theory, vigorously cultivated by the Skinnerians, with their own journals, courses, and societies.

In scientific work in education, perhaps the model of evaluation developed by Ralph Tyler qualifies as such a system of ideas. As will be recalled, that model emphasized the importance of defining educational objectives in terms of student behavior as the first step in evaluating educational outcomes. A whole generation of measurement workers in education has devoted itself to the application, refinement, extension, and elaboration of this paradigm, enunciated and promulgated in the early 1930's. Taxonomies of educational objectives, evaluation procedures and programs, and applications of the concept of behavioral definition to instructional problems have followed from this paradigm.

Three Kinds of Paradigms

Do we have paradigms in research on teaching? If so, we assume that it is desirable to examine them. It may be that nothing in this field at present merits the status of paradigm. The field may well be in a pre-paradigmatic stage of development, where no scientific approach has yet compelled the allegiance of research workers.

It is possible to conceive of three kinds of paradigms: substantive, methodological, and logistical. Substantive paradigms deal with the concepts (in research on teaching, these are educational, psychological, and sociological variables) and their relationships that constitute the subject matter of the field. These paradigms are the field's way of abstracting and focusing on a certain set of the enormously varied phenomena in the natural world. For example, methods of teaching and types of achievement are substantive concerns of research on teaching.

Methodological paradigms apply to ways of measuring variables and determining relationships between them. In research on teaching, these are the tests and statistical methods, the ways of collecting and analyzing data, the schemes of observation, rating, judging, testing, experimenting, and the ways of correlating, analyzing variance, factor analyzing, and so on.

Logistical paradigms refer to the structures, sources, and supplies of men and money. They also refer to the organizational arrangements entailed in getting research planned, executed, interpreted, communicated, applied, and improved.

These three kinds of paradigms do not, of course, exist in isolation. They interact; each affects the others. Substantive paradigms interact with methodological ones, and these in turn have implications for the kinds of logistics that will facilitate research. Kuhn was right in viewing paradigms as tightly intertwined systems of concepts, theories, instruments, and methods, and any separate treatment of them does some violence to the realities of research work. Nonetheless, it is possible to focus, as is done in the next chapter, on the substantive paradigms for research on teaching.

THE USES OF THEORY

Theories as Ends

Research workers use theories as means and also set them up as ends. As ends, or goals, theories are not mere pleasant adjuncts to the facts; rather, they are the *raison d'être* of scientific work, the crux of the matter. Not mere prediction or control, but understanding in the light of theoretical formulation and explanation, is in this view the central aim of science. Prediction may rest on empirical correlations that do not necessarily make sense. Control can be achieved with techniques that we actually miscomprehend. We can predict the mean score on achievement tests of the high school seniors of a state from the mean per capita expenditure for alcohol of the teachers of the state; this prediction, although it will have far better than chance accuracy, may not be based on any genuine understanding of the connection between the two variables. Or a medicine man may successfully control the behavior of a fellow tribesman by means of hypnotic suggestion while believing a wildly erroneous explanation of how he achieves his effects.

Similarly, understanding, or theoretical formulation, itself may not enable us to predict or control. We can understand evolution as a natural process although no one has yet been able to predict or control an actual instance of evolution; the same may be said of earthquakes or volcanic eruptions.

Hence, these three objectives of science—understanding, prediction, and control—are to some extent independent and distinct. Theory as an end belongs to the first of the three, namely, understanding. To be able to interrelate a set of variables on the basis of the rules of logic is to have a theory concerning those variables. To build such theory is the goal of many scientists. To build such theory around variables concerning the behavior or characteristics of teachers may be regarded as a prime end of research on teaching.

Theories as Means

As means, or tools, theories allow the research worker to straighten out his thinking, to bring order into his concepts and hypotheses, and perhaps to rationalize what he is doing. As Guba and Getzels (1955) put it, a theoretical framework sharpens research objectives, suggests what variables should be eliminated as nonmeaningful and hence wasteful, increases the likelihood of significant findings, simplifies the complex task of interpreting results, aids in interpreting meaningful even if nonsignificant results, and makes research cumulative from one study to the next.

How do research workers actually behave in using theory, or in theorizing, as they go about their job? There are at least two views on this question. Sometimes the research worker is described as proceeding in a logical fashion from established facts and relationships, or premises, to the derivation of new hypotheses, which he then tests empirically. It is even better, in this view, if the research worker states a complex theory, formulating the state of knowledge in his area, rather than merely a "single-idea" theory, based on a single postulate. Accordingly, the research worker carefully reviews the literature, gathering together the various ideas in the field, to reveal the gaps in knowledge. It was in keeping with this view of research behavior that the following advice was offered:

> The review of the literature, if it is conducted in the way described here, should provide an overview of the current framework of theory in the area in which it is proposed to undertake an investigation. The student may be expected to abstract from his review of the literature a theory in terms of which he plans to work. A minimum requirement should be that he draw up a statement covering the essential features of the theory, but preferably he should be more ambitious and draft the theory as a set of postulates. He should then show how his hypotheses represent a series of deductions from these postulates. This he will find to be a worthwhile exercise in clear thinking (Travers, 1958, pp. 75–76).

In contrast with this approach, we can find experienced research workers testifying that they go through no process so logical and orderly. They disclaim systematically reviewing the literature, designing crucial experiments, collecting data, analyzing results, and drawing conclusions. Instead, they admit to engaging in a much less orderly process. Here is how a seminar composed of distinguished, productive research workers in psychology described their working methods:

> Actually, the process of doing research . . . is a rather informal, often illogical and sometimes messy-looking affair. It includes a great deal of floundering around in the empirical world. . . . Somewhere and somehow in the process of floundering, the research worker will get an idea. In fact, he will get many ideas. On largely intuitive grounds he will reject most of his ideas and will accept others as the basis for extended work. . . . If the idea happens to be a good one, he may make a significant positive contribution to his science—"may" because between the idea and the contribution lies a lot of persistence, originality, intuition, and hard work. It is in this sort of activity, rather far removed from the public, more orderly and systematic phases of scientific work, that the productive research worker spends much of his time and effort (American Psychological Association, Education and Training Board, 1959, p. 169).

According to these research workers, the more formal picture of research work arose from the logical nature of the finished product. The picture also arose because it is easier to describe the design, statistics, and scholarship aspects of research than the origination, choice, and development of ideas.

The process of getting and developing ideas is undoubtedly a confused mixture of observation, thinking, asking why, cherishing little unformed notions, etc. Some people . . . work very effectively with ideas that have an iceberg quality, that is, most of the content is submerged . . . and not made explicit until a very late stage of the research. . . . As a consequence, it is easy in the training of research workers to overemphasize highly formal rigorous theory where the rules of logic can apply. It is equally easy to decry "theory". . . .

We doubt whether either of these extreme positions, if adopted seriously, can be anything but a hindrance to the research worker. The importance of the vague notion, difficult as it is to explain, should be emphasized. . . . But it should also be emphasized that the notion cannot be allowed to remain forever vague; ideas must eventually achieve clarity and testability if they are to receive serious attention from other researchers (American Psychological Association, Education and Training Board, 1959, pp. 172–173).

In short, the use of theory as a tool in research cannot be reduced to a formula. But it can be accepted as a valuable adjunct to the research process at some stage of the work in one way or another. Some familiarity with the theories of other research workers, and their implicit or explicit paradigms in particular, will make for more sophisticated effort. Awareness, and even planning, of his choice of a paradigm may help the research worker.

But some scientists do not accept this premise. In particular, Skinner (1959), in a witty but earnest case history of himself as a scientist, has thrown doubt on the value of theory. In view of his resounding success in research—not only on the behavior of subhuman organisms but in recent years on teaching with machines—his position should be known to any prospective research worker. Only a few quotations of his "unformalized principles of scientific practice" can be given here to intimate the spirit of his approach; the reader must go to the full case history for an adequate grasp of it.

1. "When you run onto something interesting, drop everything else and study it" (p. 81).

2. "Some ways of doing research are easier than others" (p. 82). (For example, automatize the collection of data and administration of experimental variables.)

3. "Some people are lucky" (p. 85). (Good ideas may come through chance occurrences in the laboratory.)

4. "Apparatuses sometimes break down" (p. 86). (The investigator may sometimes discover a new and important experimental variable in what goes wrong.)

This account of my scientific behavior . . . is as exact in letter and spirit as I can now make it. The notes, data, and publications which I have examined do not show that I ever behaved in the manner of Man Thinking as described by John Stuart Mill or John Dewey or in reconstructions of scientific behavior by other philosophers of science. I never faced a Problem which was more than the eternal problem of finding order. I never attacked a problem by constructing a Hypothesis. I never deduced Theorems or submitted them to Experimental Check. So far as I can see, I had no preconceived Model of behavior—certainly not a physiological or mentalistic one and, I believe, not a conceptual one (Skinner, 1959, p. 88).

Skinner's argument needs consideration even beyond the fact that, as he says, "We have no more reason to say that all psychologists should behave as I have behaved than that they should all behave like R. A. Fisher" (p. 99). Apart from his sustained concern with "the eternal problem of finding order," we should note that Skinner must have known some paradigms, e.g., the paradigm for Pavlovian conditioning, as the basis for his own distinction between respondent and operant behavior. Whether the knowledge of the Pavlovian paradigm helped him formulate his own in advance, or rather merely after his research had been done, may not matter. Either as tools or as products, paradigms may be found in Skinner's work. If paradigms are not useful in discovering a new truth, they may at least be useful in communicating it. The recipient of the communication may then find the paradigm serviceable in his own work.

In some ways, of course, Skinner is indisputably right. The research worker should not set up a paradigm in advance and then persist in following it through, come what may. As alleys turn blind, they should be abandoned. As promising leads appear, they should be followed up. What seems to be needed in research, and what Skinner's testimony bears upon, is a kind of artistry about which we still know little. Knowing the paradigm for a concerto will not empower a composer to write a good one. And knowing his way around paradigms for research on teaching will not empower the research worker to contribute to scientific knowledge about teaching. Yet, even if use of a paradigm is never sufficient to ensure fruitful research, it will usually be necessary.

Usages of "Theory"

One widely noted usage of the term *theory* should be distinguished from the one employed here. Skinner (1950) used the term to refer to "any explanation of an observed fact which appeals to events taking place somewhere else, at some other level of observation, described in different terms, and measured, if at all, in different dimensions" (p. 193). With respect to the study of learning, Skinner questioned whether such theories are necessary. Such theories—whether neurophysiological, mental, or conceptual—were considered by Skinner to have the effect of diverting us from the search for and exploration of relevant manipulable variables on which behavior might be dependent. Attributing behavior to a neural or mental event, real or conceptual, tends in Skinner's view to make us forget that we still need to account for the neural or mental event and also to give us an unwarranted satisfaction with the state of our knowledge.

In another sense of the term, however, Skinner does admit the possibility of fruitful theory: "a formal representation of the data reduced to a minimal number of terms" (p. 216). Such theories possess the advantage of generality beyond particular facts but do not refer to another dimensional system and hence do not obstruct the search for functional relations. It is this sense of the term that most writers intend. Hence Skinner's well-known antitheoretical position does not apply to the kind of theory of teaching considered here.

Generally, we use the term *theory* in a modest sense—to refer to any systematic ordering of ideas about the phenomena of a field of inquiry. We use the term in antithesis to ad hoc, disorderly planning or interpretation of research, and in contrast to what has been called "dust-bowl empiricism," in which the investigator looks for facts wherever he may find them, with little prior consideration of where it may be most valuable to look and with little idea of how he will interpret what he finds.

There has been much research of the kind against which our concern with theory is aimed. As one committee stated:

> Throughout both reports of this Committee has run the conviction that the present condition of research on teacher effectiveness holds little promise of yielding results commensurate with the needs of American education. This condition has two significant characteristics: disorganization and lack of orientation to other behavioral sciences. By disorganization, we mean the condition in which, at present, research too often proceeds without explicit theoretical framework, in intellectual disarray, to the testing of myriads of arbitrary, unrationalized hypotheses. The studies too often interact little with each other, do not fall into place within any scheme, and hence add little to the understanding of the teaching process (American Educational Research Association, Committee on the Criteria of Teacher Effectiveness, 1953, p. 657).

Our concern with theories and paradigms is therefore aimed at furthering more systematic and orderly approaches to the formulation of the variables and hypotheses that enter into research on teaching. We urge no movement away from facts. It is merely the ill-considered collection of facts against which we argue. We should not aspire to any large-scale deductive system, with theorems rigorously derived from postulates and axioms. But neither should we remain content with mere factual data—averages, differences, or correlations—on which the research worker has imposed little rationale.

Chapter 6   Substantive Paradigms

We come now to substantive paradigms for research on teaching. Our effort here has little precedent; there is no literature that goes openly by the name we have adopted for this chapter. Yet we shall not be completely at a loss for references. Like Moliére's bourgeois gentleman, who had been speaking prose all his life without knowing it, research on teaching has inescapably had its paradigms. We shall first examine the kind of paradigm that has dominated such research: what we call "criterion-of-effectiveness" paradigms. Then we shall turn to a variety of other paradigms that do *not* concern themselves, first and last, with the effectiveness of teachers.

CRITERION-OF-EFFECTIVENESS PARADIGMS

If we ask Anyman, "Why do research on teaching?" his answer is likely to be: "To discover what makes a good teacher." He can easily elaborate on his reply. We need such research in order better to select candidates for teacher training, to design teacher education programs, to provide a basis for teacher certification, to make possible better hiring and promotion policies, to enlighten the supervisors of teachers in service. There is no lack of practical justification for research on the questions of how teacher effectiveness can be measured, predicted, and improved.

Not only the layman has given this answer. Concern with teacher effectiveness has also held almost complete dominion over the conceptions that most research workers have brought to the field of teaching. The major bibliographies, reviews, and summaries of research on teaching (e.g., Barr, 1948; Barr, et al., 1961; Castetter, Standlee, & Fattu, 1954; Domas & Tiedeman, 1950; Mitzel, 1960; Morsh & Wilder, 1954; Ryans, 1960b; Tomlinson, 1955a, 1955b; Watters, 1954) have reflected this concern with the unfailing inclusion in their titles of such terms as "effectiveness," "competence," "evaluation," and "appraisal." The same is true of much of the research reviewed in the *Handbook of Research on Teaching* (Gage, 1963).

As soon as the idea of effectiveness enters the research, the question of a criterion of effectiveness is raised. The paradigm has then taken the following form: Identify or select a criterion (or a set of criteria) of teacher effectiveness. This criterion then becomes the dependent variable. The research task is then (1) to measure this criterion, (2) to measure potential correlates of this criterion, and (3) to determine the actual correlations between the criterion and its potential correlates. In short, variables in research on teaching conducted according to the "criterion-of-effectiveness" paradigm have typically been placed in two categories: criterion variables and potential correlates. Figure 6–1 schematizes this paradigm in its simplest form. It is noteworthy that the two articles on "Teacher Effectiveness" in the third edition of the *Encyclopedia of Educational Research* were organized in just this way: "Criteria of teacher effectiveness" (Mitzel, 1960) and "Prediction of teacher effectiveness" (Ryans, 1960b).

Often, for the sake of convenience in exploratory work, the measurements of both potential correlates and criteria have been made at about the same time. The resulting correlations are then considered to reflect the "concurrent validity" of the potential correlates. Sometimes the potential correlates have been measured some months or years prior to the measurement of the criterion variable. In such research, the correlations are considered to indicate the "predictive validity" of the potential correlates.

The correlations between other variables and criterion variables need not be simple "zero-order" ones, i.e., correlations involving only two variables, one a criterion variable and the other a predictor variable. Partial and multiple correlations may be computed between sets of *two or more* predictor variables and a criterion variable. Factor analysis (e.g., Schmid, 1961) may be applied to the intercorrelations of whole batteries of variables, consisting of sets of predictor and criterion variables. But, for our present concerns, these are merely elaborations of the same basic criterion-of-effectiveness paradigm.

The reader familiar with personnel selection research will recognize the criterion-of-effectiveness paradigm as indigenous to that field. Whether the purpose has been to select college students or clerical workers, clinical psychologists or airplane pilots, the same paradigm has prevailed: Get a criterion and then find its predictors. The widespread use and practical value of such research has been characterized

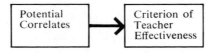

Fig. 6–1. The Criterion-of-Effectiveness Paradigm for Research on Teaching.

(Cronbach, 1949, p. 3) as an "outstanding achievement of the social sciences in recent decades." It is easy to understand the devotion to this paradigm—so successful in so many realms—on the part of researchers on teaching.

Types of Criteria of Effectiveness

In research on teaching, as in its other fields of application, the criterion-of-effectiveness paradigm has taken special forms. Apart from the whole question of what potential correlates to try, much analysis has been devoted to the criterion question itself. We turn now to paradigms that have been developed for the criterion problem.

The Wisconsin Studies. Perhaps the most extended employment of the criterion-of-effectiveness paradigm was that of Barr, who conducted and led studies of this kind at the University of Wisconsin over several decades (Barr, et al., 1961). As shown in Table 6–1, Beecher (1961) listed seven categories of criteria of teacher effectiveness used in the Wisconsin studies along with the frequencies with which they were used.

Beecher also presented a table showing the findings on 104 of the 182 "data-gathering devices," or potential correlates, used in the Wis-

TABLE 6–1.   CRITERIA AND THEIR FREQUENCY OF USE IN THE WISCONSIN STUDIES[a]

CRITERION	FREQUENCY
1. In-service Rating	
a. By the superintendent	9
b. By the principal	24
c. By other supervisory officials	51
d. By teacher educators	20
e. By departmental personnel in areas of specialization	4
f. By state departmental personnel	11
g. Self rating	11
2. Peer Rating	6
3. Pupil Gain Score	70
4. Pupil Rating	16
5. Composite of Test Scores from Tests Thought to Measure Teaching Effectiveness	14
6. Practice Teaching Grades	13
7. Combination or Composites of Some or All of the Above Criteria	83
Total	332

[a] After Beecher, 1961, pp. 30–31.

consin studies. For each correlate, he gave the reliability (as estimated by methods unspecified in the table) and validity in terms of correlation with one of the foregoing types of criteria or in terms of mean pupil gain on a measure of achievement. Beecher starred 74 of the 104 measures as having correlated .36 or more with the indicated criteria. In this sense, at least, the Wisconsin studies brought forth positive results. The compendium of findings provided by Beecher impressively displays the fruits of the criterion-of-effectiveness paradigm. This approach to research, in the Wisconsin program alone, apart from many other studies in which it has been used, has not lacked thorough exploitation. Any shortcomings in its scientific and practical yield cannot be attributed to a failure to give it a try.

The Domas-Tiedeman Categories. A further paradigm for criteria of teacher effectiveness may be derived from what is implicit in the index of the 1,000-item annotated bibliography prepared by Domas and Tiedeman (1950). Upon analysis, this paradigm turns out to depend primarily on the following distinctions:

1. Between (a) *in-service* and (b) *in-training* teachers;

2. Between criteria based on (a) *pupil achievement,* (b) *judgments* by administrators, teachers themselves, fellow teachers, student teachers, pupils, or laypersons, and (c) *performance on tests* of "teaching ability," etc.;

3. Between pupil achievement criteria (a) *"objectively"* observed and (b) those *"subjectively"* evaluated by administrators or teachers. Figure 6–2 shows an organization chart of criteria based on these distinctions. It will be noted that these criteria embody different points on the "ultimacy" and "levels" continua to be described below. The letters and numbers in the boxes in Fig. 6–2 are those used in the Domas-Tiedeman index.

The "Ultimacy" of Criteria of Teacher Effectiveness

The concept of "criterion of teacher effectiveness" connotes educational or social values of some kind. By teacher "effectiveness" is usually meant the teacher's effect on the realization of some value. Usually, the value takes the form of some educational objective, defined in terms of desired pupil behaviors, abilities, habits, or characteristics. Hence, the ultimate criterion of a teacher's effectiveness is usually considered to be his effect on his pupil's achievement of such objectives. The terms *pupil gain* and *pupil growth* are used to refer to this kind of ultimate criterion. Adjusted measures of pupil achievement after coming under a teacher's influence have been used to define such gain operationally. Ackerman (1954) and Mitzel and Gross

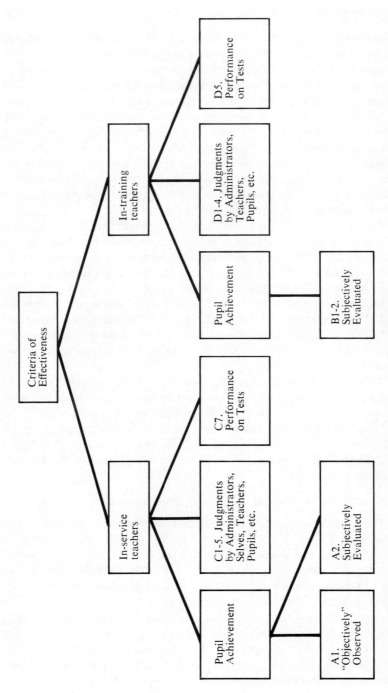

Fig. 6–2. Paradigm of Criteria of Teacher Effectiveness Derived from Classification of Annotations by Domas and Tiedeman (1950, pp. 214–215).

(1956) have reviewed studies in which pupil-gain criteria of teacher effectiveness have been used.

Many difficulties, both conceptual and practical, beset the use of pupil-gain criteria for either research or administrative purposes. These difficulties have been elaborated elsewhere (e.g., Mitzel, 1960; Ryans, 1960a, pp. 44–45). Here we note merely that they have led to the employment in much research of criteria that are not "ultimate." It was the realization that other criteria are seldom entirely escapable in research based on the criterion-of-effectiveness paradigm that led the Committee on the Criteria of Teacher Effectiveness (American Educational Research Association, 1952) to formulate an ultimacy paradigm for such criteria. This paradigm arranged criteria of teacher effectiveness on a continuum descending from the "ultimate" to the "proximate." At the top of the hierarchy of "ultimacy" might be such a criterion as "the teacher's effect on his pupils' achievement and happiness in life." Next might come "the teacher's effect on his pupils' achievement in subsequent schooling." Third might be "the teacher's effect on his pupils' achievement of current educational objectives." Much lower in the scale would be "parents' satisfaction with the teacher," "teacher's grades in student teaching courses," and "teacher's score on an intelligence test." Figure 6–3 shows an adaptation of this paradigm.

By this paradigm, each criterion depended for its validity on its correlation, or better, its functional relationship, with criteria higher on the continuum. Much criticism of research on teaching has been based on the critic's dissatisfaction with the position of someone else's

ULTIMATE CRITERION

Teachers' effect on:
    pupils' achievement and happiness in life
    pupils' achievement in subsequent schooling
    pupils' achievement of current educational objectives
    pupils' satisfaction with the teacher
    parents' satisfaction with the teacher
    superintendents' satisfaction with the teacher
Teachers' "values" or evaluative attitudes
Teachers' knowledge of educational psychology and mental hygiene
Teachers' emotional and social adjustment
Teachers' knowledge of methods of curriculum construction
Teachers' knowledge of the subject matter
Teachers' interest in the subject matter
Teachers' grades in practice teaching courses
Teachers' grades in education courses
Teachers' intelligence

Fig. 6–3. The Hierarchy of Criteria According to "Ultimacy" (After American Educational Research Association, 1952, pp. 243–244).

criterion on this continuum. The rank of some of these criteria has been hotly argued, as one might expect. For example, some educators have held that the superintendent's satisfaction with the teacher made the big difference in a teacher's career; therefore this criterion should be higher on the scale, and research should be directed toward the prediction of it. Others have held that, regardless of its "real-life" importance to teachers, this criterion has been shown to be uncorrelated with pupil gain and hence should be disregarded.

"Career Levels" and Criteria of Effectiveness

The list of criteria shown in Fig. 6–3 applies primarily to teachers already employed. Yet there are other stages of the teacher's career at which criteria are needed in research on teaching by the criterion paradigm. In its second report, the Committee on the Criteria of Teacher Effectiveness (American Educational Research Association, 1953) presented a paradigm of criteria organized on the basis of the different levels, or stages, in the progression from candidate for teacher training to on-the-job operation as a full-fledged teacher. Figure 6–4 shows this paradigm.

Four different levels, or stages, of a teacher's career were identified: (1) the prospective teacher-in-training; (2) the student in a teacher education program; (3) the student just completing teacher training; and (4) the teacher on the job. Decisions concerning persons at each of these levels take different forms. At Level 1, we make decisions concerning applicants for admission to teacher education programs, or we attempt to provide guidance for high school graduates as to the suitability of teaching as a vocation for them. At Level 2, we make decisions concerning programs for preparing teachers on the basis of evidence or assumptions concerning the hoped-for eventual effects of these programs on the teachers' subsequent effects on pupils; or, we make decisions concerning the guidance of students who are in teacher education programs. At Level 3, decisions as to the certification of teachers or the selection of teachers for jobs from among graduates of teacher education programs are in order. At Level 4, decisions are made as to the granting of tenure to teachers or the selection of teachers from among teachers who have taught, either for new positions or for special assignments or special treatments, such as salary increases. Obviously, the "predictors" at higher levels can serve as criteria for the predictors at lower levels.

A Refinement of the Criterion-of-Effectiveness Paradigm

As presented thus far, the effectiveness paradigm has only two classes of variables: predictors and criteria. The "ultimacy" and

---

ULTIMATE CRITERIA
Changes in pupils (while in school, or upon completion of formal
school, or some years later)

IN-SERVICE PREDICTORS
(Teachers' behaviors and characteristics)
[Need for in-service predictors: hiring teachers; granting tenure;
selection for special consideration]

IN-TRAINING PREDICTORS
(Behaviors and characteristics in training, achievement in student
teaching and professional education)
[Need for in-training predictors: hiring teachers; certification of teachers]

PRE-TRAINING PREDICTORS
(Behavior and characteristics prior to training, achievement in
pre-training courses, knowledge, skills, attitudes)
[Need for pre-training predictors: admission to teacher education program;
retention in the program; in-training guidance; planning, conduct, and
revision of teacher education programs]

Fig. 6–4. Schematic Representation of Career Levels of Criteria and Their
Use (After American Educational Research Association, 1953, p. 649).

"levels" paradigms for criteria imply no necessary change in this simple
picture. At whatever points on the ultimacy or levels continua the
criteria may be chosen, the research worker proceeds with only these
two kinds of variables in his paradigm. As Mitzel (1957) put it,
". . . during the past 50 years it has been characteristic of the research
on teacher effectiveness to jump directly from predictor variables to
the criterion variables . . . " (p. 2).

Research by this paradigm has been abundant; hundreds of studies,
yielding thousands of correlation coefficients, have been made. In the
large, these studies have yielded disappointing results: correlations
that are nonsignificant, inconsistent from one study to the next, and
usually lacking in psychological and educational meaning.

Under these circumstances, it was to be expected that research
workers would begin to seek refinements in the simple, but relatively
fruitless, effectiveness paradigm. One such attempt at refinement, by
Mitzel (1957), is presented here to illustrate the lines along which

such efforts have been made. This paradigm, illustrated in Fig. 6–5, contains four types of variables, or "classifications of information." These classifications were identified by Mitzel as necessary concerns of "any investigator who seeks fundamental knowledge in the general research area that is frequently called 'teacher effectiveness' . . . " (p. 1):

Type I. Human characteristics on which teachers differ and which can be hypothesized to account, in part, for differences in teacher effectiveness.

Type II. Contingency factors which modify and influence the whole complex of behaviors that enter into the educational process. "If Type II variables play a commanding role in the achievement of educational objectives, then we will be required to replicate studies of teacher effectiveness in a great many different situations. . . . "

Type III. Classroom behaviors of teachers and pupils.

Type IV. Criteria or standards, consisting of "intermediate educational goals," i.e., the measurable outcomes at the end of a period of instruction as distinguished from "the ultimate criterion which might be phrased as 'a better world in which to live.' "

Some notion of the possible interrelations among the four types of variables is shown by the connecting lines in Fig. 6–5. . . . In general, solid lines are indicative of direct effects and dotted lines suggest indirect or tangential effects. In such a scheme teacher variables (Type I) and pupil variables (Type II) are direct determinants of teacher behavior and pupil behavior respectively. Environmental variables (Type II) indirectly influence both teacher and pupil behaviors. In the view presented here, the complex of pupil-teacher interactions in the classroom is the primary source to which one must look to account for pupil growth (Mitzel, 1957, p. 1).

It is through the intercession of his Type III variables that Mitzel saw the best hope of improvement in teacher effectiveness research. To show how the paradigm could be implemented, Mitzel described the study diagramed in Fig. 6–6, in which various actual measures, or operational definitions, of the variables named in Fig. 6–5 are entered. The study thus formulated was subsequently published (Medley & Mitzel, 1959).

Other Comprehensive Models

Biddle (1964) offered a "seven-variable model" for the investigation of teacher effectiveness. In this model, (a) formative experiences, (b) teacher properties, (c) teacher behaviors, (d) immediate effects, and (e) long-term consequences serve as main sequence variables; (f)

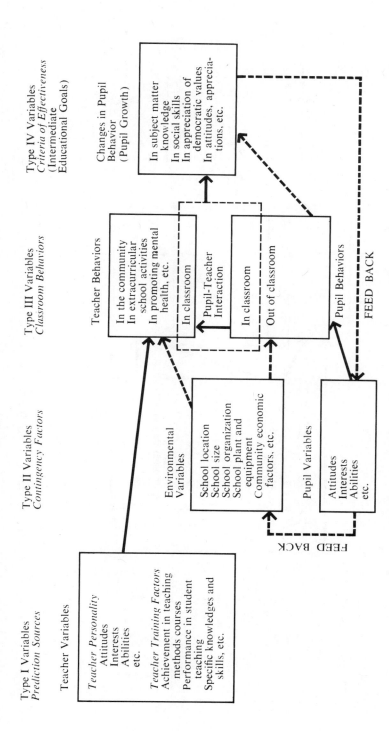

Fig. 6–5. Generalized Schema for Research in Teacher Effectiveness (Mitzel, 1957, p. 5).

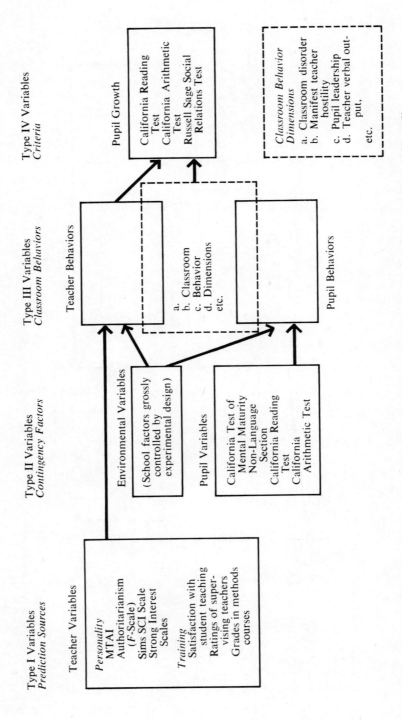

Type I Variables
Prediction Sources

Teacher Variables

Personality
MTAI
Authoritarianism
(*F*-Scale)
Sims SCI Scale
Strong Interest
Scales

Training
Satisfaction with
student teaching
Ratings of super-
vising teachers
Grades in methods
courses

Type II Variables
Contingency Factors

Environmental Variables

(School factors grossly
controlled by
experimental design)

Pupil Variables

California Test of
Mental Maturity
Non-Language
Section
California Reading
Test
California
Arithmetic Test

Type III Variables
Classroom Behaviors

Teacher Behaviors

a. Classroom
b. Behavior
c. Dimensions
d. etc.

Pupil Behaviors

Type IV Variables
Criteria

Pupil Growth

California Reading
Test
California Arithmetic
Test
Russell Sage Social
Relations Test

*Classroom Behavior
Dimensions*
a. Classroom disorder
b. Manifest teacher
   hostility
c. Pupil leadership
d. Teacher verbal out-
   put,
etc.

Fig. 6–6. Adaptation of Fig. 6–5 Concepts in Division of Teacher Education Assessment Program (Mitzel, 1957, p. 6).

classroom situations and (g) school and community contexts serve as contextual variables. The main sequence variables form a linked chain, while the contextual variables provide the situations and environments of these variables and interact with them.

A comprehensive model of factors affecting school learning was set forth by Carroll (1965) in terms that provided for (a) "quality of instruction" as one of five major variables, the others being (b) aptitude, expressed as the amount of time required by the learner to attain a specified criterion; (c) perseverance, measured by the amount of time the learner is willing to spend at learning; (d) opportunity to learn, defined as amount of time actually allowed for learning in the particular setting; and (e) ability to comprehend instruction, or perhaps verbal intelligence. Such a model, applied to the study of teaching, would require that the other four variables be controlled, held constant, or adjusted for. Statistical methods (e.g., analysis of covariance or factorial design), matching, or random assignment to experimental and control groups could be used to compare one instructional method with another. Carroll saw such factors as listenability, readability, the structure and logic of the concepts presented, reinforcement schedules, and incentive systems, as determiners of the quality of teaching itself.

Siegel and Siegel (1967) suggested a paradigm for studying the relationship to learning of several independent variables at a time and also studying interaction among the independent variables. Their approach embraces four classes of independent variables (learning environments, instructors, learners, and courses) and their interactions; the dependent variables include both effectiveness and process criteria of achievement, thought, attitude, and extra-class behavior.

"Micro-criteria" of Effectiveness

One solution within the "criterion-of-effectiveness" approach may be the development of the notion of "micro-criteria." Rather than seek criteria for the over-all effectiveness of teachers in the many, varied facets of their roles, we may have better success with criteria of effectiveness in small, specifically defined aspects of the role. Many scientific problems have eventually been solved by being analyzed into smaller problems, whose variables were less complex.

Physicists did not attempt to predict all aspects of the undulating motion of a feather as it fell in an everyday breeze. They refined the problem into the prediction of the fall of a frictionless body in a vacuum and derived laws for this phenomenon. Such laws, combined with other laws applying to similarly pure situations, can account for the vagaries of the motion of actual objects under field conditions.

Similarly, a sufficient number of laws applying to relatively pure aspects of the teacher's role, if such laws could be developed, might eventually be combined, if it were considered desirable, in such ways as to account for the actual behavior and effectiveness of teachers with pupils under genuine classroom conditions. Hence, rather than studies of teacher effectiveness, and criteria therefor, we may make better progress if we develop "micro-criteria" of effectiveness. At the very least, such an approach would imply that effectiveness should be sharply specified in terms of subject matter and grade level. (In Chapter 7, we elaborate this idea.)

TEACHING PROCESS PARADIGMS

Mitzel's paradigm, with its provision for "Type III," or classroom behavior, variables, provides a transition to paradigms that are not centered on "criteria of teacher effectiveness." Let us first at least mention the reasons for turning away from the criterion-of-effectiveness paradigm. Too often, it led to ignoring what went on in the classroom. Measures of some criterion of effectiveness were obtained, and measures of potential correlates or determiners of that criterion were obtained, and then the relationship between the two sets of measures was determined. The potential correlates or determiners were usually measures of teacher characteristics or behaviors observed outside the classroom, e.g., measures of intelligence or authoritarianism obtained with tests and questionnaires. This approach did not yield sufficiently significant or positive results. Furthermore, the events occurring inside the classroom during the teaching process were of scientific interest in themselves. It was for these two reasons—to improve the yield of positive and consistent findings and to examine intrinsically important phenomena—that process paradigms for research on teaching were developed.

Research workers (e.g., Ryans, 1960a, pp. 26–56) continued to use the term *criterion* but not with the commitment to *effectiveness*. In this sense *criterion* becomes synonymous with *dependent variable*. Other writers (e.g., Mitzel, 1960, p. 1483) used the term *process criteria*, or "aspects of teacher and student behavior which are believed to be worthwhile in their own right," and these were the Type III variables included in Mitzel's paradigm, described above. Such process criteria would all fall lower than effects on students in the scale of ultimacy.

If process variables are to be sought, what orientations can guide the search? Here we come into contact with paradigms of teaching behavior. These may be of two kinds: (a) teaching as information processing, and (b) teaching as interaction.

Teaching as Information Processing

Teacher behavior was formulated as information processing by Ryans (1963). Information processing was considered to involve a five-phase sequence of activities: (a) sensing, identifying, and classifying inputs; (b) evaluation of possible courses of action; (c) the making of decisions by the teacher; (d) ordering and arranging of information output in some logical or psychological sequence; and (e) transmission of appropriate information to the student. The whole process was considered to be influenced by the teacher's information inputs and information-processing capabilities, on the one hand, and by external information inputs, or interacting conditions external to the teacher, on the other.

A criticism of the formulation of teaching as information processing and decision-making was made by Jackson (1966a) in distinguishing between the preactive and interactive phases of teaching. Preactive behavior is that in which the teacher engages before he comes face to face with his students; such behavior may indeed "resemble, albeit crudely, the stereotype of the problem-solver, the decision-maker, the hypothesis-tester, the inquirer" (p. 13). But—

In the interactive [i.e., face-to-face] setting the teacher's behavior is more or less spontaneous . . . lately it has become popular to think of the teacher's activity in terms that describe the problem solver or the hypothesis tester. . . . There may be some advantage in using these logical and highly rational models to describe the teacher's in-class activities, and there may even be some moments when the teacher feels like a decision maker in the interactive setting, but these moments, I would wager, are few and far between (pp. 13, 14).

The interactive phase was similarly characterized by Cronbach (1967). In adapting instructional method to the individual, the teacher—

barely acknowledges the comment one pupil makes in class discussion, and stops to praise a lesser contribution from another who (he thinks) needs special encouragement. He turns away from one pupil who asks for help—"you can find the answer by yourself if you keep at it"—and walks the length of the classroom to offer help to another, because he has decided to encourage independence of the former pupil and minimize frustration of the latter. . . . The significant thing about these adaptations is their informality (pp. 28–29).

The uncontrived character, speed, and uncontrollability of teaching moves in the "interactive" phase make the formulation of teaching as information processing seem to some students of teaching to be merely metaphorical, not to be taken literally. Yet human information processing need not, perhaps, be a deliberate, slow, consciously controlled matter, and it may be that future attempts to apply information-processing conceptions of teaching will lead to fruitful research.

Teaching as Interaction

Most of the teaching process paradigms have used approaches taken from the concept of social interaction. In this concept, two or more persons serve alternately as stimuli for one another. One person's response became another's stimulus, and the latter's response became a stimulus for the first, and so on.

Smith's Paradigm. Smith (1960) has offered a paradigm, "which draws upon the psychological paradigm developed by Tolman. . ." (p. 233). As shown in Fig. 6–7, he classified all the variables involved in and related to teaching into three categories: independent (teaching actions), intervening (learning), and dependent (pupil actions) variables. In the model, the arrows indicate the direction of causal influences. The teacher's actions are

followed by postulated states, events, or processes in the pupil and are represented by the intervening variables. Then, as a result of these variables, the pupil behaves in one or more of the ways indicated in the dependent variables column. The teacher can see the pupil's behavior, but he cannot see the postulated events and processes; that is, he cannot observe interests, motives, needs, beliefs, and the like. But these psychological entities and processes are present by implication in the behavior of the pupil. The teacher may therefore infer these psychological factors from the pupil's behavior, and in some instances he actually does infer them, although he may not be aware that he is doing so. Thus the teacher often infers from the reactions of the pupil that he is interested, or that he wants to do so and so, or the contrary (Smith, 1960, p. 234).

To depict the "ebb and flow" of teaching, or the "cycle of giving and

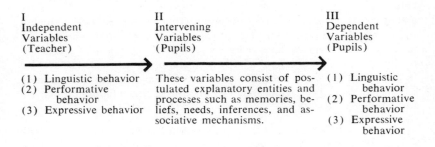

I Independent Variables (Teacher)	II Intervening Variables (Pupils)	III Dependent Variables (Pupils)
(1) Linguistic behavior (2) Performative behavior (3) Expressive behavior	These variables consist of postulated explanatory entities and processes such as memories, beliefs, needs, inferences, and associative mechanisms.	(1) Linguistic behavior (2) Performative behavior (3) Expressive behavior

Fig. 6–7. A Pedagogical Model (Smith, 1960, p. 234).

taking instruction," Smith extended the model to that shown in Fig. 6–8,

where P_t is the teacher's perception of the pupil's behavior; D_t is the teacher's diagnosis of the pupil's state of interest, readiness, knowledge, and the like, made by inference from the behavior of the pupil; and R_t is the action taken by the teacher in light of his diagnosis; and where P_p is the pupil's perception of the teacher's behavior; D_p is the pupil's diagnosis of the teacher's state of interest, what he is saying, and so on, as inferred from the teacher's behavior; and R_p is the reaction of the pupil to the actions of the teacher (Smith, 1960, p. 235).

The double vertical lines in Fig. 6–8 mark off the teaching cycles. The single vertical lines within each cycle mark off "the acts of teaching" from "the acts of taking instruction," the latter of which Smith sharply distinguishes from "learning," since learning may or may not be taking place. On the basis of analyses of tape recordings of classroom discourse (Meux & Smith, 1961), Smith has stated that "our symbolic schema and verbal performances in the classroom are isomorphic" [i.e., correspond to one another] (1960, p. 235).

Ryans' Paradigms. Lewin's formula for explaining behavior was $B = F(P, E)$, or "behavior is a function (F) of the person (P) and of his environment (E) . . ." (Lewin, 1946, p. 791). Ryans (1960a) applied this formula to the development of a "paradigm illustrating the integration of teacher behavior," shown in Fig. 6–9. In this paradigm, the boxes on the left-hand side correspond to Lewin's P variables; those on the right-hand side, to Lewin's E variables. Ascending, one goes from the most general features, through different levels of generality, to the most specific teacher and pupil behaviors at the top. The dotted arrows connecting the right- and left-hand boxes denote interaction between them. The paradigm shows the various levels of abstraction at which a research worker may operate.

In a second paradigm, stemming from his "Postulate A: Teacher behavior is social behavior," Ryans (1960a, p. 16) adapted the schema of "dyadic units" set forth by Sears (1951), as shown in Figs. 6–10 and 6–11. Sears had shown how a typical learning-theory model might be expanded to embrace interaction between two persons, each of whose instrumental acts would influence the factors antecedent to the other's instrumental acts and also the consequent environmental events

$$||P_t \rightarrow D_t \rightarrow R_t| \rightarrow P_p \rightarrow D_p \rightarrow R_p|| \rightarrow P_t \rightarrow D_t \rightarrow R_t| \rightarrow P_p \rightarrow D_p \rightarrow R_p||$$
$$\rightarrow P_t \rightarrow D_t \rightarrow R_t| \rightarrow P_p \rightarrow D_p \rightarrow R_p|| \ldots . \rightarrow \text{achievement.}$$

Fig. 6–8. Paradigm of a Series of Teaching Cycles (Smith, 1960, p. 235).

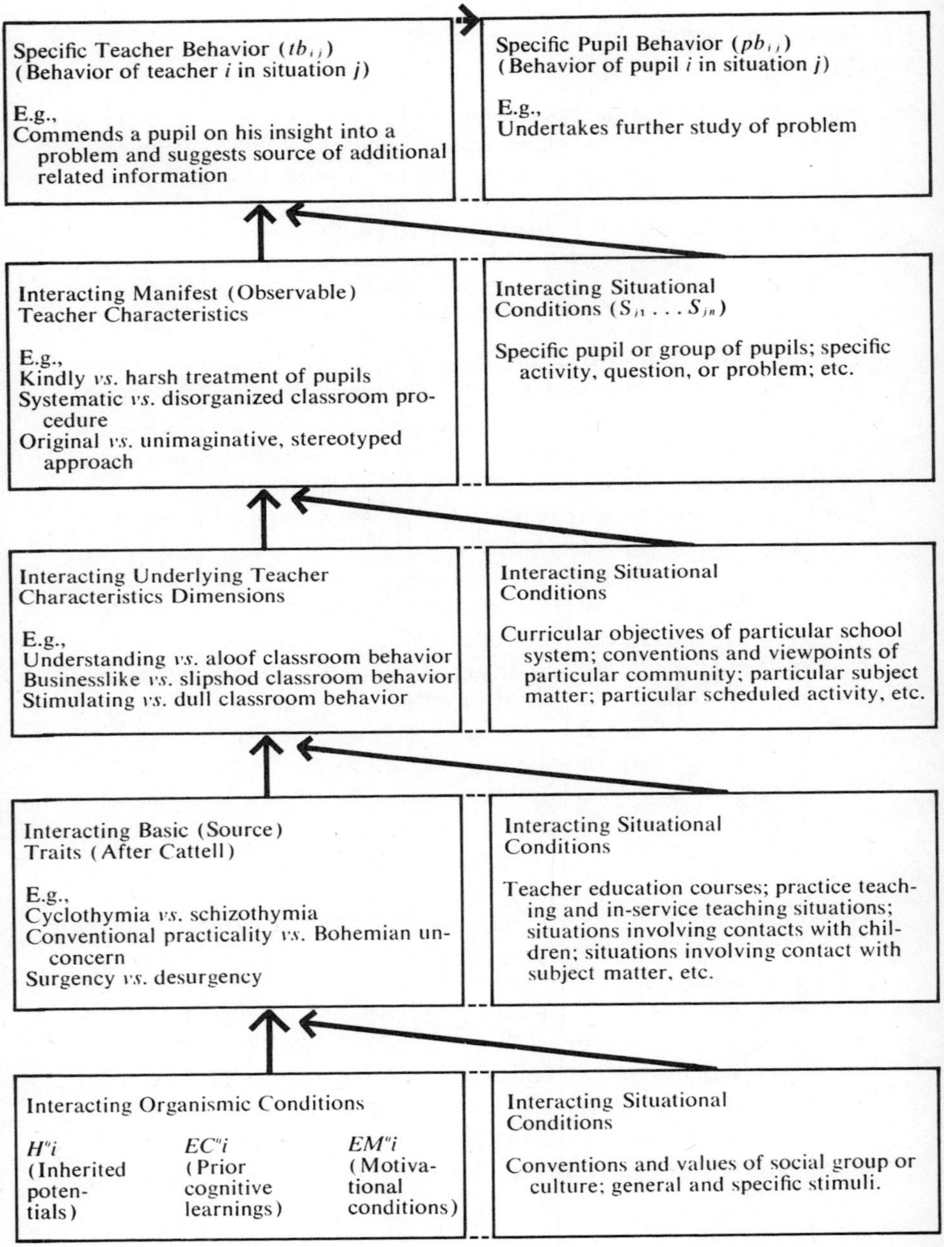

Specific Teacher Behavior (tb_{ij})
(Behavior of teacher i in situation j)

E.g.,
Commends a pupil on his insight into a
problem and suggests source of additional
related information

Specific Pupil Behavior (pb_{ij})
(Behavior of pupil i in situation j)

E.g.,
Undertakes further study of problem

**Interacting Manifest (Observable)
Teacher Characteristics**

E.g.,
Kindly *vs.* harsh treatment of pupils
Systematic *vs.* disorganized classroom pro-
cedure
Original *vs.* unimaginative, stereotyped
approach

**Interacting Situational
Conditions ($S_{j1} \ldots S_{jn}$)**

Specific pupil or group of pupils; specific
activity, question, or problem; etc.

**Interacting Underlying Teacher
Characteristics Dimensions**

E.g.,
Understanding *vs.* aloof classroom behavior
Businesslike *vs.* slipshod classroom behavior
Stimulating *vs.* dull classroom behavior

**Interacting Situational
Conditions**

Curricular objectives of particular school
system; conventions and viewpoints of
particular community; particular subject
matter; particular scheduled activity, etc.

**Interacting Basic (Source)
Traits (After Cattell)**

E.g.,
Cyclothymia *vs.* schizothymia
Conventional practicality *vs.* Bohemian un-
concern
Surgency *vs.* desurgency

**Interacting Situational
Conditions**

Teacher education courses; practice teaching and in-service teaching situations;
situations involving contacts with children; situations involving contact with
subject matter, etc.

Interacting Organismic Conditions

| $H''i$ (Inherited poten- tials) | $EC''i$ (Prior cognitive learnings) | $EM''i$ (Motiva- tional conditions) |

**Interacting Situational
Conditions**

Conventions and values of social group or
culture; general and specific stimuli.

Fig. 6–9. Paradigm Illustrating the Integration of Teacher Behavior (Adapted
from Ryans, 1960a, p. 18).

The teacher

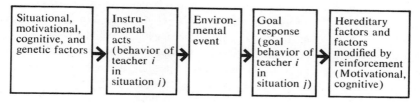

Fig. 6–10. The Monadic Instigation, Action Sequence (Adapted from Ryans, 1960a, p. 20, and Sears, 1951).

The teacher

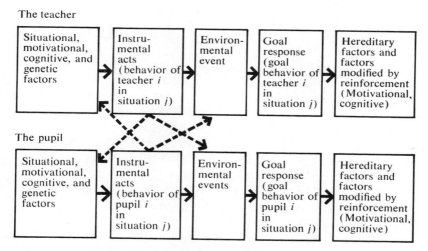

The pupil

Fig. 6–11. The Dyadic Sequence (Adapted from Ryans, 1960a, p. 20, and Sears, 1951).

of the other. In such interaction, by definition, an individual's behavior can no longer be accounted for by what we know about him alone, i.e., his personality and environment, on the one hand, and the consequences of his own acts, on the other; the acts of another person now also shape these antecedents and consequences of his behavior.

Applying Sears's conception to interpersonal perception data, Cronbach sharpened the definition of interaction by noting that "interpretations dealing with interactions can be advanced meaningfully only after the simpler main effects associated with the perceiver or the object of perception have been given separate consideration" (1958, p. 355). In teacher-pupil interaction, this caution means that we should refer to interactional explanations only after we have exhausted all the explanatory power of individual teacher and pupil personality-environment combinations. An authoritarian teacher's behavior may thus differ when he has "inner-directed" pupils from what it will be when they are "other-directed," and the pupils' behavior and learning may also vary according to the authoritarianism of their teacher. The dyadic paradigm calls attention to these possibilities and leads to research on social interaction in the classroom.

The Stone-Leavitt Paradigm. Still another social interaction paradigm was prepared by Stone and Leavitt in their "schematic analysis of teacher-pupil interaction" (personal communication, 1955). This analysis suggests that any "interact" between a teacher and a pupil consists of the following steps:

1. *Pupil provides stimuli.* Pupils enter the teacher's environment as sources of stimuli.

2. *Teacher selects stimuli.* The teacher is influenced by a sample of these stimuli. This sample, determined by the teacher's implicit personality theory . . ., by her previous formulation of the pupil's personality, and by her purposes in interacting with the pupil, constitutes the extrinsic basis (input) for the teacher's perception of the pupil.

3. *Teacher perceives pupil.* This input is organized, by the implicit personality theory of the teacher, into a formulation (or reformulation) of the pupil's characteristics and behavior.

4. *Teacher adopts ideal action pattern.* This formulation interacts with the teacher's self-concept and definition of her role so as to result in her ideal pattern of action.

5. *Teacher adopts proposed action pattern.* The teacher's proposed pattern of action is modified by her estimation of the situation (facilities, resources, attitudes of others) so as to result in her proposed pattern of action.

6. *Teacher carries out actual action pattern.* The teacher's proposed pattern of action interacts with the teacher's abilities and the actual situation so as to result in the actual pattern of action.

7. *Teacher provides stimuli.* The teacher's actual pattern of action impinges on the pupil as a source of stimuli.

8. *Pupil selects stimuli.* The pupil is influenced, consciously and unconsciously, by a sample of these stimuli. This sample of stimuli constitutes information (input) which provides the extrinsic basis for the pupil's perception of the teacher.

9. *Pupil perceives teacher.* This input is organized by the implicit personality theory of the pupil into a perception of the teacher's characteristics and behavior.

10. *Pupil adopts ideal action pattern*. This formulation interacts with the pupil's self-concept and definition of his role so as to result in his ideal pattern of action.

11. *Pupil adopts proposed action pattern*. The pupil's ideal pattern of action is modified by his estimation of the situation (attitudes of others) so as to result in his proposed pattern of action.

12. *Pupil carries out actual action pattern*. The pupil's proposed pattern of action interacts with the pupil's abilities and the actual situation so as to result in the pupil's actual pattern of action.

13. The pupil's actual pattern of action serves as a source of stimuli for the teacher.

In selecting a sample of these stimuli, the teacher may be influenced by a perceived connection between her own action and the pupil's action; i.e., the pupil's action may be seen as "feedback." In any case, at this point the conceptualization of teacher-pupil interaction has come full circle and this specific "interact" is complete.

This process can be completed in an instant or can take much longer. It can refer to a "molecule" of interaction or to the summation of many such "molecules."

Research can be directed at any one of the phases of this process or at the relationship between any two of them.

Steps 1–7 may be regarded as a sequence of sensation-perception-thought-action on the part of the teacher; Steps 8–13, a similar sequence on the part of the pupil. This analysis is reminiscent of Smith's teaching cycle, but analyzes the behavior on each side more finely. Whether the analysis could be implemented, i.e., assigned operational definitions, is unknown in the absence so far of any attempt to do so. It seems, however, in the light of currently known techniques of observation and measurement, that formidable problems would arise in distinguishing between, say, Step 1 (Pupil provides stimuli) and Step 2 (Teacher selects stimuli), or between Step 2 and Step 3 (Teacher perceives pupil).

Runkel's Paradigm. A final example, used by Runkel in his classes, is his "brief model for pupil-teacher interaction," the phases of which are listed below, with references to Figs. 6–12 and 6–13 (Runkel, personal communication, 1958).

1. The teacher brings to the classroom her own personal needs and goals developed during her *own personal history*. In combination with the particular classroom situation in which she finds herself, these lead to

2. the *teacher's choice of a goal* involving the pupil. She might want the pupil to learn how to add 3-digit numbers, to appreciate Rem-

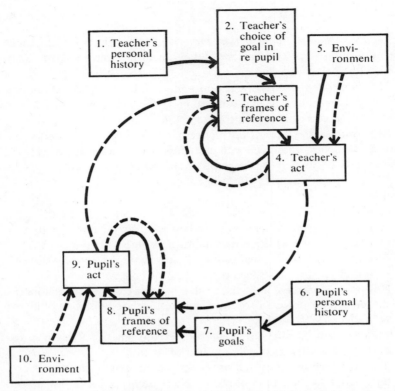

Solid lines represent intrapersonal communication via the nervous system, etc.
Dashed lines represent interpersonal communication via vision, speech, etc.

Fig. 6–12. A Brief Model for Pupil-Teacher Interaction (P. J. Runkel, personal communication, 1958).

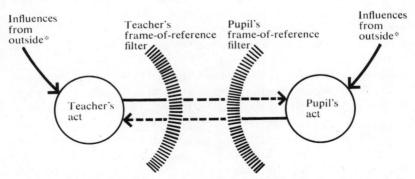

* Influences from outside the immediate interpersonal "system" such as the individual's personal history, the immediate environmental happenings, etc.

Fig. 6–13. A Brief Model for Pupil-Teacher Interaction (P. J. Runkel, personal communication, 1958).

brandt, to be a good boy, to know when Columbus discovered America, to strive valiantly in competitive athletics, etc.

3. The goal chosen by the teacher is circumscribed by her *frames of reference*, and so is the particular series of actions on which she embarks in order to approach the goal. These determinants lead to

4. *the teacher's act.* Examples would be telling the pupils to read Chapter III, sending a boy to the principal's office, explaining how to take square root, taking the class on a trip to the museum, etc. Aside from the influences already listed, however, the particular acts chosen are shaped by

5. the *environment* in which the acts are carried out. The speed of the bus affects the time spent at the museum; the size of the blackboard affects the explanation of square root; the noise of passing trucks affects the remarks made about Rembrandt; the admonitions concerning striving in sports are tempered to suit the respective sizes of the combatants, etc.

The part of the teacher's environment we wish particularly to scrutinize is the pupil. As the teacher chooses the particular actions which mark her path toward her goal, she will devote particular attention to the pupil who is involved in the goal. The pupil's act (Phase 9) therefore appears on the chart separately from other aspects of the teacher's environment (Phase 5). Similarly, the teacher's act (Phase 4) is charted separately from the rest of the pupil's environment (Phase 10).

6. Similarly, the *pupil's personal history*

7. helps determine the *pupil's goals* which he brings with him to the classroom or which he develops there. These, along with his perception of the teacher's act, must fit with at least a minimum degree of consistency the

8. *pupil's frames of reference.* Having assimilated these extrapersonal and intrapersonal influences, the pupil can now act.

9. The *pupil's act*, like that of the teacher, is also molded by the

10. *environment* in which it takes place. And the pupil's act, in turn, becomes one of the determinants of the next act on the part of the teacher, after it has been interpreted by the teacher through her frames of reference.

We must also remember that the teacher observes herself acting, and so does the pupil. "Feedback" lines are therefore drawn on the chart from Phase 4 back to Phase 3, and likewise from Phase 9 back to Phase 8. This feedback can accelerate either positively or negatively the existing processes.

The large circle itself represents a feedback circuit, although it is indirect and not self-contained. (It contains "noise.") After the teacher acts (Phase 4), the act has some effect on the pupil (Phases 8 and 9).

TABLE 6-2. COMMON ELEMENTS IN PARADIGMS OF TEACHER-PUPIL
INTERACTION

TYPE OF ELEMENT	SMITH	RYANS
1. Perceptual-Cognitive Elements, Teacher	Teacher's perception of pupil's behavior Teacher's diagnosis of pupil's state	Teacher's situational, motivational, cognitive, genetic factors
2. Action Elements, Teacher	Teacher's action	Teacher's instrumental acts Teacher's environmental event Teacher's goal response Teacher's hereditary factors and factors modified by reinforcement
3. Perceptual-Cognitive Elements, Pupil	Pupil's perception of teacher's behavior Pupil's diagnosis of teacher's state	Pupil's situational, motivational, cognitive, genetic factors
4. Action Elements, Pupil	Pupil's reaction to teacher's action	Pupil's instrumental acts Pupil's environmental event Pupil's goal response Pupil's hereditary factors and factors modified by reinforcement

TABLE 6–2. (CONTINUED)

STONE-LEAVITT	RUNKEL	STOLUROW
Pupil provides stimuli Teacher selects stimuli Teacher perceives pupil	Teacher's personal needs and goals, personal history Teacher's choice of a goal Teacher's frames of reference The teacher's environment	4. Comparator unit 6. Collator-recorder 8. Library unit 9. Program 10. Computer
Teacher adopts ideal action pattern Teacher adopts proposed action pattern Teacher carries out actual action pattern	Teacher's act	1. Display unit 3. Pacing unit 7. Selector unit
Teacher provides stimuli Pupil selects stimuli Pupil perceives teacher	Pupil's personal history Pupil's goals Pupil's frame of reference The pupil's environment	5. Knowledge of results, or feedback
Pupil adopts ideal action pattern Pupil adopts proposed action pattern Pupil carries out actual action pattern	Pupil's act	2. Response unit

The pupil's act is in turn perceived by the teacher (via Phase 3), who may then modify her subsequent actions. But the "information" conveyed in this roundabout circuit may be altered in various ways by exterior influences (Phases 1, 2, 5, 6, 7, and 10) and by the intrapersonal feedback.

Common Elements in the Process Paradigms

The reader will by now have noted common elements in the various paradigms of teacher-pupil interaction. As Table 6–2 shows, it is possible to list the elements in these paradigms in rows cutting across the paradigms, so that each row contains roughly equivalent elements. Each paradigm can thus be seen to begin with (I) an element, or several elements, referring to perceptual and cognitive processes on the part of the teacher. The processes eventuate in (II) action elements on the teacher's part. The teacher's actions are followed by (III) perceptual and cognitive processes on the pupil's part, and these in turn lead to (IV) action elements on the pupil's side.

In one paradigm, i.e., Ryans', the elements of Type I, perceptual-cognitive, are represented by only one inclusive entry. In another paradigm, e.g., Smith's, this type of element is broken down into two parts, perception and diagnosis. Similarly, while Smith and Runkel have only one element for the teacher's action, Ryans' paradigm analyzes this rubric into four parts, consisting not only of the act but also of the teacher's subsequent environmental events, goal responses, and reinforcement-induced changes. For the same type of element, Stone and Leavitt have a three-part analysis consisting of ideal, proposed, and actual action patterns.

Despite differences in their terminology, fineness of breakdown of elements in the process, and methods of portraying interaction, all the paradigms have (1) a cyclical, repetitive quality and (2) an oscillatory character. In these paradigms, teacher-pupil interaction is seen, somewhat like tennis, to consist of action first on one side, then on the other. While one side is in action, the other is perceiving, anticipating, getting set.

But these paradigms neglect the fact that the roles of the two sides differ in teaching, if not in tennis. In tennis, each side is identically and competitively motivated, while in teaching, the motivations are, ideally at least, complementary and cooperative. Although each side gets feedback on its actions from the behavior of the other side, these processes are different for teachers and pupils, even if not for two tennis opponents. The paradigms also, in their symmetry, neglect the enormous differences in what is considered appropriate behavior for teachers and pupils. In their excessive generality, these interaction paradigms make teaching and "pupiling" look identical.

None of these models has come to grips with the complication that teachers typically deal with more than one pupil at a time. In classroom lecturing, of course, the pupil side must be "averaged" in some way by the teacher, who engages in most of the action, or overt behavior, shown in the paradigms. In classroom discussion, the pupil on the other side of the "net" from the teacher may change from volley to volley, and stable conceptions of the characteristics of the changing pupil may be hard to envisage.

Finally, let us note that the unit of interaction connoted by these paradigms is a "small" one, a single "interact," analogous to only one complete passage of the tennis ball back and forth across the net. In tennis, of course, significant strategies, like getting one's opponent out of position, or playing to his weak side, often consist of more than one exchange. And the strategy can seldom be described by mere addition, or some similarly simple combination, of several exchanges. Further, the significant outcomes, like winning games and sets, depend on several exchanges, although in this case simple addition of the exchanges may suffice to characterize the outcome. Just how interacts between teachers and pupils should be combined to characterize significant processes and outcomes in the classroom has not been dealt with in the foregoing paradigms. At the present stage of paradigm development, this gap does not seem to be an urgent one. When more experience has been gained in providing operational definitions for the paradigms, the problem of combining interacts into educationally significant units will become more realistic.

A MACHINE PARADIGM

The design of teaching machines was originally guided by the characteristics and processes of human learners. It is conceivable that this approach can be reversed, i.e., that the design of research on human teachers can be guided by the characteristics of teaching machines. Such an attempt might well be made in accordance with the critical requirements of a teaching machine formulated by Stolurow (1961) and illustrated in Fig. 6–14. Stolurow's "adaptive teaching machine system" may thus be regarded as a paradigm for research on teaching.

1. The paradigm begins with a *display unit* which presents subject-matter information to the learner. In the machine, this might be done via pages, tapes, discs, slides, films, or recordings; the human teacher may use his voice, a textbook, or the blackboard. The presentation ends with a question or a cue to which the learner is asked to respond.

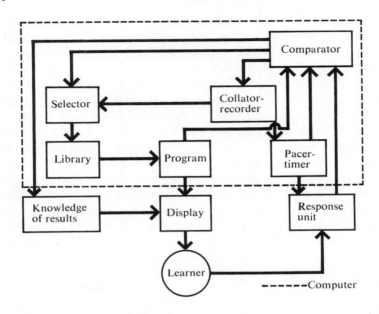

Fig. 6–14. Adaptive Teaching Machine System (Stolurow, 1961, p. 7). (The terms are explained in the text.)

2. Next there is a *response unit* which receives and implements the learner's action, whether it be a recognition, a recall, a composed sentence, or whatever. In the usual classroom, the response unit might be the pupil's vocal equipment for making an oral reply to a question, or his writing equipment.

3. *The pacing unit* times the intervals between (a) question and correct answer, and (b) each question. Both *a* and *b* intervals may be fixed, both may vary according to the learner's response, or *a* alone may vary while *b* remains fixed. In the classroom, this is merely (a) the teacher's speed of reaction to pupils' responses and (b) his rate of proceeding from one statement-question unit to the next, presumably according to how well his class is learning.

4. *The comparator unit* compares the learner's response with the correct or desired one, either explicitly or merely by presenting the correct response to the learner and letting him make the comparison. The teacher does this by saying to himself, "Right," or "Wrong," or by stating aloud the correct or desired answer.

5. *Knowledge of results or feedback* is then made available to the learner, either through his own inference from his own comparison of his response with the correct response, or by the machine's giving him

a correct response, or by the machine's giving him a light or sound or other clue. In the classroom the teacher can allow the pupil to infer his feedback or give it to him explicitly by audibly stating, "Right" or "Wrong."

6. *The collator-recorder* measures and records the learning process, collecting data on number and type of errors, time intervals required for response, etc. The collating unit feeds this information into the part of the unit to which it pertains. In the human situation, the teacher remembers the correctness and style of the pupil's successive responses and uses this memory to make the teaching process more appropriate to the learner's ability and rate of progress.

7. *The selector unit* chooses the next item in the program. Depending on whether the preceding response was wrong or right, it presents the same item or a new one. It may also take into account the learner's whole previous record, as received from the collator-recorder unit. In the classroom, the teacher chooses the next item.

8. *The library unit* stores the information, concepts, etc., to be taught. Its effectiveness depends on its capacity, access time, and form of storage. In the classroom, the teacher's own knowledge, textbooks, and other sources serve this function; how much the teacher knows, or knows how to find, with what speed, and in what form (books, films, etc.) are the analogous characteristics.

9. *Programming* is the sequence of items, either predetermined (linear, or noninterpretive) or flexible according to the learner's responses (branching, or interpretive). Programming is equivalent to the teacher's implicit or explicit conception of the best pedagogical structure of the discipline being taught, and in the classroom, of course, teachers typically do adapt the sequence of ideas to their pupils, except when lecturing or when individual differences among learners cannot be taken into account.

10. *The computer* is the high-speed electronic digital device that can perform all the functions enclosed in the dotted rectangle in Fig. 6–14. The teacher's "mind" is the best analog of this function in the human teacher.

Note that the components themselves tell much less than the whole story of how teaching machines, and teachers, ideally function according to Stolurow's paradigm. The sources of input and the destinations of output of each component must be considered for any full grasp of what the paradigm represents. These connections among components are shown by the arrows between boxes in Figs. 6–14 and 6–15.

Does this paradigm of an idealized teaching machine suggest variables and relationships that have been neglected in research on human

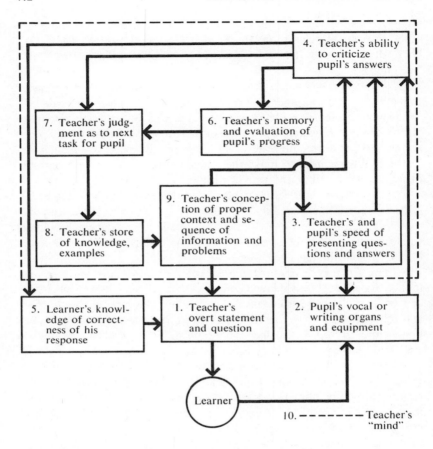

Fig. 6–15. Human Equivalent of a Teaching Machine System (Based on Stolurow, 1961).

teaching? Table 6–2 shows how the "units" of Stolurow's teaching machine system fit into the previous classification of elements in teacher-pupil interaction paradigms. Appropriately enough, most of the components belong in the teacher's side of the interaction, since this is a *teaching* machine and not a learning machine. Stolurow's components are particularly suggestive as to the perceptual-cognitive parts of the teaching process, i.e., the pacing, comparator, knowledge of results, and collator-recorder functions of teachers. How fast teachers proceed, how well they evaluate students' responses in the ongoing classroom discussion, how clearly and fully they give students knowledge of their own correctness, and how well they keep track of the progress of students' learning, are matters that can be variables in research on teaching. When such variables are used in research, they can be averaged or manipulated over large blocks of behavior, or units of subject matter. Thus, students can be given total scores on tests some time after they have taken the test, or knowledge of the correctness of responses to individual items immediately after making each response. If the latter kind of knowledge of results is important to learning, it should be studied as a variable in human teaching as well as machine teaching. Experiments in machine teaching (e.g., Coulson & Silberman, 1960) have called into question the value of some variations of some of Stolurow's components (e.g., branching). Would human teachers' branching, i.e., adaptation of content to individual differences among students in learning, yield the same finding?

The heart of machine teaching is the program, and indeed many of the benefits may be available without any machine at all, e.g., with only a programmed textbook. Apart from all the research problems inherent in the programming concept, the teaching machine paradigm suggests that the programs teachers carry around "in their heads" need analysis. Such "implicit programs," or the at least partly unconscious structures and sequences of subject matter that teachers employ, might be revealed with unstructured and open-ended interviewing techniques, among others.

We have made a series of analogies between teaching machine functions and teachers' behaviors and characteristics. These analogies may serve, more than anything, to reveal the inadequacies of human teachers. Hardly a teacher is alive who can do all the things that teaching machines are supposed to do according to Stolurow's schema. Here lies the reason for contemporary interest in teaching machines and programmed learning. Systematic comparison of machine functions and those of human teachers, function by function, may reveal the proper and unique role of each. Paradigms for human teaching comparable to those for teaching machines will help in making such analyses.

Chapter 7

An Analytic Approach

The early years of research on teaching have not paid off in solid, replicable, meaningful results of considerable theoretical or practical value. Positive and significant results have seldom been forthcoming, and they have survived replication even less often. The research has yielded many findings that do not make sense, that do not hang together in any meaningful way.

Under these conditions, as Kuhn (1962) has pointed out, research workers are impelled to re-examine their first principles, the paradigms by which they guide their efforts. The model problems and solutions of the community of researchers on teaching are accordingly subjected to more and more reappraisal. Licking the wounds inflicted by their negative results, investigators have built up a modest literature on conceptual frameworks, approaches, and paradigms for research on teaching, of the kind reviewed in Chapters 5 and 6.

To illustrate, let me refer to one of the dominant ideas that even today leads much discussion and research into the wilderness. This is the view that what we need above all, before we can select and train better teachers, or even do research on teaching, is *the* criterion of teacher effectiveness. Here is one example of that kind of approach:

The lack of an adequate, concrete, objective, universal criterion for teaching ability is thus the primary source of trouble for all who would measure teaching. One typical method of attack used in rating scales is to compile a list of broad general traits supposedly desirable for teachers, with respect to which the rater passes judgment on each teacher. This amounts to an arbitrary definition of good teaching, which is subjective and usually vague, but it does not necessarily lead to an identification of it. Only if the traits themselves can be reliably identified can their possessor be identified as a "good teacher" according to the definition laid down in the scale. Even when the scale is made quite specific, relating not to general traits but to concrete procedure, the fundamental difficulty remains, that there is no external and generally accepted criterion against which the scale can be validated to establish the significance of its items (Walker, 1935, pp. x-xi).

This kind of writing implies that there is some magic variable that applies to all of teaching, for all students, at all grade levels, in all subject matters, and for all objectives. The phrase "the criterion of teacher effectiveness" betokens a degree of generality that has seldom been found in any branch of the behavioral sciences. It also reflects the mistaken notion that such a criterion, largely a matter of values, can be established on the basis of scientific method alone.

The so-called criterion problem misled a whole generation of investigators of teaching, embroiled them in endless and fruitless controversy, and lured them into hopelessly ambitious attempts to predict "teacher effectiveness" over vast arrays and spans of outcomes, teacher behaviors, time intervals, and student characteristics, all on the basis of predictive variables that had only the most tenuous theoretical justification in the first place. It is little wonder that, when Berelson and Steiner (1964) dealt with the subject of teachers' behaviors and characteristics in their inventory of scientific findings in the behavioral sciences, they dismissed the "large number of studies" with the single dismal sentence that "there are no clear conclusions" (p. 441).

AN ANALYTIC APPROACH

If the global criterion approach proved to be sterile, what was the alternative? The answer was to take the same path that more mature sciences had already followed: If variables at one level of phenomena do not exhibit lawfulness, break them down. Chemistry, physics, and biology had, in a sense, made progress through making finer and finer analyses of the phenomena and events they dealt with. Perhaps research on teaching would reach firm ground if it followed the same route.

Apparently, a number of students of the problem had this general idea at about the same time. In one form it is represented by the notion of "micro-criteria," set forth in Chapter 6, page 95.

Technical Skills

In another form, it can be discerned in what, during the early 1960's, the Stanford program for training secondary school teachers (directed by Robert Bush and Dwight Allen) termed "technical skills." Technical skills are specific instructional techniques and procedures that a teacher may use in the classroom. They represent an analysis of the teaching process into relatively discrete components that can be used in different combinations in the continuous flow of the teacher's performance. The specific set of technical skills adopted in the teacher education program at Stanford is arguable. Indeed, the list of skills has been revised a number of times over the years. What is important is the approach— the attempt to analyze teaching into limited, well-defined, components that can be taught, practiced, evaluated, predicted, controlled, and understood in a way that has proven to be impossible for teaching viewed in the larger units that occur over a period of a day, a week, or a year.

When teaching analyzed into technical skills is made the focus of concern, it becomes possible to do fairly satisfying research on both teacher education and teacher effects. The satisfaction comes from being able to measure or manipulate relevant independent variables, perform true experiments, or make careful analyses and measure relevant dependent variables.

The idea of technical skills may be illustrated by the terms used in a recent list of such skills. (1) "Establishing set" is the establishment of cognitive rapport between students and teacher to obtain immediate involvement in the lesson; one technique for inducing a positive set is the use of relevant analogies. (2) "Establishing appropriate frames of reference" deals with giving the students various points of view. (3) "Achieving closure" is the ability to pull together major points, linking old and new knowledge, at appropriate junctures within a teaching episode and at the end. (4) "Using questions" refers to questioning in such a way as to elicit the kinds of thought-processes and behaviors desired, such as simple recall, or concept-formation, or evaluation. Other technical skills are termed (5) "Recognizing and obtaining attending behavior," (6) "Control of participation," (7) "Providing feedback," (8) "Employing rewards and punishments," and (9) "Setting a model."

Microteaching

The technical skills into which important aspects of teaching have been analyzed are not merely the subjects of lectures and discussions in the teacher education program. Rather, they form the basis for the intern's practice teaching prior to his entrance into actual classrooms. This procedure, well known by now as "microteaching" (Allen & Ryan, 1969), consists in getting the trainee to teach a scaled-down teaching exercise. It is scaled down in terms of (a) time, because it lasts only five to ten minutes, (b) class size, because the intern teaches a group of not more than five students, who are brought in and paid to serve as students in the microteaching clinic, (c) the task, since the trainee attempts to perform only one of the technical skills in any single microteaching session. The sessions are recorded on video tape, and the trainee gets to see and hear himself immediately after the session. While he looks at and listens to himself, he receives criticisms and suggestions from supervisors trained to be both perceptive and tactful. Then he "re-teaches" the same lesson to a new small group of students

in an attempt to improve on his first performance of the specific technical skill that is his concern in that session.

Obviously, the general idea is subject to many variations. The size
of the class can be manipulated, the number of trainees teaching a
given group of children can be increased, the duration of the lessons
can be lengthened, and the nature of the teaching task can be made
more complex so as to embrace a *group* of technical skills in an approximation of their real-life combinations. But the idea of analyzing
teaching into technical skills remains the heart of the method and provides its power as a paradigm for research.

The research on microteaching and technical skills in the Stanford
teacher education program has taken the form of experiments in which
various treatments administered to the trainee are manipulated. Dwight
Allen and Frederick McDonald organized a program of research on
variables hypothesized to influence the learning of the technical skills
of teaching. Their independent variables fell into three categories:
practice variables, feedback variables, and demonstration variables.
A practice variable may consist in microteaching vs. teaching in an
actual classroom. A feedback variable may be the positive or negative
character of the feedback, or the mediation of the feedback by another
person rather than the trainee himself. Finally, a demonstration variable may take the form of symbolic demonstration, consisting of
written or spoken words, or perceptual demonstration, consisting of
either live or videotaped portrayals of the desired behavior; each of
these can consist either of self-modeling or modeling by others. Other
independent variables have been identified, such as the timing of a
reinforcement, the amount of practice, and the amount of feedback.
This brief description of the Allen-McDonald research program illustrates the use of the analytic approach to research on teacher education. But the technical skills approach can also be applied to the study
of teacher effects.

RESEARCH ON EXPLAINING

One such research program has dealt with a technical skill termed
"explaining," or the skill of engendering comprehension—usually
orally, verbally, and extemporaneously—of some process, concept, or
generalization. Explaining occurs in all grade levels and subject matters. A fifth-grade teacher explains why the time in New York differs
from that in San Francisco. A geologist explains how the ice age may
have been caused by volcanic eruptions. Everyday observation tells
us that some people explain aptly, getting to the heart of the matter
with just the right terminology, examples, and organization of ideas.

Other explainers, on the contrary, get us and themselves all mixed up, use terms beyond our level of comprehension, draw inept analogies, and even employ concepts and principles that cannot be understood without an understanding of the thing being explained. To explore the problem area we have made some studies (Gage, et. al., 1968) of explaining ability, including attempts to determine some characteristics of effective explanations.

Generality of Ability to Explain

The first study (Fortune, Gage, & Shutes, 1966) was made in the microteaching clinic at Stanford. It was intended to determine the generality of explaining ability. To what degree was the ability to explain one topic correlated with the ability to explain another topic? Also, to what degree was the ability to explain a topic to one group of students on one occasion correlated with the ability to explain the same topic to another group of students on another occasion? We were also able to design the study so as to determine the degree to which there was generality over both students and topics, i.e., the degree to which the ability to explain one topic to one group of students on one day correlated with the ability to explain another topic to another group of students on another day.

Because there were only 60 students to be shared in groups of 5 among approximately 40 interns in the microteaching clinic, the design became quite complex. We had to avoid having any intern teach the same topic to the same group of students more than once and, of course, to avoid having the same group of students receive an explanation of a given topic more than once. Accordingly, the 40 social studies interns—we worked with the social studies interns because there were more of them than any other kind of intern—were divided into five clusters of eight interns each. The lectures dealt with 20 different topics, each consisting of an "Atlantic Report" from the *Atlantic Monthly*. The correlations that we obtained were thus medians of five correlations, each based on four, six, six, six, or eight interns, respectively (10 of the 40 interns being lost to the study for one reason or another).

What I would like to call the micro-criterion of teacher effectiveness in explaining was the students' mean score on a 10-item test of their comprehension of the main ideas of the Atlantic Report, which were presented by each intern in 15 minutes under somewhat standardized conditions. This mean score was adjusted for the mean ability of the students in the given group as measured by their scores on all of the other topics. Similarly, any given mean score was adjusted for the difficulty of the topic as measured by the mean score of all groups of students on that topic. Thus, the variance of the adjusted mean posttest comprehension scores was attributable not to the ability of the students or the difficulty of the topic, but rather to the differences among the teachers. We then investigated the various kinds of generality by determining the median intercorrelations among the various means. The upshot was that generality over topics was non-existent, and generality over groups was reflected in a correlation coefficient of about .4. In other words, the interns were moderately consistent in their ability to explain the same topic to different groups on different occasions, but they were not consistent in their ability to explain different topics.

This study also dealt with the correlations between explaining effectiveness and the students' ratings of various aspects of the explanations. The students rated the interns' performance with respect to 12 items, such as clarity of aims, organization of the lesson, selection of material, and clarity of presentation. It seemed to us that some of these dimensions should correlate with explaining ability more highly than others. In particular, such discriminant validity would be manifest in the form of a higher correlation between the mean rating of the lecture for "clarity of presentation" than for any of the other items. Our expectation was borne out; the correlation of the adjusted mean posttest comprehension scores with students' ratings of "clarity of presentation" was .56, higher than that with any of the other rating scale items. This result seems to support the validity of both the index of effectiveness and the mean ratings by the students.

Belgard, Rosenshine, and Gage (Gage, et al., 1968, pp. 9–20) replicated and extended this study using high school teachers and students. Because there was no lack of students in the high school classes, taught by their own teachers, we did not become involved in the complexities of design necessary in the microteaching clinic. We asked each of 40 eleventh-grade social studies teachers to deliver a 15-minute lecture on an Atlantic Report on Yugoslavia taken from the *Atlantic.* Each teacher was given the article several days in advance, and was told to prepare a lecture that would enable her students to answer a 10-item multiple-choice test of comprehension of the article's main ideas. To guide them in preparing their lecture, they were given five of the multiple-choice questions that would be asked, while the other five questions were withheld. During the lecture, the teachers were permitted to use the blackboard but no other aids. Then their students took the 10-item test and also rated the teacher's lecture on items similar to those already described. The next day, the same teachers and classes did the same things, except that the subject matter was an

Atlantic Report on Thailand. On the third day, all classes heard the same third lecture, an audiotape-recorded verbatim reading of an Atlantic Report on Israel. Then they took a 10-item test based on that article.

The class mean on the Israel test was used to adjust the class means on Yugoslavia and Thailand for between-class differences in ability. Our reasoning was that the score on such a test would be useful in controlling relevant kinds of ability. The variance that still remained in the adjusted comprehension test means of the classes would reflect differences between the teachers in what we were concerned with, namely, the intellectual style and process of the teacher's lecture. In this study, the teacher's adjusted effectiveness index on Yugoslavia correlated .47 with his effectiveness on Thailand. Thus, there was considerable generality of effectiveness over topics, even after student ability had been partialed out.

We were using the microteaching idea in this investigation. The teaching was restricted to just one aspect of the teacher's role, namely, ability to explain the current social, political, and economic situation in another country. The curriculum was also scaled down. We also used another major feature of the microteaching clinic, the videotape recorders, which made it possible for us to study the teacher's behavior, verbal and nonverbal, at leisure.

Modality of Cues to Effectiveness

Was teacher effectiveness in explaining manifested in something about the lecture that was visible or audible? What kinds of evidence enabled the most accurate discrimination between good and poor explanations?

First the mean scores of the classes were adjusted for both mean student ability and also for "content-relevance." The latter adjustment in the class means on Yugoslavia and Thailand was made by scoring the transcript of the lecture for relevance to the 10 items on the comprehension test. Then Unruh (1967; also in Gage, et al., 1968, pp. 21–35) picked four lectures on Yugoslavia that fell in different fourths of the distribution of the criterion measure of effectiveness. He picked four lectures on Thailand by different teachers, on similar grounds. Then he had seven groups of eight judges each read the article on Yugoslavia and take the comprehension test, in order to become familiar with the "curriculum." Each of the seven groups of eight judges received one of the seven kinds of evidence listed in Table 7–1. Each group based their ratings of the lesson's effectiveness on the cues received from this evidence. Then the judges ranked the lectures in

TABLE 7–1.   RANK-ORDER CORRELATION COEFFICIENTS BETWEEN POSTDICTED AND ACTUAL RANKS IN EFFECTIVENESS FOR FOUR YUGOSLAVIA AND FOUR THAILAND TEACHER-LESSONS PER RATER[a]

PROTOCOL (TYPE OF EVIDENCE ON WHICH TO BASE RATINGS)		MEDIAN CORRELATION FOR EIGHT RATERS OF FOUR LESSONS	
		Yugoslavia	Thailand
Typewritten transcript only	T	−.6	−.2
Audio record only	A	.1	.1
Video record only	V	.2	.2
Typewritten transcript plus audio record	TA	−.8	−.2
Typewritten transcript plus video record	TV	−.1	.2
Audio record plus video record	AV	.6	.7
Typewritten transcript plus video record plus audio record	TAV	.3	.1

[a] Based on Unruh in Gage, et al., 1968, p. 23.

terms of perceived effectiveness in engendering comprehension as measured by the 10-item test. For each judge, the correlation between his ranking and the actual ranking of the four teachers in effectiveness was determined. Then the average correlation of the eight judges in the group was computed. As shown in Table 7–1, it turned out that the judges' average accuracy in judging effectiveness on the basis of the *audio-video* record was quite substantial (median $rs = .6$ and .7) on both lectures. It was also much greater than the accuracy of judgments based on other combinations of kinds of evidence. Apparently the mean achievement microcriterion was reflected in something that could be seen and heard in the lecture.

Behavioral Predictors of Effectiveness

The 30 videotape records of the Yugoslavia and Thailand lessons were used by Rosenshine (1968; also in Gage, et al., 1968, pp. 36–45) to determine the cognitive and stylistic correlates of the lecture's effectiveness. He used extreme groups to minimize the labor of scoring a host of variables about which he had no great conviction. So the 10 most effective explanations on Yugoslavia were identified and also the 10 least effective. From these, he chose at random five of the most effective and five of the least effective. Then, groups of trained judges and content analysts worked over the transcripts of the lectures, determining the frequencies and rates per minute or per 100 words of a host of variables. Among these variables were "sentence fragments," "average sentence length," "number of prepositional phrases per sentence," "number of words per minute," and "number of self-references by the teacher." The variables reflected various aspects of syntax, instructional set, familiarization, uses of previous knowledge, mobilizing set, attention focusing, organization, emphasis, amount of repetition and redundancy, and so on.

The variables that discriminated between the five best and the five worst lectures on Yugoslavia were then tried out on the other set of five best and five worst lectures on Yugoslavia to see if they still discriminated. Those that survived this first cross-validation were then tried out on the five best and five worst lectures on Thailand.

Which characteristics of the lectures survived these validation and cross-validation procedures? One of these variables was what Rosenshine called "explaining links," or the degree to which the teacher uses words such as "because," "in order to," and "so that," which describe the how, why, or effect of something. A second was the "rule-example-rule" pattern, or the degree to which the teacher states a generalization, gives examples of it, and then summarizes the examples at a higher level of generality than the examples themselves. A third variable was the amount of gesture and movement displayed by the teacher. These variables not only were reliably counted by independent judges but also discriminated consistently between sets of more and less effective lectures. Nonetheless, these must not be considered to be firmly established findings; they are merely examples of the kinds of conclusions to which research of this kind can lead.

Computer Analyses of Lesson Style

Because the counting of words and phrases in transcripts is laborious, computers were applied to the task by Daryl Dell and Jack Hiller (Gage, et al., 1968, pp. 46–54; Hiller, 1968). The transcripts of selected lectures were punched on IBM cards, and the computer was used to determine the frequencies of words appearing both in the transcripts and in various "dictionaries." In the latter, words are classified as to type, affect loading, or other dimensions. In addition to three dictionaries developed, respectively, for research in political science (Holsti), social psychology (Stone, et al.), and readability (Dale), this study employed three dictionaries especially developed by Hiller: (a) "vagueness," i.e., words like "almost," "generally," or "many," reflecting uncertainty of the speaker about his material; (b) "adherence-to-detail," i.e., all proper nouns and place designations in the original articles; (c) "problem-issues," i.e., words such as "conflict," "divergent," and "issue." Further, a dictionary was developed to approximate a count of "explaining links" as defined by Rosenshine. This computer count did not, of course, take account of context in the way that human coders did this originally.

The computer's word-counts were correlated with the effectiveness indices (mean scores of students on the comprehension test, adjusted for student ability and content-relevance) of 15 teachers' lectures on Yugoslavia and 15 other teachers' lectures on Thailand. The correlations for some of the counts were at least .30 in the same direction in both samples. Thus, as shown in Table 7–2, "Space Reference," "Avoid," "Affective-2," "Problem-Issue," "Explaining Links 2," "Explaining Links Total," and "Adherence to Detail" yielded suggestive results in this sense. Some of these findings are easily interpreted, after the fact, of course. The positive correlations for "Problem-Issue" words may reflect their attention-arousing function. Those for "Adherence to Detail" may indicate that less effective teachers lost clarity by using more pronouns in place of proper nouns.

As for "vagueness," a subsequent study by Hiller, Fisher, and Kaess (1969) obtained positive results with an expanded dictionary capable of counting phrases as well as single words. Tested on 30 Yugoslavia and 23 Thailand lectures, the new dictionary yielded measures of proportion-of-vagueness-words-and-phrases that correlated −.59 and −.48 with the effectiveness indices for Yugoslavia and Thailand, respectively. All in all, these results should encourage further investigation of the usefulness of computers in analyzing classroom discourse and determining correlates of microcriteria of effectiveness.

TOWARD EXPERIMENTAL ANALYSIS

What I have been describing are, of course, correlational studies. Along with their advantages in permitting the exploration of a wide variety of possible correlates of explaining ability as they occur under fairly normal conditions, they also have the disadvantage of making causal interpretations hazardous. For this reason, studies of this kind ought to proceed fairly rapidly into experiments in which the different ways of explaining will be based, at least in part, on leads obtained from our correlational studies. Such experimental research may lead toward quite novel methods of teaching that could never be developed on the basis of studies of teaching the way teaching is. An example of such an experiment (Miltz, 1971)—one involving a manual on explaining—is described in Chapter 13.

The basic theme of the research on teaching here described is *analysis*, breaking down the complexities that have proven to be so unmanageable when dealt with as a whole. We must no longer be misled by the notion that, because there is one word called teaching, there is one, single, over-all criterion of effectiveness in teaching that will take essentially the same form wherever teaching occurs. Even if none of the analyses that we have now yields consistently positive results, they

TABLE 7–2. MEAN FREQUENCIES OF VARIOUS CATEGORIES OF WORDS AND CORRELATIONS OF THESE FREQUENCIES WITH EFFECTIVENESS IN EXPLAINING OF 15 LESSONS ON EACH OF TWO TOPICS[a]

CATEGORY OF WORDS	SOURCE AND DEFINITION	WORD SAMPLE	YUGOSLAVIA (N = 15) MEAN FREQUENCY	r	THAILAND (N = 15) MEAN FREQUENCY	r
1. Space Reference	Harvard Psy. III Reference to spatial dimensions	about, ahead, back	75.9	.51	67.7	.34
2. Avoid	Harvard Psy. III Movement away from	abandon, absent	8.7	.41	11.5	.54
3. Affective-2 (proportional)	Holsti (words with middle rating on affective negative scale)	complain, embarrass, slander	26.1	−.34	23.5	−.37
4. Problem-Issue	Hiller: Words used by teachers in presenting issues	conflict, divergent, issue	9.7	.29	11.0	.55
5. Explaining Links 2	Rosenshine	Contains only the words: if, then, to	55.3	.41	56.2	.41
6. Explaining Links Total	Rosenshine	All of Explaining Links 2, plus 15 other words: e.g., consequently, because, since	119.4	.38	112.5	.37
7. Adherence to detail	Hiller: All proper nouns and place designations in original article	Thailand, Tito, Hitler	121.4	.32	111.6	.48

[a] Based on Dell & Hiller, in Gage, et al., 1968, pp. 50–51.

will not be replaced by the global, conceptually complex variables which have been used in much of the barren research on teaching in the past. Instead, they will be replaced by other analyses, perhaps even finer ones, until we obtain the sets of lawful relationships between variables that will mark the emergence of a scientific basis for the practice of teaching. It may well be that a 15-minute explanation of a 5-page magazine article is still too large a unit of teaching behavior to yield valid, lawful knowledge. The mean score on a 10-item test of comprehension, adjusted for student ability and content relevance of the lecture, may still be too complex a dependent variable. But, compared with the massive, tangled, and unanalyzable units that have typically been studied in the past—in research on the lecture method, the discussion method, and class size, for example—such units seem precise and manageable indeed. And eventually, of course, they will permit putting teaching back together again in syntheses that are better than the teaching that goes on now.

Chapter 8   Cognitive Aspects

By research on cognitive aspects of teaching, I mean something fairly restricted. Research, of course, is the quest for relationships between variables, preferably causal relationships, or functional relationships, but if not these, then mere correlations of any kind. Research on teaching, as I have stated earlier, is that in which at least one of the variables consists of a behavior or characteristic of teachers—something that the teacher does or is. It might be the teacher's way of explaining something, or his characteristic of being warm or logical.

The term cognitive refers to those aspects of teaching that are directly concerned with furthering the learner's achievement of the so-called cognitive objectives of education, as distinguished from affective and psychomotor objectives. The cognitive objectives are various kinds of knowledge—defined as ability to recall or recognize facts, definitions, laws, and so on—and various intellectual arts and skills, such as ability to analyze, evaluate, synthesize, translate, interpret, and so on. This chapter deals with research on teacher effects which is directly, expressly, and obviously concerned with cognitive objectives, as distinguished from social and emotional aspects or objectives of teaching.

We should not exaggerate the distinction between cognitive and affective. As Murphy (1961) said, "if there is love to begin with, love can reach out and entwine within itself all of the things, acts, and relationships of this world. It can even come to love the very process by which it differentiates, analyzes, and makes meaningful reality out of this turbulent world" (p. 23). And the authors of the *Taxonomy of Educational Objectives in the Affective Domain* (Krathwohl, Bloom, & Masia, 1964) also noted the connection between cognitive and affective concerns. They observed that "under some conditions the development of cognitive behaviors may actually destroy certain desired affective behaviors. . . . For example, it is quite possible that many literature courses at the high-school and college levels instill knowledge of the history of literature . . . while at the same time producing an aversion to . . . literary works" (p. 20). Nonetheless, it is possible to distinguish between cognitive and affective aspects of teaching; and here I propose to restrict the discussion to the former.

THE RELATIVE NEGLECT OF COGNITIVE ASPECTS

Strangely enough, this restriction is a very severe one. Much of the literature of research on teaching is not cognitively oriented. Many if not most of the best known programs of research on teaching have been aimed at social and emotional aspects of how teachers behave and how students respond and develop. Indeed, it is probably also fair to say that the more successful programs of research on teaching have been noncognitively oriented. I can illustrate this point with reference to testing, rating, and observational studies of teaching.

First, we consider the research centered around the development, validation, and exploration of the Minnesota Teacher Attitude Inventory (Getzels & Jackson, 1963, pp. 508–22; Yee, 1968). This research has yielded positive results as consistently, perhaps, as any other kind of research on teaching and makes it possible to predict with better than chance success how well an elementary school teacher will be liked by her students, or how well she will get along with them. But this research does not deal with how much knowledge or understanding those students will achieve.

The massive Teacher Characteristics Study (Ryans, 1960) used a rating approach. That program dealt with how warm teachers are, how systematic and orderly they are as managers, and how enthusiastic and ebullient they are. So far as I know, these variables, which Ryans developed with great circumspection and diligence and which he explored in relation to many other characteristics of teachers, have not been shown, by him or anyone else, to be promising points of entry into the relationship between what teachers do and their students' achievement of knowledge or comprehension.

For an observational approach, let us refer to a third productive and still very active line of research on teaching, well exemplified by Flanders' research (1965) on classroom interaction. The observer writes a number every three seconds in 1 of 10 categories to record whether the teacher or a student is talking and whether what is being said is approving, extending, questioning, or criticizing. These numbers are then converted to tallies in a 10 x 10 matrix which shows what kind of behavior, as indicated on the vertical axis, was followed by what kind of behavior, in the next three seconds, as indicated on the horizontal axis. By summing columns and various groups of cells in such matrices, one can learn a great deal about how "directly" or "indirectly" teachers behave, how students behave, and how the teacher and his students interact. Although he has studied the relationships between various measures derived from his interaction analysis and how much students learn in mathematics and English classes, it seems to me that Flanders' direct concern, as reflected in the categories of behavior he observes, is not with cognitive aspects of teaching.

The MTAI research, the Ryans research, and the Flanders research are highly representative of a large part of the research on teaching that has been done thus far, and are among the most fruitful research undertakings of their kind. But it should be noted that we have only recently begun to see work of comparable scope, significance, and influence in the field of research on cognitive aspects of teaching.

It would be interesting for a historian of ideas to attempt to explain this relative neglect. Perhaps he would find that, prior to the middle 1950's, American educational psychology and educational research as a whole, and not merely research on teaching, were relatively little concerned with cognitive learning, as against emotional and social development, in the classroom, school, and community. Perhaps American educational psychology was handicapped by too much reliance upon the kind of global learning theory cultivated by animal and laboratory psychologists, which yielded too little when it was applied to the problems of school learning. Perhaps advances in dealing with instruction had to wait for the emergence of a substantial cadre of experimental psychologists from the training laboratories of the military; for it was in those military training installations that many of our most productive experimental psychologists were required to handle concrete problems of cognitive and psychomotor learning and, in the process, became educational psychologists with a flair for analyzing instructional problems.

Whatever the historian might find, the fact remains that in research on teaching for cognitive objectives we have had, until recently, relatively little of the descriptive, analytical, theoretical, experimental, or correlational work that can be found in relative abundance in research on the social and emotional phenomena in classrooms. We have had substantial enterprises on curricula for teaching reading, arithmetic, science, languages, and so on. And, to some extent, this research has become more analytical and more detailed than such gross variables as lecture-vs.-discussion method would indicate. But we have not had any major effort, until recently, aimed at producing *general* principles of teaching behavior related to achievement of cognitive objectives.

RECENT RESEARCH ON COGNITIVE ASPECTS

Now let us turn to various recent studies of cognitive aspects of teaching. Those we shall consider are only a fraction of those made, but they are quite representative of recent developments.

Smith and Meux (1962, 1964) analyzed transcripts of tape recordings of oral discourse in 17 high school classes, in English, mathematics, science, and social studies. Assuming that the influence of instruction is primarily logical—and this is, of course, a crucial assumption—they identified the units of verbal discourse which can be sorted into different logical categories, each one coordinate with such a logical operation as "defining," "explaining," "evaluating," and "classifying."

In addition to these logical "tactics" in classroom discourse, Smith and his co-workers also worked with larger units called "strategies," by which they mean the large-scale maneuvers that give general direction to student behavior. Underlying their strategies are intermediate units of discourse which Smith and his co-workers called "ventures"; these are "segments of discourse consisting of a set of utterances dealing with a single topic and having a single overarching content objective."

This description of the work of Smith and Meux is cursory, but it suggests the nature of their approach. They have been concerned, in essence, with a detailed analysis of logical, cognitive, intellectual aspects of classroom discourse. They have not intervened in, interfered with, manipulated, or changed the phenomena prior to recording them. Nor did they impose programmed instruction or give tests. Hence their raw data reflect classroom intellectual life as it is lived without the influence of the investigator.

Bellack and his collaborators (1966) also analyzed transcripts of linguistic behavior—that of 15 high school classes studying the same unit in international trade in four class periods. Their analysis yielded four categories of pedagogical moves: structuring, soliciting, responding, and reacting. They also identified a variety of teaching cycles, or groups of moves. They identified four types of meanings in the content of discourse and termed these the "substantive," "substantive-logical," "instructional," and "instructional-logical" meanings of the content. Their results consisted of detailed descriptions of the discourse in the classrooms studied, in terms of each of the major categories of meaning and some of the more important relations among categories. It is noteworthy that they found much more variability among their teachers in the substantive meanings covered in the classroom than in the teaching techniques used, despite the fact that all classes were supposed to be dealing with the same subject matter, carefully delimited. These investigators also took a step beyond the Smith-Meux research in that they investigated the amount of learning that occurred in each of their 15 classes. They did not find what they expected; namely, they did not find greater learning about topics most discussed than they did about topics least discussed in the classroom. They drew from this finding the lesson that "instead of setting up certain bits of knowledge as those which *should* be learned . . . , it would undoubtedly be more useful to formulate future research in terms of the question, 'What kinds of classroom events are related to what kinds of learning outcomes?' "

It should be noted that Smith regards his work as "neither an evaluative nor an experimental investigation of teaching." The same may be said of Bellack's studies. Little or no attempt was made to determine the effects of teaching behavior upon students, or to establish correlations among variables, or to search for causes of teacher behavior. Analytic and descriptive in the natural history sense, theirs was an effort to analyze verbal teaching behavior into pedagogically significant units and to analyze the units in logically meaningful ways.

It seems to me that a major difficulty with the descriptive approaches taken by Smith and by Bellack is that they have no way of knowing whether the variables they are studying are relevant to learning. Not everything that teachers do is relevant to one major purpose for which we study teaching, namely, to improve learning. We typically do not concern ourselves with how teachers scratch their heads, hold their chalk, or cross their legs, for the simple reason that we assume such behaviors to be irrelevant to the kinds of learning the teachers bring about in students.

Is not the naturalistic description of teaching a worthwhile undertaking in itself? It is, indeed. Some geologists find Northwestern Canada, or any other area on earth, an important object of study in its own right, and they describe it carefully in terms of the constructs and variables of geological science. But other geologists go into Northwestern Canada for a different purpose; they want to find oil or gold, and they guide their search accordingly. At any moment, it seems likely that most research workers concerned with teaching feel like the latter kind of geologist: they want to study teaching for the purpose of improving learning.

If so, we must be impatient for evidence that the logical aspects of classroom discourse with which Smith has been concerned or the categories of meaning in classroom language with which Bellack has been concerned are indeed relevant to changes in the knowledge or understanding of students. But, as we note in Chapter 11, it may not be necessary to require such evidence. Asking for it may impose an unrealistic and overly stringent standard for the relevance or validity of any specific kind of teacher behavior. By all that is plausible, the logical and substantive content of classroom discourse ought to have some connection with what knowledge and comprehension students acquire. We have been fooled before in educational research, and so we shall rest uneasy until the evidence on these connections is in. But perhaps that evidence can be based on established principles of logic and psychology, rather than on correlations with criteria based on student achievement. It would be regrettable indeed if the prodigious labors in content analysis that Smith and Bellack and their co-workers have expended were judged irrelevant merely because their counts are unrelated to measures of what students learn. Just as not every item of good medical practice in, say, performing a physical examination has been demonstrated to be correlated with patient health, so not every item of good teaching should necessarily be shown to be correlated with student achievement.

ACTIVE VS. PASSIVE RESEARCH ON TEACHING

These studies of classroom discourse bring to the fore a distinction between two basically different strategies in research on teaching. Smith and Bellack, with their cognitive categories, and the MTAI, Ryans, and Flanders researches, with their noncognitive variables, have one major characteristic in common. These research programs study teaching and teachers as they are. If these approaches someday find substantial differences between good teachers, defined as those who foster much knowledge and comprehension, and poor teachers, who foster little, they will have discovered something about teaching only as it now goes on. They would then have a basis for improving teaching, to be sure, by educating more teachers to be like the good teachers of today and educating fewer teachers to be like the bad teachers of today. But the upper limit on quality of teaching, by this strategy, is today's best teachers. Such research cannot, in principle, go beyond the best we now have, unless one synthesizes a superior model by combining features from several existing teaching patterns or strategies.

Now suppose we assume, not too implausibly, that even the best that we now have for teaching toward cognitive objectives is not very good. Then the strategy of studying "the way teaching is," even if it yields dependable knowledge concerning the differences in behavior between good and poor present-day teachers, is not going to get us very far.

Furthermore, let us look at the chances that it will yield such knowledge. As Stolurow (1965) and many others have noted, teaching behavior is complex, and consequently, it is difficult to interpret what one observes in it. It is difficult to attribute student learning to particular teacher behaviors. Also, it is not unlikely that ineffective teaching behaviors could be identified even in master teachers. All these factors serve to make the approach of what Stolurow calls "modeling the master teacher" ineffective. That is, says Stolurow, "this idea of modeling the master teacher has not worked" (p. 225). He goes on to say that

The most significant conclusion that can be drawn from efforts to use teachers as a basis for information about teaching is that effective instruction can be produced by a variety of combinations of characteristics and conditions rather than by one unique combination. If this were not the case, efforts to enumerate the characteristics of good teachers would have resulted in the identification of at least one or two critical characteristics. However, neither the observation of master teachers nor that of a large number of effective teachers . . . has led to findings that are either substantial or sufficient for the understanding of teaching as a process. Thus, an alternative approach is needed (p. 226).

Stolurow's alternative approach is "mastering the teaching model." He begins by making the point that "it may be possible to do a better job of teaching than that which has been observed" (p. 226). If so, "then it is unwise to *restrict* one's concern to what teachers are doing now" (p. 227). Rather, we should set out to develop, de novo more or less, models of the teaching process designed to predict learning outcomes. Such models will force the investigator to make explicit the elements and relationships needed to account for the phenomenon in which he is interested, namely, the student's achievement of a learning task. Such models entail commitment to a position. If properly designed, the models can be tested and corrected.

PROGRAMMED INSTRUCTION

In general, the new kinds of models proposed by Stolurow and others seeking to master the teaching model are those embodied in computer-assisted or other forms of programmed instruction. Such models provide for (a) the presentation of cognitive content, on a screen or typewriter or some other device, (b) the student's responding in some way, (c) immediate comparison of the response with a criterion, (d) immediate feedback of knowledge of results, (e) rapid searching of the library for frames or materials to be presented next, and so on, along lines described in Chapter 6, pp. 109–11.

Such models have already materialized in hardware and programs. They exist at half a dozen research centers around the nation, and substantial funds and research staffs are being devoted to them. The centers are moving rapidly, and pilot studies have yielded no results to dim the optimism of their developers (Atkinson & Wilson, eds., 1969).

Complexity

Arguments for programmed instruction, already noted in Chapter 3, may be reviewed here. Adequate analyses of teaching for cognitive objectives show that, properly done, such teaching is extremely complex. Such analyses reveal demands on the teacher that look well-nigh impossible for ordinary mortals, like teachers, to meet. Consider the following statements by Taba (1963), similar to those quoted in Chapter 3, concerning the implications of her study of what the teaching of concept formation entails:

Decisions must be made regarding the adaptation of the sequential steps required for a particular cognitive task to the possibilities of the group: how to pace each step, or to combine certain processes, such as alternating specification and classification of information and generalizing; deciding when it is possible to shift the focus, or to lift the level of thought, such as shifting from description ("What") to explanation ("Why"), and so on. Attempts to lift thought prematurely to a higher level result either in confusion or regression to the more primitive level. The chief difficulty with the current teaching procedure is that while the subject moves on, there is no corresponding movement in the maturity of thought. Providing for cumulative growth in cognitive skills is a requirement against which the current teaching practice commits the greatest errors. . . .

Decisions regarding the pacing and progressive lifting of thought levels naturally depend on accurate diagnosis of the group's quality of performance. Depending on both their ability and previous habits of thought, some groups require a more prolonged enumeration before they can group similar items successfully, while others can do with less. Some students can readily grasp the idea that grouping must be done according to some definite basis, while others may need to "mess around" for a while until they "discover" this idea. . . . Since the particular response patterns differ radically from class to class and even from individual to individual, these matters inevitably must be decided "on the spot," so to say. While the general principles of sequence can be established beforehand, their particular application and the ways of coping with the divergent student performance can be mastered only "in the process" and aided through analysis of feedback.

This is only an example of the kind of complexity that teaching for certain kinds of cognitive objectives must face. If Taba's analysis is valid, we face the question of whether teachers can ever be trained to cope with such complexities on anything approaching a scientific basis.

Individualization

Apart from the problem of complexity, we face the problem of individualization. Even if a teacher can do the job properly for *groups* of students—and notice that Taba speaks of such groups—how can he ever adapt the process to the needs of 30 *individuals* at a time? As we know, students differ among themselves and within themselves in many important determiners of their readiness to learn. On any given day, in any given class, some students are brighter in general, better in some prerequisite skill or knowledge, better motivated, better adjusted to the group, and so on, than other students. To cope with this fact, and with the implication that teaching ought therefore to be individualized, educators have developed such administrative arrangements and teaching methods as homogeneous grouping, special classes for slow learners and superior learners, supplementary classes and tutoring, nongraded schools, retention and acceleration procedures, frequent promotion plans, parallel-track plans, contract and unit plans, team teaching, teacher aides, and special activities and assignments for groups and individuals within the class (Thomas & Thomas, 1965).

These individualization techniques have their possibilities. But we are finally beginning to grasp, through such analyses as Taba's, the full demands of instruction for certain kinds of cognitive objectives. Even if a group of students is made homogeneous in stable characteristics, such as general ability or achievement in reading, they will not be homogeneous in certain of their *momentary* yet important characteristics, such as the stage they have reached in learning a given concept.

The problem of individualization is neglected in most research on teaching. Even in recent research, we find little concern with the behaviors of teachers in attempting to cope with individual differences in the classroom. Programmed instruction seems to have much greater potential, both in theory and in practice, for coping with such complexities in ways adaptable to the requirements of individual students. So it is understandable that Thomas and Thomas (1965) treat programmed materials as a major approach to meeting intellectual differences.

Many writers see the main hope of progress in thoroughgoing efforts to individualize instruction. Ericksen (1967, pp. 156–157) hoped to "release and give greater freedom to individual-difference variables. . . . The student-linked factors . . . are the key factors that will open up new resources for making significant changes in the quality of the educational process." Gagné (1965) and Skinner (1968) hold that instruction in graded classrooms is, in large part, a drawback. "Individually prescribed instruction" (Lindvall & Bolvin, 1967) and Project PLAN (Program for Learning in Accordance with Needs) (Flanagan, 1967) represent attempts to do away with the teaching of whole classes at a time by permitting students to work at their own pace on tasks prescribed by teachers on the basis of frequently administered measures of learning on small, carefully planned units of instruction.

But even if this general position concerning classroom teaching were accepted, few would deny that, for some objectives, the teaching of students in groups, even whole classes, is advantageous or essential. The question, "What are these objectives?" has not yet been subjected to rigorous analysis. At the least, of course, "ability to participate in group discussions" is such an objective at all levels of education. Similarly, various kinds of ability to explore ideas through intellectual interaction may require classroom teaching. Or teaching those things that can be learned best by observing the teacher's modeling of how an educated person behaves requires live teachers in classrooms.

Yet much of the contemporary argument in favor of individualizing instruction, or adapting teaching to individual differences among learners, for many kinds of objectives, is extremely plausible. Learners do differ in ways relevant to their ability to profit from different kinds of instruction, content, incentives, and the like. Almost by definition, instruction adapted to these individual differences should be more effective.

If so, why has not the evidence from attempts to individualize instruction yielded more dramatic results? Why are not the mean scores on achievement measures of pupils taught with due respect for their individual needs and abilities substantially higher, in unmistakable ways, than those of students taught in the conventional classroom, where everyone reads the same book, listens to the same lecture, participates in the same classroom discussion, moves at the same pace, and works at the same problems? For the fact is that, despite several decades of concern with individualization, few if any striking results have been reported.

Perhaps the time is ripe for a re-examination of assumptions about what goes on in the conventional classroom. Despite the kinds of apparent uniformity noted above, students in the conventional classroom may somehow individualize instruction for themselves so that each takes from it what is fairly well suited to his needs. A search for explanations of this kind may be more fruitful than continued recourse to the plea that, so far, the individualization has not been good enough. Is it inconceivable that the kind of "spraying" of stimuli, ideas, questions, and answers that goes on in a relatively unplanned (unprogrammed) way in the conventional classroom does succeed nonetheless, by virtue of its near randomness, in hitting most students where they are? Careful determination of who gets what out of instruction in the conventional classroom may reveal a much greater degree of appropriate individualization than has been thought possible.

But beyond such a possibility there lies the promise, at least in principle, that improved individualization will make a major difference. Such improved individualization could be based upon what Cronbach (1967) described as "aptitude-treatment" interactions. Such interactions, similar to those outlined by Siegel and Siegel (1967), occur when one teaching method turns out to be more effective for students with one kind or level of aptitude (or other characteristics), while another teaching method proves to be more effective for other kinds of students. "And it will be a long time before we have adequately validated rules of adaptation that take into account even a half-dozen differential variables" (Cronbach, 1967, p. 37). If so, instruction that is not explicitly individualized will for a long time be just as effective as that which is. Research on teaching in the conventional classroom will not, in that event, be unrelated to educational needs.

IMPLICATIONS FOR RESEARCH ON HUMAN TEACHING

In any case, research on how teachers now attempt to foster certain kinds of knowledge and comprehension may need to be re-examined as programmed instruction gains momentum, especially as computer-based programmed instruction matures. As of now, the advocates of programmed instruction have a theoretical advantage in regard to certain problems in learning and instruction. Teachers are less able than programmed instruction to present ideas in meticulously planned patterns, to require the student to make specified responses, to provide him with individualized feedback or correction, to adjust themselves to the pace and needs of every individual student, to adapt themselves to cues from all students in the form of various kinds of correct or incorrect responses.

If the promise of computer-based instruction is not illusory, then for some kinds of cognitive objectives the teacher can be enormously supplemented by programmed instruction. But, in any case, programmed instruction provides a highly controllable and replicable means of seeking and inventing better ways of instructing.

We shall need live teachers engaged in instruction for cognitive objectives of the many important kinds with which programmed instruction cannot cope. But the role of such teachers will need to be re-examined. We must, of course, remember that the teacher is not merely aiming at cognitive objectives. Briggs (1964) noted that teachers are needed in arranging for problem-solving by groups, guiding social development, providing enrichment and special projects based on individual needs and interests, and providing training that requires supervised practice—such as laboratory procedures, report-writing, interviewing, or playing a musical instrument. He also pointed out that the teacher is needed for "recognizing and rewarding creativity, administering achievement tests, answering the odd question not covered in the program, updating the information if necessary, and assigning units of work based on student abilities and goals" (p. 274). As is the case with other inventions, the new methods of instruction, programmed and otherwise, will not supplant the old methods so much as they will supplement them.

Part II

Research on Teacher Education

Chapter 9

The Promise of Research on Teacher Education

Research on teacher education is that in which teachers' behaviors and characteristics are dependent variables, and ways of recruiting, selecting, and educating teachers are independent variables. At this point in the history of American teacher education, it should not be necessary to talk about the need for such research. So much excellent argument has been offered in favor of research on teacher education for so many years that the thesis must now seem stale. Reasoned and impassioned appeals have been made by Washburne (1952), Gross (1959), Stinnett and Clarke (1960), Carroll (1961), Sarason and his co-authors (1962), Wattenberg (1963), and Reynard (1963). Over the years, we have at least yearned for research on teacher education, even if we have not done enough of it.

CONANT, FLEXNER, AND RESEARCH ON TEACHER EDUCATION

And then we had the widely noted book on teacher education by Conant (1963). In that book, research on teacher education was indeed mentioned, although indirectly, as in sentences about the promise of research in psychology. Conant exercised judgment, applied common sense, examined current practice, and consulted expert opinion. Of course, he was concerned primarily with what could be done now, or in the next few years. Hence, he did not place great emphasis on the long-range values that might be gained from research pertinent to teacher education. From his 27 recommendations, we can infer that improving teacher education requires changing the policies of state and local governments, of colleges and universities, and of private accrediting agencies—but not with respect to research. He seemed to be concerned mainly with a better utilization of what we already know about ways to educate teachers. He gave most of his attention to problems arising from allegedly injudicious political, administrative, and curricular arrangements.

So there is room for one more plea for research on teacher education. And let me enter that plea by making some comparisons between medical education in 1910 and teacher education in 1963, by looking at the Conant report in the light of the famous Flexner report.

Within a year after its publication, the Flexner report had caused half of the medical schools then operating to close their doors. Most of the surviving independent institutions hastened to improve themselves, in many obvious and also subtle ways. In quick and devastating fashion, the Flexner report caused tremendous improvements in medical education (Miller, 1962, p. 104).

It seems unlikely that the Conant report will have as sharp an effect. And why not? For one thing, teacher education is probably not as sick today, even in the opinion of its most scathing critics, as medical education was in 1910.

But an additional reason suggests itself. Even in 1910, the content of medical education had a strong scientific base. Flexner (1910, p. 53) began his four chapters on the medical course of study with the statement that

... medicine is part and parcel of modern science. ... The normal course of bodily activity is a matter of observation and experience; the best methods of combating interference must be learned in much the same way. Gratuitous speculation is at every stage foreign to the scientific attitude of mind.

This brave statement by Flexner does not mean that he naively overrated the condition of medical science in 1910. He went on to say,

Scientific medicine is, however, as yet by no means all of one piece; uniform exactitude is still indefinitely remote; fortunately, scientific integrity does not depend on the perfect homogeneity of all its data and conclusions. Modern medicine deals, then, like empiricism, not only with certainties, but also with probabilities, surmises, theories ... it does not cure defects of knowledge by partisan heat; it is free of dogmatism and open-armed to demonstration from whatever quarter ... (p. 53).

Conant (1963, p. 142) saw a need for "giving institutions freedom to experiment with different ways of training teachers" and this need clearly implies a need for research to determine the results of the experiments. Hence, we may infer that Conant viewed educational research and its parents, the behavioral sciences, with some hope, with something more than amused tolerance. He was willing to let us try, and he gave us some encouragement. It seems that Keppel (1962, p. 91) did not have Conant in mind when he wrote that some Americans have grave doubts that one can depend on the findings of scholars in the behavioral sciences.

The efforts to use scientific methods to study human behavior seem to them ridiculous if not impious. The result, they say, is a ponderous, pseudo-scientific language which takes ten pages to explain the obvious or to dilute the wisdom long ago learned in humanistic studies . . . to build an art of teaching on the basis of the "behavioral sciences," they suggest, is to build on sand.

The Flexner and Conant reports differ markedly in the extent to which the professions they dealt with rest on scientific research. The rottenness that Flexner found in medical education could be contrasted with the strength of the scientific knowledge that medical research had built. The weaknesses that Conant finds are not so glaring, because the light of scientific knowledge about education is less strong. If educational research had yielded as much knowledge about teaching by 1963, as medical research had yielded about healing in 1910, the Conant report might have had the tremendously compelling force for improvement that the Flexner report produced. As it is, too much of the Conant report must stand as "one man's opinion." And we then witnessed the kind of debate on the Conant report to which lack of scientific knowledge leads—the attempt to "cure defects of knowledge by partisan heat" of which Flexner spoke.

Research is the procedure that will base both the content and method of teacher education less on opinion and more on scientific knowledge. The source of knowledge about the science and technology of teaching must be research—and research on teaching in particular.

OBVIOUSNESS IN EDUCATIONAL PSYCHOLOGY

Conant did give some attention to one branch of the behavioral sciences—general and educational psychology—which ought to furnish much of the content and method of teacher education. And in characterizing contemporary psychology, Dr. Conant described it as consisting in large part of common-sense generalizations about human nature. These are "for the most part highly limited and unsystematized generalizations, which are the stock in trade of everyday life for all sane people." Conant saw this common-sense component as providing the main connection or boundary between educational psychology and the art of teaching. He agreed that educational psychology has something to offer teachers, especially elementary school teachers, but for the most part what it has to offer is obvious, merely representing common sense.

It is important to understand this point of view, and it may be helpful to consider a few propositions of the kind which might be found in

a textbook of educational psychology. Here is a short list of such statements, with brief interpretive comments:

1. More intelligent children tend to receive less social acceptance
from their peers in the classroom; that is, there is a negative correlation
between IQ, or scholastic achievement, and sociometric status. (This
is easy to understand, because as is well known, children resent the
greater success, higher grades, and teacher acceptance of the more
able pupils.)

2. If a group of pupils is given a considerable amount of practice
and instruction in developing a skill, the pupils will become more alike
in that skill. (Certainly, if a group of persons is subjected to a uniform
experience, their homogeneity on dimensions relevant to this experience
will become greater.)

3. If a teacher wants to measure how much her pupils have learned
from a given kind of instruction, she should subtract the pupils' score
on a pretest from their score on an equivalent posttest on the given
kind of achievement. (Nothing could be simpler than following the
same procedure that a parent uses in measuring how much his children
have gained in height over a period of time.)

4. When growth in achievement is measured by the "posttest minus
pretest" method just described, it will usually be found that the brighter
pupils have gained more than the pupils who had less of this kind of
achievement to begin with. (Of course this is true, just as taller children
at a given age become taller by growing faster, and until they approach
the end of the growing period, they will continue to grow faster.)

5. If you want to strengthen a kind of behavior, you should reward
it, and if you want to eliminate an erroneous kind of behavior, you
should punish it. And if the pupil repeats his error, he should be pun-
ished more severely than for the first error. (And, of course, many
parents successfully control their children's behavior in exactly this
way.)

6. The only way to secure transfer of learning from one situation to
another is to increase the similarity, or the number of so-called identical elements, between the learning situation and the application situation. (Ever since William James and E. L. Thorndike, we have known
that there is no general transfer and that schooling should therefore
be made as much like real life as possible.)

I have tried to give a brief list of the kinds of common-sense generalizations that might be found in a textbook of educational psychology. Since these principles are so obvious, why do educational
research workers expend so much effort to ascertain and validate
them? And why should such common-sense notions be taught to pros-

pective teachers in unctuous elaboration of the obvious? These would be legitimate questions except for one noteworthy fact about this list: *Every one of these statements is the direct opposite of what actually has been found by educational psychologists.* More intelligent pupils are *better* accepted by their classmates. Individual differences *increase* with training. One should *not* measure growth in achievement by merely subtracting pretest from posttest scores. Owing to regression effects that need to be taken into account, brighter pupils will seem to gain *less.* One does *not* eliminate undesirable behavior most effectively by punishing it. One *can* foster transfer by getting pupils to learn general concepts and principles in an intellectual discipline.

As has been remarked by Lazarsfeld (1949, p. 380), on whose discussion of obviousness I have patterned my own, if we had mentioned the actual results first, the critics would have labeled these "obvious" also. "Obviously, something is wrong with the entire argument of 'obviousness.' It should really be turned on its head. Since every kind of human reaction is conceivable, it is of great importance to know which reactions actually occur most frequently and under what conditions. . . ."

STATUS AND PROSPECTS OF RESEARCH ON TEACHER EDUCATION

Let us turn now to somewhat more positive ideas about the status and prospects of research on teacher education.

To organize these ideas, I wish to introduce two sets of distinctions. In the first place, we can distinguish three stages of knowledge derived from psychological theory and empirical research for teacher education. In the first stage, knowledge is already being used in programs of teacher education. In the second stage, knowledge is already available, but not being used. And, in the third stage, desirable knowledge is not yet available. We can liken these three stages to three conditions of money: In the first condition, money is already invested; in the second, money is being kept in a safe-deposit box rather than put to use; and in the third, the money has not yet been obtained. Like money, research-based knowledge of value in teacher education exists under each of these conditions. That is, some we already possess and use, some we merely possess but do not use, and some we do not possess yet but need to acquire.

The first stage concerns us primarily as an illustration of the kind of yield from research that critics of research on teacher education seem to ignore. I deal with the second stage to call the attention of practitioners to research products waiting to be used. And I discuss the third in an effort to sketch areas that might well concern future research on teacher education.

The second set of distinctions deals with substantive, methodological, and logistical aspects of educational research. By "substantive" I mean the concepts and principles, educational and psychological variables and their relationships, that constitute the subject matter of research on teacher education. In research on teacher education the substantive concerns are the behaviors and characteristics of teachers, the procedures of recruitment, selection, and training, and the content of teacher education courses.

By "methodological" concerns I mean ways of measuring variables and determining the relationships between them. These are the tests and statistical methods, the ways of collecting and analyzing data, that are used in research on teacher education. Such methodological concerns deal with schemes for observation, content analysis, rating, judging, testing, experimenting, correlating, analyzing variance, factor analysis, and so on.

Finally, by "logistical" I mean the host of concerns with men and money, organization and administration, entailed in planning, executing, interpreting, communicating, applying, and improving research. These are the research grant and contract programs, the fellowship and scholarship programs, the university bureaus and centers, the federal, state, and local agencies, the faculty time allotments and computer facilities—in short, the supplies and channels of brains and materials that we devote to research.

If we take the three conditions of research-based knowledge (namely, available and used, available but not used, and not yet available) and combine these with the three categories of concern in research on teacher education (namely, substantive, methodological, and logistical), we can identify nine different combinations of condition and concern. The remainder of the discussion is based on these nine combinations in an attempt to illustrate what is, and what could be, throughout the whole domain of research on teacher education.

Substantive Results

What substantive results of research are already available and being used in teacher education? Here we can cite the research on correlations between the intellectual abilities of students, as measured by standard scholastic ability tests, and their performances in their college courses; such tests are often used in selecting college students, including prospective teachers. In the same way, much has been learned and used about ways of measuring achievement in teacher education courses through objectively scorable tests, essay examinations, and methods of describing performance in student teaching, including the properties and values of students' ratings of their teachers. We markedly influence prospective teachers' conceptions of their roles; teachers from one college differ markedly in such conceptions from those trained at another college with a different orientation toward the teacher's role.

As measured by simple inventories, teachers' attitudes correlate significantly with how well they get along with students and with such personality-determined, real-life variables as rates of failing (nonpromoting) students. We know that teachers should be taught to reinforce behavior that reflects progress toward or achievement of an educational objective. Teachers need to take their students' motivations into account and either arouse appropriate motives or channel those already present in desired ways. We know something about the importance of cognitive structure for some kinds of learning, of imitation for other kinds, and of conditioning for still other kinds. And these kinds of knowledge are widely used in the education of teachers.

Another substantive outcome, already available and beginning to be widely used, is that from studies of feedback to teachers from observers' interaction analyses, from video tapes, or from ratings by their students (see Chapter 12). The evidence seems good enough to warrant even more exploitation of such feedback than it has thus far received in teacher education.

But, since I wish to characterize the used substantive yield of research in a valid way, I must state at this point that no one has an adequate basis for saying what knowledge is used in teacher education. We simply do not have the data about what goes on in our hundreds of teacher education programs, courses, or classrooms. Perhaps we should find out about this in greater detail than the occasional visitor like Conant possibly could. Or still better, we ought to develop and implement the kind of design for teacher education of which Broudy (1963, p. 88) spoke, one that "will organize, systematize, and stabilize the training of all educational workers." Perhaps such designs will result from the model programs for the education of elementary school teachers recently developed with the support of the U.S. Office of Education.

What knowledge is already available from research on teacher education, of a substantive kind, that is not being adequately used in teacher education? I can illustrate here with the knowledge acquired by Ryans (1960a) concerning the dimensions of teachers' classroom behavior and the correlates of those dimensions in teachers' attitudes, information, background, working conditions, and so on. For example,

we know from that study (pp. 350–351) that teachers who rank high
in all three of his dimensions of teacher behavior tend to be persons
who take a favorable view of other people, who find it difficult to say
anything unfavorable about other persons. This type of finding also is
consistent with much of what we know about teachers from research
with the California F Scale and the Minnesota Teacher Attitude Inventory. But so far as I know, these findings have not been coordinated
with theories of social development and person perception or put to
work in programs for teacher education, selection, and counseling. We
do not adequately explore the meaning of such research findings with
the students in our teacher education programs.

Substantive findings not yet available but worthwhile and possible
would include special ways of educating teachers for the great cities.
That research would include studies of (a) the effect of improving the
teacher's knowledge of the deprived child's social world, (b) the effect
of the deprived child's models and identification figures on his behavior,
(c) the effect on teacher performance of group appointments of new
teachers to a given slum school, and (d) the value of training in clinical
methods of remedial reading for teachers in urban areas. Many such
research problems of considerable importance can be identified, and
they need to be investigated.

Methodology

Methodological achievements of research on teacher education already in use would cover all the methods of observation, rating, content
analysis, correlational analysis, experimental design, and analysis of
variance and covariance. As Cogan (1963) and Biddle (1967) pointed
out, the use of videotape recorders has raised the analysis of classroom
behavior to new levels of reliability, objectivity, and replicability. The
videotape recorder has also made possible greatly improved techniques
for training teachers in ways of classroom behavior. Research on
teacher education has fairly standard sets of research tools with which
advanced graduate students become familiar.

Examples of methodology available but insufficiently used would
include new methods of factor analysis and other kinds of multivariate
analysis. Similarly, many of the "quasi-experimental" designs that
Campbell (1967) has expounded have not yet been used. Where the
true, more rigorous experimental designs are impossible, these designs
can yield useful research-based knowledge, despite the limitations of
non-laboratory, real-life conditions. Campbell (1967) also has contributed a promising analysis of the possibilities of administrative experimentation on teacher education, using institutional records and

other unobtrusive measures. These methodological ideas allow us to do experiments, not mere correlational studies, in important settings—wherever it is possible for an administrator to influence sustained interactions among large groups of persons. Campbell (1967, pp. 258–259) noted that

... if we are to have an experimental social science, the social scientist must develop a liaison with the people who have the power. It is not we [the social scientists], but [the administrators] who have the experimental laboratories, through being at the site, if not in the decision-making seat, when abrupt administrative policy changes are made. What we social scientists must do is to convince [administrators] of the necessity of keeping books on the experiments [they] make, and organizing your record systems and . . . publication practices so that [they] let us know what you tried and how it came out.

An example of an independent variable is a plan (Rivlin, 1962) for using team teaching and related devices to prepare and recruit prospective teachers for challenging urban areas. The dependent variable would be the "percentages of graduating teachers choosing to teach in the difficult urban areas." We could use what Campbell calls the "interrupted time series" design and collect percentages of graduating teachers choosing difficult schools over a period of, say, five years. Then we would have good evidence on the effectiveness of the new program. This type of experimental design of considerable validity can be carried out under real-life conditions with just a few changes in ways of record-keeping. A considerable number of such designs have great potential and thus far have been little used.

An example of a methodological development that is not yet available but may be possible is the need for a logic and a design for evaluating complex training programs or experimental treatments. Such an evaluation should be made both over-all and in detail, that is, in terms of the effectiveness of the many specific components of the complex program. Suppose we made a maximum effort to recruit additional students into programs of teacher education for slum areas. We might introduce a host of new treatments in a single package called the new recruiting program, or the internship program, or the fifth-year program. How could we evaluate the effect of each of the component innovations that enter into the new program? That is, how can we determine which part of the package has what effect? If the various components could be varied in a planned design, the problem would not exist. But the components often cannot be isolated from one another and varied independently in anything like a neat Latin square or factorial design. This kind of wholistic yet analytical evaluation would allow us to learn things important for theory without having to break up a socially significant program into its components.

Logistics

What logistical arrangements for research on teacher education are already available and being used? Here, the Cooperative Research Program of the Office of Education, the National Defense Education Act Title VII program, and the research grants of the National Institute of Mental Health come quickly to mind. The Small Contracts Program has fired the imagination of hundreds of graduate students in education (probably including many concerned with teacher education) with the possibilities of getting financial support for better dissertations than have been possible before. The Office of Education has also created research and development centers and regional laboratories that have brought together relatively substantial resources for integrated attacks on problems in teacher education. As already noted, the Office has also supported the planning of a dozen model programs for the education of elementary school teachers, and these programs typically include provisions for research on their own effectiveness. Also, the Office has initiated research training programs that are beginning to produce qualified investigators of educational problems, including teacher education.

When it comes to logistical developments that are available and not used, it is hard to find examples. Our logistical resources for research on teacher education are scarce. And we have built up an enormous appetite for such resources.

Finally, we come to examples of logistical developments for research on teacher education that are not yet in hand but are important and possible. Such problems may be the most important. Krathwohl (1969) proposed a National Institute of Education that would conduct research on education in the same way that the National Institutes of Health in the U. S. Public Health Service conduct medical research.

The critical shortage is one of men. We do not have an adequate number of research workers of the necessary quality to begin to grapple seriously with the problems that beset American education. The problem is that of attracting, selecting, and training a much larger and better generation of research workers. We need to establish educational research as a career about as well-populated and recognized as the careers for chemists, physicists, biologists, and engineers in American industry, medicine, and agriculture. We should stop looking to charismatic figures to solve our problems. Such men help enormously, but with or without them, we still need thousands of men and women actively engaged in educational research on something like a full-time basis, just as we have masses of research workers in other major institutions of our society.

At present, we do not have such thousands. The American Educational Research Association now has about 10,000 members, but only a fraction of them do research, and most of them do it for only a fraction of their time. We have many research projects in education in the form of master's and doctor's theses. But most of this research is done by persons for whom it is the first and last research enterprise. They come to this research out of traditions alien to it—out of teaching or administration—and they go back into those traditions after the dissertation hurdle has been cleared. Most graduate education related to teacher education does not produce workers who continue to do research.

We need what other scholarly and technical disciplines have—a tradition of graduate work into which young persons move directly from the bachelor's degree. Without first spending years as teachers (any more than young people do in psychology, chemistry, anthropology, or history), these persons would get a thorough grounding in research methodology, including statistics, measurement, and experimental design. At the same time, these students would participate actively in the research projects of their professors. Thus, early in their graduate careers, they would begin to gain research experience, rather than first passing the qualifying examinations and then writing a thesis proposal. The best part of research training—and on this point research workers seem to be unanimous—is the experience of working with another, more mature research man. It is during this experience that the student becomes imbued with the values, the itch to discover order in phenomena, the ability to tolerate negative results, the taste for subtle hypotheses and well-reasoned expectations, the patience to conduct pretests and pilot studies, the respect (but not too much respect) for the literature, and the addiction to publishing that characterize and distinguish the typical productive research worker. It is these attitudes that research workers need as much as they need knowledge about analysis of covariance or the semantic differential.

To produce persons of this stripe, who will carry out research on teacher education, we seem to need new logistical arrangements or paradigms in American education. We need a way to tap the resources of bright undergraduates who might be attracted, not merely to research in the behavioral sciences, but to research in the behavioral sciences as they apply to education. At present these young people go into psychology and sociology and find careers in many social contexts and institutions other than education. We have not been getting an adequate supply of educational research workers through these avenues. The school of education that first invents an arrangement for enticing bright young persons directly from their undergraduate work into graduate school for training as educational research workers will become for educational research what Johns Hopkins was for medical research, what Teachers College was for school administration, what Cambridge under Rutherford was for physics. Other universities would follow its lead. In a decade, we might begin to have the research on teacher education that would make obsolete our present controversial ways. We would begin to have the scientific basis for teacher education that Flexner found in 1910 for medical education.

Chapter 10

Educational Psychology in Teacher Education

The objectives of educational psychology are to provide educators with psychological concepts, principles, and facts on which reasoning about educational problems can be based. Such objectives differ from those of providing direct solutions to problems. Instead, educational psychology improves the basis for sound judgments and interpretations of experience.

Educational psychology is a "foundation" course in the same sense that physics and chemistry are foundation courses for engineers. These courses do not tell engineers how to build bridges or design refineries, but they do provide the concepts, principles, and facts upon which engineers must base their solutions to particular problems. In ancient times, substantial engineering projects were carried out without modern physics and chemistry. In the same way, much teaching has been well done over the centuries without the help of educational psychology. But engineering improved as its foundational sciences developed. Similarly, teaching should improve as educational psychology advances.

Considerations other than physical and chemical ones enter into the engineer's work; similarly, considerations other than psychological ones enter into the work of a teacher. In education, the other considerations take such forms as social values, economic necessities, and political factors. But educational psychology gives the prospective teacher the facts, concepts, and principles about human behavior and psychological characteristics that he should keep in mind as he teaches, i.e., as he formulates educational objectives, designs activities and experiences that will foster achievement of those objectives, arranges for learners to carry out those activities and undergo those experiences, and then evaluates the degree to which his students have achieved the objectives.

It may be helpful here to look at four uses of knowledge that have been distinguished by Broudy, Smith, and Burnett (1964):

1. The *associative* use of schooling, made when one responds to a question by calling up from memory something or other suggested by a cue. So-called concomitant learnings can often be classified as associative uses of schooling.

2. The *replicative* use of learning, which permits one to repeat an operation much as it was performed in school. Skills of reading, computing, and reciting belong in this group.

3. The *applicative* use of schooling, which consists in applying knowledge to particular problems of practice, such as the problems of how to teach reading or fractions. Courses in educational psychology do not usually give much actual practice in this applicative use of knowledge. Most educational psychologists seem to hold that this use of educational psychology should be relegated for the most part to subsequent stages of the teacher education program—to student teaching and courses in teaching methods and curriculum. But many critics hold that educational psychology ought to provide much more practice in applicative uses.

4. The *interpretative* use of schooling, whereby one categorizes, conceptualizes, or classifies experience to make it intelligible. This use of knowledge represents well the kinds of purposes and values that educational psychologists see in their course. To bring order out of the confusion that a neophyte experiences when he enters a classroom in the role of teacher—that is, to give him a set of psychological concepts and principles by which he can make sense out of classroom occurrences—is the use of educational psychology apparently considered pre-eminent by those who teach, and write the books for, the course. It may well be that the course ought to be geared more for action and problem-solving rather than merely for orientation and perspective. But as the course now stands, the latter objectives predominate.

The field of educational psychology has been structured and restructured repeatedly over the years by various committees of professional associations and by review publications. But these efforts at restructuring by fiat have had much less influence than the textbook writers, whose formulations are used by hundreds of instructors and thousands of prospective teachers. From an examination of the section headings of several leading textbooks, one can form an impression of the major categories of the course's content.

Although the textbooks differ in the organization, phrasing, and emphasis of their major headings, they unquestionably have much in common. On the basis of the amount of consideration it receives, the topic of *learning* must be put at the heart of the subject. Since learning is a complex process, it is usually broken down into components. After learning, as a theme of almost equal prominence, comes *growth and development in readiness*, i.e., in abilities, interests, and the like. Third, there is the ubiquitous chapter or section on *measurement and evalua-*

tion. Finally, a section or at least a chapter on *emotional and social adjustment,* or mental health, including character development, is usually present.

LEARNING

Learning, the pre-eminent topic of present-day educational psychology, is usually divided into a set of components. Motivation, perception, response, and reward, as set forth by Miller and Dollard (1941), are representative. In order to learn, a person must want something, notice something, do something, and get something. The Miller-Dollard analysis is still useful as a summary of common elements in textbook treatments of learning.

The general conception of learning contained in the Miller-Dollard scheme belongs to reinforcement theory. But, as noted in Chapter 2, educational psychologists now often make use of identification theory and cognitive theory as well. We shall not repeat here our sketches of those approaches to the description of learning, except to say that most educational psychology textbooks are still eclectic. They do not pay sole allegiance to any one of the major families of learning theory. An occasional book takes a firm stand on "cognitive theory" as against "stimulus-response conditioning theory" (e.g., Ausubel, 1968; Bigge & Hunt, 1968) or vice-versa (De Cecco, 1968), but most books, including the dominant survey of learning theory (Hilgard & Bower, 1966), pick and choose from all approaches the ideas and findings about learning that seem helpful in education. In the latter volume, 20 "principles potentially useful in practice" are classified according to whether they are emphasized within S-R theory, cognitive theory, or motivation and personality theory.

GROWTH AND DEVELOPMENT

Growth and development is a second major topic in educational psychology. It deals with physical, emotional, social, and intellectual changes in persons as a result of influences other than those explicitly arranged in the school. The great independent variable in studies of growth and development is time, or chronological age. But cultural factors are also considered major independent variables.

The study of growth and development reveals what students are like at a given age, and what they are capable of learning at that age. Such knowledge helps teachers plan their work and guides their expectations. But it cannot take the simple form of parallel lists of age levels and corresponding characteristics and behaviors normal for each age. The definition of normal is not that simple, and many factors influence whether a student will be ahead of or behind what is average for his age group.

Another concern in this area is the issue of nature and nurture. To what extent are the determiners of differences in ability to benefit from schooling to be found in heredity, rather than environment? To the degree that hereditary factors predominate, there may be little that can be done to improve children's ability, and schooling should merely be adjusted to individual differences in IQ. But insofar as environment can influence IQ and other factors in learning, something can be done about them. The whole problem was given renewed attention after Jensen (1969a) published a widely noted, detailed, and controversial analysis in the *Harvard Educational Review*. Most authors assume that teachers ought to know the nature of the issue, the ways in which evidence on it is sought, and the implications of present knowledge.

So the educational psychology course may contain material on the physical basis of heredity in chromosomes and genes, the distinction between fraternal and identical twins, and the ways in which twins and persons in other relationships have been studied to throw light on the nature-nurture issue. Students are told about the sizes of the correlation coefficients between persons of different degrees of blood relationship in such characteristics as height, IQ, temperament, and values. They are given the evidence on the ways in which impoverished environments, on the one hand, and emotional and intellectual enrichment of the child's environment, on the other, can make a difference in how he develops.

Another concern in studying growth and development may be termed social class. The ideal is that American education should serve all children. In recent decades American educational psychologists have become much more aware that lower-class children differ from middle-class children not only economically but in cultural variables that determine development. Hence, such children also differ in the intellectual nurturing provided by their environments, and in attitudes, values, aspirations, and other characteristics that affect readiness for school learning.

One other topic often comes under the heading of growth and development—sex-linked differences, or in the differences between boys and girls in abilities, interests, and skills. Here again, the aim is to eliminate erroneous preconceptions on the part of prospective teachers and to inculcate accurate expectations. Such concerns may help American education to reduce the vast waste of female intellectual resources.

EDUCATIONAL MEASUREMENT AND EVALUATION

Measurement and evaluation is a third major topic of present-day educational psychology. Conant (1963) in his discussion of the proper educational psychology for prospective secondary school teachers, classed it as the only topic that all such teachers needed. Tests and measurements are used by teachers in two ways: to measure a student's readiness before a learning experience and to measure his achievement after it. In the first function, measures of intellectual ability and skill, attitude and interest, and previous achievement are used in appraising the readiness of students for some kind or level of new learning. The placement of students in various grade levels, or in fast or slow sections within a given grade level, is often based in part on tests. The search to understand why a student may not be learning well enough may employ standardized tests of mental ability and other factors.

To use the results of such tests properly, teachers need to understand how the tests are made, given, and interpreted. They need to know something about how definitions of mental abilities are derived, how test questions are written and evaluated, how subtle changes in testing procedure can influence and even invalidate test results, and how the norms of mental tests are developed. They need to know something about the theory and method of estimating test reliability (the degree to which a test yields consistent measures) and especially validity (the degree to which a test score has meaning or measures what it is intended to measure). And finally, they need a background of knowledge about the results obtained in testing groups differing in age, sex, occupation, social class, urban and rural residence, and so on.

The technology of testing, especially standardized mental ability testing, is a solid achievement of the behavioral sciences in this century. Testing goes considerably beyond the commonsense folk wisdom to which Conant relegated a great deal of the content of educational psychology. This area contains a good share of the best-established content to be found in the course. Indeed, at one university the course was often begun with material on tests and measurements in an effort to gain the respectful attention of students as soon as possible.

The second major function of testing, as already noted, is to help teachers evaluate student achievement. The rationale and content in this area are also fairly well agreed upon. Teachers should know how to define the objectives of their instruction in terms of observable behavior on the part of students. To elicit this behavior, teachers must know how to write valid test questions. Hence prospective teachers are sensitized to the difference between test questions that elicit mere knowledge of unrelated bits of information, and questions that require higher mental processes, such as analysis, judgment, and explanation. Although not enough can be done along these lines in the first course in educational psychology, students are at least taught that the so-called objective types of test item can be used for getting at kinds of achievement other than unstructured knowledge. They are also taught that essay tests have distinct advantages when they are properly constructed and graded.

EMOTIONAL AND SOCIAL ADJUSTMENT

The fourth major topic of educational psychology is emotional and social adjustment. Some books call it personality integration, the self-concept, or mental health, and it also includes such topics as character development, discipline, or social-emotional problems in the classroom.

Emotional and social aspects of adjustment are important not only in their own right, as objectives of child-rearing and education, but also because they determine how well students learn the intellectual matter that everyone agrees should be a focus of the school. During the 1930's–1950's, these emotional and social concerns of educational psychologists were strongly emphasized. But in recent years there seems to have been a countertendency to pay more attention to cognitive, intellectual aspects of learning and teaching. In any case, concern with adjustment has led to the inclusion in educational psychology of material on sociometry, group dynamics, student-centered teaching methods, counseling, role-playing, inventories of students' problems, and research with projective techniques.

Although attention to these matters may be counterbalanced with emphasis on academic learning, it is unlikely that educational psychologists will cease to be deeply interested in how students feel and how they get along with other people. Some writers on education want to reduce to a minimum the school's concern with emotional and social matters on the ground that the school should stick to what it alone can do in our society, namely, nurture the intellect through contact with the basic academic disciplines. The home, the neighborhood, and the church should, in this view, take responsibility for character and personality development. But other writers view any such tendencies with strong misgivings. They point to the millions of children in our great cities whose homes, neighborhoods, and churches—whatever ought to be their function—are not doing the job of fostering mental health and good character. And not only the dwellers in slums, the so-called culturally disadvantaged, arouse such misgivings. Newspapers carry stories of adolescents from middle-class and wealthy homes who commit vandalism and other delinquencies. The hippie and drug cultures are also symptomatic of emotional and motivational problems. Attempts are made to eliminate such anomalies in the behavior of children whose homes and communities seem, at least superficially, to be as good as American society affords. These attempts raise anew the question of what the schools should do to give students a sense of purpose and a desire to lead a good life as defined by the best in the American heritage.

In the debate on the functions of schools, most educational psychologists will be found on the side of those who want teachers to understand and do something constructive about the mental health and character of their students. Teachers are thus viewed as agents of society responsible for something more than the inculcation of the intellectual virtues. Our intellectual equipment for understanding emotional and social aspects of students may not be good enough. There may not exist a clear enough conception of what teachers can do with such an understanding once they have it. Nevertheless, educational psychologists for the most part are unwilling to abandon the effort to give such tools and ideas to prospective teachers.

One practical consideration—classroom discipline—serves to keep such topics in the forefront of the concerns of educators of prospective teachers. This matter always turns up prominently in studies of the causes of failure of beginning teachers. Teachers are dismissed from their initial position most often because of failures to maintain classroom discipline and not for failures to help students achieve the cognitive objectives of schooling. Whatever the arguments in favor of concentrating on intellectual matters, school administrators and teachers continue to be troubled about discipline. Since discipline turns out to be a matter of emotional and social adjustment and of mental hygiene and character development, educational psychologists may be expected to continue to teach about such matters.

Underlying the approach to emotional and social adjustment that is taught to prospective teachers is a view of human behavior as caused, or determined. The working principle offered teachers is expressed in such terms as these: " . . . children behave in about the only way they can considering the factors in their backgrounds and present conditions surrounding them . . . " (Blair, Jones, & Simpson, 1968, p. 409).

Thus, teachers are taught to look for the causes of adjustment problems not in the pupil's intrinsic weakness, or bad character, but in the relationship between the student's characteristics and his environment. Misbehavior or withdrawal may result from school tasks inappropriate—too hard or too easy—for a student's abilities. The school tasks may seem to the student to be irrelevant to his needs, interests, or outlook on life. The amount of sitting still that a teacher requires may be inappropriate to a young child's need for sheer physical moving around. A teacher's behavior may seem to a student to be outrageously unfair in relation to the student's notions of legitimate teacher power. According to Skinner (1968), teachers fail because they rely too much on "aversive," i.e., unpleasant or painful, stimulation and control.

The Adjustment Process

Given a concern for social and emotional adjustment, and a view of behavior as caused, what does the educational psychologist offer the prospective teacher? The answer can be built around the following model of the adjustment process that, in one form or another, has been taught for many years: Adjustment begins with a need that the person then undertakes to satisfy. If his first effort to satisfy the need is frustrated, he resorts to varied kinds of behavior or to so-called adjustment mechanisms of various kinds. Eventually, the person achieves satisfaction of the need or continues to suffer frustration. In this way he builds up a kind of emotional or social adjustment.

Basic psychological needs are acquired in the process of growing up in society. There is no universally accepted scheme or list of such needs, but the following are often mentioned: status, security, affiliation, independence, and achievement.

Under ordinary circumstances, the student finds ways to satisfy these needs in his everyday life. He achieves the kind of status that he has come to expect. He enjoys the kind of affiliation that he has learned to need. He gains the kind of independence that seems to him appropriate to his age. He satisfies his need for achievement and his need to avoid failure. His family, his peers, and his teachers in the home, neighborhood, and school interact with him in ways that leave him fairly well satisfied.

But for some students, on some occasions, conditions arise to frustrate such needs. It may be a personal defect or physical ailment, poverty, social customs and restrictions, conflict between competing needs, or conflict between the individual's conscience and his needs. When the individual is frustrated, he is tense, uncomfortable, restless —in a state of imbalance.

To reduce this frustration, he may resort to a direct and rational attack on the obstacles to the satisfaction of his needs. Or he may use one of the "adjustment mechanisms": aggression, compensation, sublimation, identification, rationalization, projection, repression, re-action formation, egocentrism, negativism, withdrawal, regression, psychosomatic ailments. He may even become neurotic or psychotic. Educational psychology courses typically deal with these adjustment mechanisms at least to the extent of defining and illustrating them. Presumably, the teacher should become able to recognize such mechanisms in his students and in his own behavior. The teacher can then cope better with the irrational ways in which his students sometimes seek to satisfy their emotional and social needs in classroom life. Or the teacher may then be better able to recognize and forestall such irrationality on his own part.

Discipline

"Discipline" generally refers to the degree or quality of control exercised by the teacher over his students. Disciplinary problems are failures in such control. They take the form of all the minor and major offenses against order, the peccadilloes and crimes, that are familiar to anyone who has attended an elementary and secondary school.

Educational psychologists regard disciplinary problems as symptoms of something wrong, rather than as the basic problems in themselves. What to do about the specific behavior called a disciplinary problem is one thing; what to do about the underlying trouble is another. A disciplinary problem may be a symptom of something either trivial or important.

Teachers are given the principle that treating the symptom is not the same as solving the underlying problem. Treating the symptom may be a matter of sending the child out of the room, keeping him after school, giving him a talking to, or in some other way imposing sanctions that he will seek to avoid in the future by not repeating the kinds of behavior that caused him to have an unpleasant experience. To determine the underlying problem, however, the teacher needs to know something about mechanisms of adjustment, behavior problems, interests and abilities, home and school environment, personality and temperament, and the dynamics of social interaction in the school.

Teachers need two kinds of equipment in dealing with disciplinary problems: tactics and strategies. They need tactics to deal with the immediate problem of restoring order in the classroom and the school. They need strategies for solving the problems of emotional and social adjustment that may underlie the immediate disciplinary problem.

The teacher's tactics for restoring order in the classroom should be determined by whatever works in the short run and does not do harm in the long run. Such tactics, analogous to aspirin, consist of removing the disorderly pupil from the group in one way or another, or restraining him physically from continuing to misbehave, or even, in some cases, applying that universally understood measure known as corporal punishment. It does not matter too much what the teacher does as long as it works for the moment and does not do any long-range harm.

Some of the tactics that are considered to do long-range harm, in all likelihood, are punishing a whole group for the misconduct of an individual, using sarcasm or ridicule, overlooking the student's physical illness or disorder, or reacting to misconduct as a personal affront. In general, it is recognized as harmful to employ hard, cruel, implacable forms of punishment. Also, as Skinner (1968) has pointed out, there are more subtle, less violent, but equally "aversive" procedures in the operation of most present-day classrooms and schools— factors that cripple learning and motivation.

Good tactics are reasonable, just, and fair; the teacher explains the reasons for the rules, allows discussion, and permits students to participate in establishing the regulations insofar as they are qualified to do so.

Educational psychologists agree fairly well on the question of punishments. For example, one book states: "Praise and social approval are more effective in promoting good standards of conduct than are censure, blame, and punishment" (Blair, Jones, & Simpson, 1968, p. 410). The author of another book writes: "If one wishes merely to suppress unwanted responses during the time pupils are under the teacher's eye, consistent punishment would be expected to do the job. If the aim is to teach pupils to regulate their own conduct so that the teacher's pressure can be removed, punishment will not work" (Cronbach, 1963, p. 493).

The general tone of educational psychologists is one that urges teachers to emphasize the positive kinds of reinforcement, insofar as such emphases are reasonable and workable. Given a choice between two alternative and effective ways of eliminating misbehavior, the teacher should generally choose the positive over the negative, i.e., try to elicit good behavior that can be rewarded rather than merely punish the undesirable behavior.

In social learning and imitation, the learner's model (e.g., the teacher) must be someone whom the learner likes and respects. Only when the student positively identifies with his teacher will the student be inclined to adopt the teacher's attitudes and values about classroom order, among many other things. And to engender such liking and respect for their teachers on the part of students, educational psychologists advocate that, whenever a reasonable choice is at hand, the teacher give preference to reward and approval—but only when the choice is available and reasonable. Thus, the teacher ought to be alert to every opportunity to give praise and approval and to avoid reproof and punishment. But this is not the same as advocating that reproof and punishment be avoided entirely; when the need for reasonable punishment is clear and distinct, it should not go unmet.

When disciplinary problems arise too often, a teacher needs to examine his strategies. Like the headache that comes back after the aspirin has worn off, a disciplinary problem may reappear after a tactic has run its course. Then something more than a momentary aberration is involved. Here the teacher is taught to re-examine what he knows about the readiness of his students for the kind of learning that he is trying to bring about. Frustration caused by repeated failure to learn or get approval, or boredom resulting from a student's failure to see connections between what he wants and what he is required to do—such conditions indicate that a teacher's whole approach needs re-examination if the problems underlying poor discipline are to be solved and something more than symptoms are to be attacked.

SPECIAL NEEDS OF EDUCATIONAL PSYCHOLOGY IN THE GREAT CITIES

It is in the great cities, with their concentrations of culturally disadvantaged families, that the problems of school adjustment and character development are especially profound. The problems are aggravated by the now well-recognized tendency of teachers to move away from positions in the big city slums, where the teaching seems harder and less rewarding. One special aspect of big-city education, accordingly, is that of teacher personnel: the recruitment, selection, education, placement, and retention of larger numbers of teachers who are better qualified for work in the great cities. Many of the problems are not psychological; rather, they are administrative, financial, political, curricular, and operational. Nonetheless, the psychological aspects of educational problems in the great cities loom large. "The incidence of mental health problems is greatest in the slums. A sociologist commented that when social class figures on mental problems are examined, the only significant increase from one class to another is between the lowest socioeconomic class and the one above it" (Great Cities Program, etc., 1963). The rate of school dropouts is highest in the slum areas of big cities. It is easy to defend the proposition that the best equipment of educational psychology ought to be brought to bear on the problems of educating the culturally deprived child.

Needed Research on Students

Teaching in the great cities is different because the students are different. Much knowledge of the characteristics of culturally deprived children and youth is already at hand, but more is needed. Such knowledge can be categorized according to whether it deals with intellectual abilities, achievement, attitudes, interests, environment and background, emotional and social adjustment, or physical aspects.

Intellectual Abilities. To what degree do the test performances of culturally deprived youth reflect their environmental disadvantages, or the biases built into the tests, or indeed, hereditary patterns? Research on social class and intelligence tests, summarized by W. W. Charters (1963), needs to be pursued further. The Davis-Eells test, intended to yield an index of problem-solving ability that was educationally significant but also fair to children from lower-class backgrounds, seems not to have succeeded well enough in eliminating social class differences or in producing scores that are valid against present-day criteria of school success.

But the search for such a test should not be abandoned. Riessman (1962) suggested that further exploration be made of the usefulness of "games" orientations, longer time limits, fewer academic and bookish problems, methods of scoring that deal with process as well as the accuracy of the final answer, items that do not discriminate between deprived and middle-class groups, pretraining students in effective methods of test-taking, and training examiners in special methods of establishing rapport with culturally deprived children.

In the 1960's, New York City and Los Angeles abandoned the use of group intelligence tests in their schools in favor of complete reliance on achievement tests. Teachers knowledgeable in the measurement aspects of educational psychology would at least know what questions to ask about this policy.

Educational psychology also is concerned with the organization of mental ability. Into what kinds of factors—e.g., verbal, numerical, spatial—can intelligence be analyzed? Such factors are known to exist along with a general factor of mental ability. Are the mental abilities of culturally deprived children organized factorially in the same way as those of middle-class children? That is, do they show the same results in factor analyses of mental ability as do middle-class children? Do batteries of mental tests have the same kind of predictive value, in regression equations, for culturally deprived children? Studies along these lines might yield improved understanding of the cognitive processes of culturally deprived children.

Jensen (1969b) has obtained evidence which he thinks suggests that disadvantaged children are not inferior in associative, or rote-learning, abilities, but only in conceptual, or higher-order abilities. If so, methods of teaching lower-class children should be designed to take advantage of the kinds of abilities in which they are not handicapped. But these are still being debated (Humphreys & Dachler, 1969a, 1969b).

Achievement of Cognitive Objectives. Culturally deprived students get lower marks from teachers and lower scores on standardized achievement tests. Perhaps there are better ways of defining and appraising the achievement of culturally deprived students; perhaps ways can be devised to help teachers eliminate their social-class biases from the marks and grades that they give students. That such biases exist has been suggested by research on teachers' perceptions of their students. Studies have shown that teachers often have less favorable attitudes toward lower-class children. Students with a lower socioeconomic position tend to have lower sociometric status among their fellow students. If "the same factors which contribute to his rejection by peers tend to arouse attitudes of rejection on the part of the teacher" (Gronlund, 1959, p. 281), then it is readily inferred that teachers' marks tend to be biased against lower-class students. Training teachers to understand and accept such students can reduce this bias in teachers' marks; similarly, curricula and objectives better suited to the needs and interests of culturally deprived students would reduce bias in defining and measuring educational achievement.

Attitudes, Interests, and Values. Riessman (1962, p. 13) found that "the under-privileged person is much more oriented to the vocational, in contrast to the academic aspect of education," and has "great respect for physical science" but is "least interested in social studies, literature and the arts, as they are now presented in schools." The teacher and the curriculum builder need to acquire and act upon much more detailed knowledge concerning the attitudes of culturally deprived children and youth toward different kinds of people, occupations, and activities. Careful surveys of these attitudes, obtained with inventories and open-ended questions, would allow the replacement of conjectures with facts.

Environment and Background. Child-rearing practices, parent-child relationships, and cultural and physical environments determine the behavioral opportunities of children. The crowded conditions, poor sanitation, and loose family structure of the homes and neighborhoods of culturally deprived students have an influence on their strengths and limitations. Reissman (1962) offered provocative hypotheses concerning the meaning of physical punishment as used by parents of lower-class children, the possible implications of parent-child relationships in lower-class homes for the significance of psychoanalytic concepts developed by middle-class persons, and the significance for sex behavior of crowded living conditions. Again, teachers in the great cities need more detailed knowledge based on careful research.

Emotional and Social Adjustment. There have already been some studies of the differences between middle- and lower-class students in their responses to lists of problems to be checked as to whether they are troublesome to the student, in their school dropout rates, and in their morale. Teachers need better knowledge in this area also, based on more careful inventories, interviews, ratings, observations, and content analyses.

The nutritional status and health problems of lower-class children need to be described and understood in relation to their schooling. Lower-class children report more health problems on checklists of their concerns and worries. The role of athletics in the life of the culturally deprived boy is different from that in the life of the suburban, middle-class son of a college-educated professional worker.

Research on Teaching Culturally Disadvantaged Students

Let us assume that teaching consists of (1) motivating students, (2) directing their perceptions, (3) eliciting their responses, and (4) reinforcing these responses. How do these functions take special forms in teaching culturally deprived students?

1. Some writers suggest that culturally deprived children respond best to strictly utilitarian justifications of the value of school learning. If so, the new mathematics and science curricula, intended to be less narrowly functional in everyday life, will either fail or need to be especially adapted for lower-class students. But evidence here is scanty. Old assumptions about the futility of motivating students through appeals to the basic structures of mathematics and science have turned out to be false as far as middle-class students are concerned. It may be that a genuine effort will show these assumptions to be false for lower-class children as well, but only further research can tell.

The family life of the culturally deprived student may force upon him a greater concern with sharing, cooperation, and group goals. If so, the teacher can make effective use of group processes for motivational purposes. Group projects, role-playing, team games, and incentives for group achievement may therefore prove to be more effective with lower-class students.

2. A whole school of theorists of perception has grown up around the notion that motives, needs, and values exert directive influences on perceptions. Poor children have been considered to have more distorted perceptions of the sizes of coins, for example, than do rich children. The emotional significance of a word appears to influence the speed with which it can be recognized. Riessman (1962, pp. 69, 73) held that deprived children "appear to think in spatial terms, rather than temporal terms (they often have poor time perspective)," and that the deprived child's style is "physical and visual rather than aural." They seem, he states, "to have a very different attitude toward abstract concepts. They need to have the abstract constantly and intimately pinned to the immediate, the sensory, the topical. This is not to say that they dislike abstract thinking. It is, rather, that they do it differently."

Educational psychologists ask whether these notions—directive states in perception and differences in preferred perceptual modes— are valid and have implications for teaching methods. These aspects of the perception-directing components of teaching seem to be worthy of investigation.

3. Teaching can vary from the lecture method, where the learner is passive (but only apparently!), to the discussion method and programmed learning, in which the learner responds frequently and actively. Do lower- and middle-class students differ in how well they learn under passive and active methods? Some current research on programmed learning has shown that the active responding makes little difference. Children have been found to learn about as well when they read the response in the program as when they make it themselves. Yet, writers like Riessman refer to "the physical or motoric style of deprived groups." If a style difference exists, overt responding may be more effective in getting such students to learn. The active response feature of teaching machines, combined with their game-like quality, may make them more effective with culturally deprived students. Participation in classroom processes through discussion, group planning, and other kinds of activities may also prove to be more valuable for lower-class than middle-class students.

4. For culturally deprived students, the value of report card grades must be questioned. Riessman (1962) distinguished between love and respect and considered the lower-class child to want the latter particularly, since "love is not a major issue in the deprived home . . . (but) respect, on the other hand, is something that the child is not likely to

have received in the culture at large" (pp. 46–47). Teachers must be able to communicate the respect they feel, and conversely, must also gain status in the lower-class students' eyes. Unless the teacher has such status, he cannot be an effective dispenser of rewards. In lower-class schools, unlike middle-class schools, the teacher does not have high status automatically, but must win it.

Research has not thus far been much concerned with whether various traits and characteristics of teachers have different educational significance for lower-class than for middle-class students. Yet, in at least one instance, the validity of a teacher attitude inventory was much higher for students who emphasized warmth in what they wanted of a teacher than for students who emphasized instructional skill (Della Piana & Gage, 1955). If lower-class students emphasize teacher warmth, the attitudes measured by the Minnesota Teacher Attitude Inventory—permissive, acceptant attitudes—should be all the more significant for teacher effectiveness in winning a favorable response from such students.

Riessman (1962) suggested that teachers of disadvantaged children should have some "identification with the underdog," should have a reformer's zeal, should be physical rather than word-ridden in their approach, and should be "dedicated." Educational psychologists would want to develop methods of measuring these dimensions and validate them against criteria of effectiveness in teacher-pupil relationships. Research on teachers' personality traits must take the pupils' social class into account.

What is known about pupils' characteristics, teaching methods, and teachers' personalities that bears on education in the great cities should be used to improve the education of teachers for those cities. Some attempts to contend with these special problems of teacher education have already been made. (See, for example, Rivlin, 1962; Yeshiva University, 1963; Great Cities Program, etc., 1963; Taba & Elkins, 1966).

Many of the teacher education problems are not, strictly speaking, problems of educational psychology. Increasing salaries, hiring more teachers to make smaller classes possible, and eliminating certain examination requirements and red tape—all these may help to improve the competitive position of the great cities in employing new teachers. Co-operative arrangements between school districts and colleges for teacher education, getting the mass media to present a better-rounded and more favorable image of what teaching in the great cities entails, and perhaps establishing special certificates for teachers of culturally deprived children have all been recommended by knowledge-able students of the problems.

Educational psychology bears not only upon the content of teacher education but also upon its methods. The best ways of teaching students should suggest better ways of teaching teachers. Educational psychology needs to be applied to teacher education as much as it has already been applied to the education of students in our elementary and secondary schools.

Chapter 11

The Evaluation of Teaching: An Analysis of Ends and Means

We can appraise teaching for any of these purposes: to provide a basis for *administrative decisions* on promotion, tenure, and pay; to provide a basis for *self-improvement* on the part of teachers; and to provide a *criterion for use in research* on teaching.

The purpose that governs an appraisal affects the usefulness of a particular approach. An approach may be valid and useful for one purpose but not for another. As a broad generalization, this is a simple idea. When spelled out, however, it leads to judgments on the usefulness of various methods for each of the purposes, and perhaps to some proposals for next steps.

EVALUATION OF TEACHING FOR ADMINISTRATIVE PURPOSES

In appraising teaching to obtain a basis for administrative decisions on promotion, tenure, and pay, one has to make sure above all that the appraisal is "fair." "Fair" here means not penalizing instructors because of teaching conditions over which they have no control. Examples of such conditions are the level of the course or class (e.g., elementary or secondary, undergraduate or graduate), class size, the elective or required nature of the subject, and its location on-campus or off-campus, in a suburb or a slum.

Students' Ratings

Consider the approach to appraising the quality of teaching by means of students' ratings. Suppose it is found that there are non-chance differences in the average rating received by teachers according to whether they teach elective or required courses, undergraduate or graduate courses, or small as against large classes. In at least one instance where students' ratings of instructors were studied, namely, in the College of Education at the University of Illinois, such significant differences did occur. Teachers of the lower-level courses consistently received less favorable mean ratings than did those of more advanced courses. Teachers in courses with 30-39 students consistently received lower ratings than did those in courses with more or fewer students. Instructors and assistant professors consistently received lower ratings than the associate professors and professors. Teachers of on-campus courses received significantly worse ratings than did those of off-campus courses. Finally, teachers of elective courses received consistently more favorable ratings than did instructors of required courses.

These differences were not only statistically but also substantively significant. For each of the differences, many basic questions can be asked. Are students in very small and very large classes better taught, because such sections are easier to teach, or are the students more lenient and generous in their rating tendencies? Are teachers of higher academic rank better teachers, or do they get the more generous and more lenient students? Do teachers operate more effectively in elective courses, or are the students in such courses easier to please, perhaps because they are better motivated?

Such questions are typically unanswerable if only the students' ratings of teacher effectiveness are available. Whatever their values in other circumstances, the question remains. Can students' ratings be made "fair," by any practicable means, in such a way that we can be certain not to penalize a teacher for working under unfavorable conditions over which he has no control? If a full professor was assigned a graduate, elective, off-campus course of intermediate size, these Illinois data indicate that he was almost certain to get relatively high ratings from his students. If an instructor was assigned to teach an undergraduate, required, on-campus course of relatively large size, he was almost certain to receive relatively low ratings from his students.

It might be possible to correct the unfairness in students' ratings by statistical means. A school system or university could make up separate tables of norms for interpreting students' ratings in all these various categories. That is, it could have separate norms for each academic rank, for elective and required subjects, and so on. To do so, however, might take much more data, subjected to more refined analysis, than any school system or university yet has acquired. It may be possible and worth the trouble, but so far as I know, the job has never yet been done.

Student Achievement

How much students have learned has obvious strength as a basis for appraising teaching. This approach is usable in large school systems or universities having many classes or courses taught by many instructors under uniform conditions. Among these uniform conditions would be the same objectives, the same textbooks, the same laboratories, the same class size, and so on. Also the factors other than the teacher that determine student achievement would need to be controlled statistically. Among these factors would be student intelligence, family background, and previous schooling. Such a basis for evaluating teachers can be objective insofar as the measures of student achievement are objective.

Typically the instructors in such many-sectioned courses at the college level are comparatively junior members of the academic staff, such as graduate teaching assistants. It may be particularly desirable to appraise teachers at this early stage in their academic careers. Those instructors whose sections *significantly and consistently* underachieve may justifiably receive administrative scrutiny. On the face of it, such evidence would certainly raise questions as to their effectiveness as teachers. Administrative steps might then be taken to remedy their shortcomings or to weed them out of the teaching staff.

But it should be remembered that this method of appraisal can be used with justification only when the achievement of students under various teachers can be objectively appraised and corrected for factors beyond the teacher's control. In all those hundreds of courses where only one or two instructors teach the same course, it is hard to see how this approach can work.

Furthermore, the side effects of this approach might harm teaching. Teachers might begin to "teach for the tests" with a vengeance and permit achievement of other objectives to suffer. Teacher morale would also, according to the testimony of many teachers and administrators, be expected to deteriorate.

Observation

Observation by expert judges of teaching probably cannot be used for administrative appraisals. Observers are hard enough to ignore when they are friends or researchers, whose impressions will not affect one's standing. But when the teacher knows he is being looked over by someone whose opinion will determine his promotion or salary, his performance may depend more on his nerve than on his teaching skill. Perhaps this alone is enough to make such a program unworkable. But there are many other obstacles—like the difficulties of adequate time sampling and staffing—to the success of such an approach, even if we assume that such observations can yield valid evidence on the effectiveness of teaching. And, so far, research support for that assumption is much too weak.

EVALUATION FOR SELF-IMPROVEMENT

For the teacher who wants to learn about his shortcomings so that he can lessen them, students' ratings need not have the faults described above. Such ratings have yielded useful evidence on teaching at levels as low as fourth grade and as high as medical school. The teacher can repeatedly give one or more of a wide variety of rating scales or questionnaires to his students, under anonymous conditions, and study the results. He may be helped in interpreting these results if he has norms showing how other teachers have been rated. He can also build up his own set of norms over the years. The sources of bias may still operate. But if the teacher interprets the ratings for himself with reference only to himself, he can obtain valid information. He can note the high and low points in the profile of how his students rate him. However bruising to his ego the low points may be, he can nurse his wounds in private and eventually do something about them. With enough motivation and ingenuity, he can diagnose his faults more exactly and find ways to remove or compensate for them. The teacher can talk things over with students or colleagues, read books on teaching, and consult his spouse. But at least he will not be risking an administrative action which is unfair because his low ratings are due to factors in his teaching situation over which he has no control. And, as we shall see in Chapter 12, the evidence suggests that teachers improve their behaviors as a result of receiving such information.

Other methods of appraising teaching as a basis for self-improvement are available. The teacher can pay more attention to the shape of his profile of ratings than to its level. He can get diagnostic information in this way without putting his ego on the block. The administrator on the other hand is bound to be interested more in the mean level of the ratings. And, as has been indicated, the level of student ratings is influenced by many factors beyond the teacher's control.

Another method has been used by some teachers. They have called in a colleague to conduct a mass interview of the class near the end of the course. The teacher, obviously, stays away from that meeting, but he then receives a report on this interview from his friend. When presented with all the qualitative detail and sympathetic understanding that only a friend can provide, this report has yielded some of the advantages of a clinical interview without sacrificing student anonymity.

Finally, the teacher bent on getting feedback for self-improvement has always been able to look at his students' achievements as evidence on his teaching. In one sense, what has not been learned has not been taught well. If so, the teacher can look at students' responses to oral and written questions, quizzes, and examinations. Where the answers are weak, the teacher can infer that his teaching has been ineffective, and can change his methods accordingly.

EVALUATION OF TEACHING AS A CRITERION IN RESEARCH

The third use of evaluation of teaching considered here is that of providing a criterion of effectiveness in research aimed at understanding, predicting, and controlling the teaching-learning process.

Styles of Research on Teaching

Three styles of research on teaching can be distinguished: experimental, correlational, and process-descriptive. In experimental studies of teaching, the independent variable is manipulated. This variable is teaching method, while the dependent variable consists of changes in the knowledge, understanding, or attitudes of students. The result of this kind of study typically takes the form of a difference between means on the dependent variable. In the second style, the independent variable is not manipulated. Typically it is some measure of the teacher's behavior and characteristics obtained by observation, testing, or rating; the dependent variable is again a measure of the students' knowledge, understanding, or attitude. Here the result of the study is typically some kind of correlation coefficient.

A third style of research on teaching is less ambitious. In this style, the emphasis is on description. The purpose is not so much to ascertain relationships between variables as to describe an aspect of the teaching process in itself. It often seems in such research as if attention is being focused on only one variable. Examples are studies (Anderson, et al., 1945, 1946) of teachers' dominative-integrative behavior in the primary grades, analyses of teachers' verbal behaviors (Withall, 1956), descriptions of students' thought processes during lectures and discussions (Bloom, 1954), and studies of logical aspects of teaching (Smith, et al., 1964; Bellack, et al., 1966).

Both of the first two styles of research often benefit from the third. Experimental studies of teaching methods and correlational studies of teachers' traits have often labored with variables too grossly defined. When one point on a teaching methods variable is labeled "the lecture method," we have not denoted in adequate detail just what the lecture method has consisted of. Lectures obviously have many dimensions and qualities. The same is true of the discussion method, recitation, assignment-making, testing, and grading. Similarly, teachers' traits need to be studied for what they mean in classroom behavior; the authoritarian teacher's actions need to be differentiated from those of the nonauthoritarian teacher (see McGee, 1955). Better descriptive studies are needed to reveal what actually goes on in classrooms during lectures, discussions, recitations, and demonstrations. Improved description will make possible more fruitful experimental and correlational studies.

Descriptive Research on Medical Practice

One such descriptive study comes from a different profession. In this study (Peterson, 1956), about 90 practitioners of general medicine in North Carolina were actually observed as they went about their work. The observers, themselves expert internists, spent three days or so with each physician, in his office, on house calls, and at the hospital. A detailed schedule of questions and of the information and observations being sought was brought along on each visit. These forms were never shown to the physician; the observer filled them in during the course of the visit or after it was over.

In the most interesting part of the questionnaire, the observer filled out detailed checklists on the general practitioner's clinical routines for diagnosis and therapy as he applied them to new patients or others for whom a careful history and examination were needed. In this checklist there were items dealing with the physician's history-taking, physical examination, laboratory procedures, sterile techniques, therapy, and obstetrical care. The physicians observed were chosen from the population of general practitioners in North Carolina so as to be a representative stratified sample. The stratification was based on area of the state, age group, urban or rural place of practice, and medical school attended. The methods of scoring the data obtained with the interviews and observations were carefully worked out. Both interobserver reliability and test-retest reliability were examined.

The authors considered one aspect of validity—does a physician being observed and followed attempt to "alter his habitual patterns of practice in order to create a more favorable impression of his performance?" Against this possibility, they stated that

it is difficult abruptly to change established habits and reactions patterns and even less likely that alterations could be consistently maintained for the three- or four-day period during which observations were carried out. As noted previously, the physician was not informed that assessment of the level of his performance was one of the objectives of this study. Although some physicians grasped this purpose, it seems very improbable that physicians significantly altered their habits greatly during the period of observation; however, it is impossible to gage [sic] the extent of the possible bias.

As might be expected, the study yielded a treasure-house of information on the quality of medical care provided by general practitioners. A large part of the report discusses the percentages of physicians that did and did not carry out specific procedures considered desirable in general practice. Remarkable variation in the performance of general practitioners was noted. The study provided valuable measures of this variation as well as of the central tendencies in general practice.

One point is simply that such a study was made. The physician-patient relationship is at least as sensitive, delicate, and complex as any to be found between teacher and student in a classroom. Yet it was possible to define what to look for in appraising the physician's general practice, to gain entry into his place of work, to watch him at his work, to describe what was seen, and to draw some provocative conclusions about medical practice. And all this was not a quick foray, like those in which a single perspicacious and wise researcher invades a few classrooms for an hour or two (e.g., Klapper, 1949), but a systematic, comprehensive, large-scale investigation of a representative sample.

It is true that some descriptive, observational studies have been made of teaching. But they have not been systematic or extensive enough. We do not know enough about what goes on in elementary school classrooms, high school classes in English or physics, or college classes in freshman rhetoric, in engineering drawing, or advanced zoology.

In short, we need better process-descriptive research in the form of major projects, using questionnaires, interviews, observations, and recordings applied to representative samples of classrooms.

A second point is that we can perhaps evaluate teachers' procedures in a way similar to that used in the North Carolina study in evaluating physicians' procedures. For example, in any valid examination of the abdomen, it is necessary for the patient to lie on his back. Yet some physicians did not have the patient lie down. The evaluation of this procedure was based on well-established knowledge in anatomy, physiology, and pathology. It is not necessary to correlate the use of the having-the-patient-lie-down procedure with ultimate criteria such as the patient's long-range physical well-being. The validity of this "item" in the evaluation of physicians' procedures could be established in terms of its immediate, or short-range, effects on next steps or accuracy in diagnosis. Similarly, aspects of treatment can be validated in terms of their short-range effects on physiological processes rather than ultimate effects on health and longevity.

Are there not such procedures in teaching whose desirability can be established on the basis of what is known about logic, learning, or mental hygiene? For example, we can vouch for the desirability of the teacher's following the rules of logic in defining a new term. Such a rule would call for specifying both the class of things to which the thing being defined belongs and the distinctive features of the thing within that class. Or we can assume that teachers should give students opportunities to apply new knowledge in a variety of contexts and feedback on the correctness of their applications. Or we can assume that teachers should avoid sarcasm and ridicule in evaluating student behavior. Then, following the model of the North Carolina study, we could score teachers on the degree to which they followed such correct procedures or avoided incorrect ones. The "correctness" would be based on our knowledge of logic, learning, and mental hygiene, just as the correctness of medical procedures was based on knowledge of anatomy, physiology, and pathology.

Much of the past approach to the evaluation of teaching has insisted that every evaluation be based on correlations between teachers' behaviors and students' relatively long-range learnings. Such correlations have been low and inconsistent. They would probably be similarly low between medical procedures and long-range patient health. Too many other factors intervene to attenuate such correlations. The connection between any single medical procedure and patient health is too loose to show up in a substantial correlation. The same is true of the connection between any single teaching procedure and the students' subsequent score on a fairly complex achievement test.

Yet physicians can argue convincingly from their basic disciplines for the desirability of many medical procedures. And also, they have seen those procedures pay off almost immediately in improved functioning of a physiological system. Educators must similarly develop the argument for the desirability of many teaching procedures, by making use of the facts and principles available in such underlying disciplines as logic, learning, and mental hygiene. And they can similarly use empirical evidence of effects on specific short-range learnings rather than general achievement measured days, weeks, or months later. Then these validated items of teaching procedure can be assembled in the form of checklists and tests for use in the evaluation of teaching.

Chapter 12   **Feedback of Ratings to and from Teachers**

Many studies on "accuracy in perceiving other persons" have been based on the simple procedure of asking one person to fill out a questionnaire as he thought a second person would fill it out. If the second person then filled out the questionnaire, the first person's "predictions" could be scored for their accuracy against the actual responses of the second person. The greater the accuracy, the greater the first person's "understanding" of the second. And the greater his understanding, the more effective the first person should be in his relationships with the second. Teachers who are more accurate in predicting students' responses should be more effective in relationships with their students.

Some of the methodological and conceptual products of research along these lines have already been sketched (Gage, 1958). That research consisted primarily of correlational studies on the generality and behavioral correlates of accuracy in such perception.

Subsequently, I undertook a different kind of research on interpersonal perception. It reflected my choices among alternatives of the kind that must be faced by anyone undertaking research on teaching. The underlying decisions, although listed below in fairly explicit form, were not nearly so consciously developed at the time. In this new research, I wanted:

1. To conduct an *experiment* rather than a correlational study. (An experiment would be a study in which I would manipulate variables rather than merely measure and correlate them. It would yield data that could be interpreted in causal terms. An experiment meant "doing something" to change conditions rather than merely measuring and correlating them.)

2. To work in natural situations rather than contrived ones. (That is, I wanted data on changes in actual, operating classrooms.)

3. To continue to deal with interpersonal perception and its connections with interpersonal relationships. (But I wanted also to avoid the artifacts and equivocalities in such data that our previous work had revealed.)

4. To improve what seemed to be the low level of accuracy in

interpersonal perception that I had been finding under unmanipulated conditions. (What would happen if, instead of measuring such accuracy as it existed, I took steps to improve it?)

5. To deal with more significant "outtake" or things-to-be-perceived. (In the previous work, I had been concerned with teachers' perceptions of such characteristics of students as their self-descriptions on personality inventories, their interests, cognitive abilities, likes and dislikes of other students. But perhaps these things-to-be-perceived were not the most significant for the teachers' behavior. Perhaps the teacher's perceptions of her students' views of the *teacher's own behavior* and the students' evaluations of that behavior might be more important.)

6. To exploit current theory about interpersonal perception and behavior, particularly that developed in 1946 by Heider (1958) and in 1953 by Newcomb (1959). (Their consistency theories, sketched below, seemed to impose order on a wide range of pertinent phenomena.)

7. To conduct research that might have some potentiality for the improvement, rather than merely the description, of teachers' behaviors vis-á-vis their students.

In line with these intentions and choices, P. J. Runkel and I carried out an experiment in feedback from students to teachers. That research has been described in full detail by Gage, Runkel, and Chatterjee (1960) and also more briefly by the same authors (1963). The following account is intended to show how what we did was related to the intentions sketched above.

EXPERIMENTS IN FEEDBACK FROM STUDENTS TO TEACHERS

Early in the fall of the school year, we asked each superintendent of schools in Illinois to give us the name of the first teacher in the alphabetical list of all sixth-grade teachers in his district. We chose sixth-grade teachers because their students are the most mature of all students who have only one teacher all day long. We wanted mature students because they could read and fill out paper-and-pencil instruments most readily. We wanted only one teacher in each district in order to keep teachers from "comparing notes."

After the teachers' names had been received, we sent each one a booklet entitled "What Do They Expect?" This booklet was attractive in both content and format. The first seven pages of the booklet—in an informal, intimate, light vein—described the project and invited the teacher to participate. The last 17 pages contained a questionnaire and instructions for filling it out.

The questionnaire had four sections, but I shall describe only the two of concern here: (a) a 12-item section which asked the teacher to describe herself on each item along a six-step scale from "very much like me" to "very much unlike me"; (b) a 12-item section asking the teacher for her perception of how her modal pupil would describe her on each item.

The teacher also indicated how many pupils were in her class. She was then furnished with a "pupil opinion booklet" for each of her pupils. In these booklets, the pupils described their teacher on each of the 12 items. The pupils also described "the best teacher you can imagine" on the same 12 items. The booklets were administered by the teacher according to detailed instructions that insured anonymity of the pupils.

As the pupil opinion booklets were received from the teachers, they were put at random into control and experimental groups. For the teachers in the experimental group, frequency distributions and medians of the pupils' descriptions of their own teacher on each of the 12 items were obtained. The same was done for the pupils' descriptions of their "best imaginable" teacher.

With all possible speed, a "Report on Your Pupils' Opinions" was prepared for each teacher in the experimental group. In each "Report," 12 charts appeared, one for each of the 12 items. A specimen chart is shown in Fig. 12–1.

The chart for each item had two parts: (a) a bar-graph showing how many of the teacher's students chose "very much like my teacher," "somewhat like my teacher," etc., (b) a bar-graph showing how many of them chose "very much like a 'best' teacher," "somewhat like a 'best' teacher," etc. On each chart, the position of the median answer was shown with an arrow.

The "Reports" were sent to each teacher in the experimental group as soon as possible, i.e., within about ten days after receiving the student opinion booklets. Similar reports were prepared for the teachers in the control group but were not sent to them until the experiment had been completed.

The 12 items of teacher behavior, on which the students described their own teacher and their "best imaginable" teacher, were

A. Enjoys a funny remark made by a pupil.
B. Praises what a pupil says in class discussion.
C. Tells pupils about some interesting things to read.
D. Explains arithmetic so pupils can understand it.
E. Suggests to pupils new and helpful ways of studying.
F. Talks with a pupil after school about an idea the pupil has had.
G. Asks a small group of pupils to study something together.

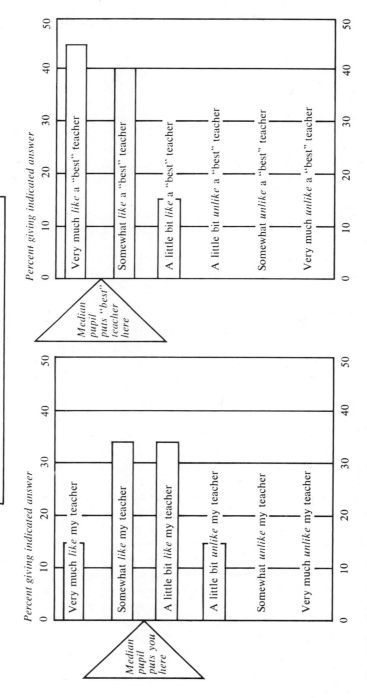

Fig. 12–1. Illustrative Chart from the "Report on Your Pupils' Opinions."

TABLE 12-1. MEANS OF ADJUSTED POST-ACTUAL AND PRE-IDEAL RATINGS[a]

($N_{exp.} = 86$; $N_{cont.} = 90$)

Item (1)	ADJUSTED POST-ACTUAL MEAN[b]		PRE-IDEAL MEAN[c]		ADJUSTED POST-ACTUAL MINUS PRE-IDEAL[d]		IS DIFFERENCE BETWEEN COLUMNS 6 AND 7 IN HYPOTHESIZED DIRECTION?
	Exp. (2)	Cont. (3)	Exp. (4)	Cont. (5)	Exp. (6)	Cont. (7)	
A. Enjoys a funny remark	2.57	2.57	2.20	2.20	.37	.37	No
B. Praises what a pupil says	3.46	3.61	3.21	3.02	.25	.59	Yes[e]
C. Tells . . . interesting things to read	2.33	2.42	2.09	1.96	.24	.46	Yes
D. Explains arithmetic	1.15	1.18	1.13	1.12	.02	.06	Yes[e]
E. Suggests . . . ways of studying	2.22	2.30	1.60	1.51	.62	.79	Yes
F. Talks with a pupil after school	4.07	4.20	3.31	3.14	.76	1.06	Yes
G. Asks . . . pupils to study . . . together	3.35	3.46	2.81	2.83	.54	.63	Yes
H. Shows . . . how to look up an answer	2.19	2.16	1.66	1.57	.53	.59	Yes
I. Asks . . . what they'd like to study	5.29	5.30	4.06	3.83	1.23	1.47	Yes
J. Acts disappointed when pupil . . wrong	4.27	4.33	4.54	4.44	-.27	-.11	No
K. Uses examples from games and sports	3.24	3.44	2.64	2.66	.60	.78	Yes[e]
L. Asks the class what they think	2.84	2.96	2.77	2.80	.07	.16	Yes[e]

[a] In this table, means refer to a scale in which a score of 1 was assigned to the "Very much like" rating scale alternative, 2 to "Somewhat like," and so on, to 6 for "Very much unlike."

[b] The adjusted post-actual mean is the mean rating of the teacher on the second occasion adjusted to eliminate differences between experimental and control groups in their mean ratings on the first occasion.

[c] The pre-ideal mean is the mean rating by pupils on the first occasion to indicate the degree to which the pupils considered the behavior to characterize their "best imaginable" teacher.

[d] Column 6 equals column 2 minus column 4; column 7 equals column 3 minus column 5.

[e] Difference between columns 2 and 3 is significant at the .05 level, on a one-tail basis, with df = 173.

    H. Shows a pupil how to look up an answer when the pupil can't find it himself.

    I. Asks the pupils what they'd like to study in tomorrow's lesson.

    J. Acts disappointed when a pupil gets something wrong.

    K. Explains something by using examples from games and sports.

    L. Asks the class what they think of something a pupil has said.

These items had been selected on the basis of interviews with teachers, pretests with students, and considerable analysis of their discriminability.

Between one and two months after receiving the "Report on Your Pupils' Opinions," all teachers again filled out the forms according to the same directions. And their pupils again described their actual teacher and their ideal teacher.

The Rationale

The feedback was intended to create what Heider (1958) would call "imbalance" in teachers' perceptions of their own behaviors. Imbalance may be said to exist whenever a person (teacher) finds that she holds a different attitude toward something (her behavior) from what she believes is held by another person or group (her students) to whom she feels herself positively oriented. A person in such a state of "imbalance" is motivated to do something to restore a balanced condition. This can be done in many ways, but we hypothesized that the following would prevail in our experiment: the teacher would seek to change her behavior so that it would more closely approximate her students' descriptions of the behavior of their "best imaginable" teacher.

According to this rationale, if teachers may be assumed to have positive attitudes toward their students, the teachers receiving feedback (the experimental group) will change their behaviors in the direction of students' descriptions of their "best imaginable" teacher to a greater degree than will teachers who do not receive such feedback (the control group).

Results

Using analysis of covariance, which is a statistical method able to adjust the teachers' posttest ratings for differences in their initial ratings by students, we compared the mean post-feedback ratings of the experimental and control groups. As shown in the right-hand column of Table 12–1, the direction of the difference between the two groups in 10 of the 12 items was in the hypothesized direction; that is, the teachers in the experimental group were rated as closer to the students' "best imaginable," or ideal, teacher. (On four of these ten items, there was a statistically significant difference between the teachers who had and those who had not received the reports on their students' opinions —the feedback.) On Item A, there was no difference at all between the two groups. On Item J, the difference was opposite in direction to that hypothesized. All in all, although the differences in the direction of our hypothesis seemed small, they tended to indicate that the feedback had the hypothesized effect. Teachers who received feedback did seem to change in the direction of students' "ideals" more than did teachers from whom feedback was withheld.

The accuracy of the teachers in predicting their students' ratings of the teacher's behavior also improved in the experimental group. These teachers should have become more accurate than the control group simply by virtue of having been told how they were rated by the students. This expectation was borne out. When accuracy was measured by the difference between predicted and actual means of the second ratings, the experimental group was more accurate on nine of the twelve items. When accuracy was measured by the correlation between teachers' predictions and their students' actual mean ratings, improvements were again greater in the experimental group.

Other Experiments

A similar experiment by Bryan (1963) also yielded encouraging results. He presented feedback of students' ratings to high school teachers on three occasions over a two-year period. Of 60 teachers in the experimental group, 57 per cent changed very significantly on one or more of the ten items rated, while only 24 per cent of 59 teachers in a control group showed similar gains.

The effects of feedback from different sources were compared by Tuckman and Oliver (1968) in an experiment conducted along lines similar to those described above. Each of four groups of teachers received feedback from one of the following sources: (a) students only, (b) supervisors only, (c) both students and supervisors, and (d) neither. Student feedback led to a positive change, as measured by change in students' ratings after a 12-week interval, while supervisor feedback did not increase this effect, and, when given alone, resulted in change opposite to the feedback. The effect of student feedback was greater for less experienced teachers.

In an experiment by Hayes, Keim, and Neiman (1967) with 80 sixth-grade teachers, several kinds of feedback were manipulated: (a) pupil reaction to their teachers obtained four times during the fall, (b) results of classroom interaction analysis using Flanders' procedures, and (c) a combination of *a* and *b*. Some of the teachers received the feedback only by mail, while others also received a face-to-face report.

When class averages were analyzed, no significant differences in student achievement or attitude were found that could be attributed to feedback variables. When individual student scores were analyzed, however, significant differences in achievement were found. These differences favored the students of teachers who had received written feedback only rather than face-to-face plus written feedback. Similar differences were found in individual student ratings of their teachers.

That is, students' ratings of their teachers were more favorable as a result of the teachers' receiving feedback on their students' earlier ratings or feedback on such ratings plus observations based on classroom interaction analysis. Such advantages were not gained as a result of feedback only of observations based on classroom interaction analysis. Nor did such gains result from feedback to the teacher of pretest results on student achievement and attitude toward subjects. (The latter kind of feedback was given to all teachers involved in the experiment.)

Where teachers received written feedback only, the feedback of (a) student ratings proved more effective in improving students' ratings than feedback of (b) observations only, (c) observations plus ratings, or (d) neither observations nor ratings. Thus, as the authors point out, the students' rating scale used as feedback "takes only a few minutes to administer and to analyze" and yet provides "a reliable, reasonably valid way to help teachers improve their teaching" (Hayes, Keim, & Neiman, 1967, p. 26).

Implications

Providing feedback to teachers of students' ratings seems useful for the practical purpose of improving teacher behavior. As described by the students, teachers did change in the direction of students' ideals as a result of getting feedback. Whether the changes were great enough to have educational significance, whether they would be found if teachers' behaviors were described and measured by expert outside observers rather than students, whether changes toward students' ideals also move toward educators' ideals—all these are questions for subsequent investigation.

Commenting on the Gage-Runkel-Chatterjee experiment, Morrison and McIntyre (1969, p. 178) observed that "few teachers will have the courage to follow [these] ingenious procedures in their classrooms. . . ." Some experience belies this statement. High proportions of teachers at the elementary, secondary, and higher levels of education have volunteered in response to research workers' invitations to teachers to let themselves be rated by students and receive confidential reports on the ratings. But more experience is needed with routine programs of collecting and reporting such ratings to determine whether they require unusual "courage" of teachers.

Additional issues would arise in any attempt to develop such feedback into a usable scheme for teacher improvement. But the amount of data to be processed would present no obstacle. A fully developed program could use computers for rapid data-processing.

EXPERIMENTS IN FEEDBACK FROM TEACHERS TO PRINCIPALS

Feedback has possibilities as a method of changing the behavior of persons other than teachers. Superintendents can be given feedback from their school boards. Principals have been given feedback from their teachers (Daw & Gage, 1967; Burns, 1969) with results indicating significant effects in improving the principals' behavior. Several refinements of the design were introduced by Daw and Gage (1967):

1. A third group of subjects was described by the raters, but only at the time of the posttest. This "posttest-only" group permitted testing the possible attenuating effect on the comparisons owing to the unintended feedback received by the control group simply because they participated in the pretest. It turned out that such an effect did not appear.

2. Half the recipients of feedback received only the median of the ratings of themselves and the ideal on each item; the other half received the median plus the frequency distribution of the ratings. Comparison of the amount of change in the two groups showed no difference in the effects of "sharp" and "blunt" feedback.

3. Each of the items of behavior was worded in both positive (desirable) and negative (undesirable) directions in alternate forms. Comparison of changes with the two forms indicated that the raters' descriptions were independent of any positional or directional response set.

4. Half of the subjects were posttested six weeks after receiving feedback, while the other half were posttested 12 weeks after. Comparison of the amount of change in the two groups yielded no evidence that the effect of feedback decays or increases with time.

In addition to finding an over-all favorable effect attributable to feedback of ratings from teachers to principals, Burns (1969) compared the effects of various kinds of feedback: ratings of the teachers' actual and ideal principal, ratings of the ideal only, ratings of actual only, and no feedback. The evidence indicated that ideal-only feedback was most effective in producing positive changes in the post-feedback ratings of the principals by their teachers.

Further, Burns had some of the principals in each feedback-treatment group indicate a "commitment" to change, i.e., to "work on" improving themselves, in one of two areas of principal-teacher interaction. The two areas were "task assistance to the teacher" and "personal support of the teacher." The results showed no difference in the effect of the feedback on principals attributable to commitment to "work on" the behavioral items in a given area.

In none of the experiments with feedback have the results been striking or statistically significant to a very high degree. It is rather the consistency in the direction of the modest effects that should encourage further development of the technique. This kind of consistency can be noted both within and across studies.

It should be noted that less significant positive effects have sometimes been obtained in experiments with the feedback of ratings. Hovenier (1966) experimented with feedback from high school teachers of social studies to their department heads; on only two of ten items were significant differences produced by the feedback, although the differences went in the hypothesized direction for eight of the ten items.

But Hovenier also examined another variable that could influence the effect of feedback. This was the amount of pressure to change on a given item, as measured by the discrepancy between teachers' ratings of their actual and ideal department head on that item. For eight of the ten items, department heads who were subjected to the most pressure to change in this sense did change most, when compared with control (no-feedback) department heads who had the same initial discrepancy between actual and ideal ratings. Apparently, department heads who satisfy their teachers least will change the most when given feedback.

Feedback of a reference group's opinions about an individual's behavior may turn out to be an effective, democratic, and practical way of changing behavior. Whether such changes also constitute improvements depends on one's values. Where teachers and their students, or principals and their teachers, are concerned, my own values make me optimistic.

Chapter 13   **Toward the
                    New Roles
                    of Teachers**

          What are the functions of research in effect-
ing the changes in teachers' roles that are required by educational
innovations? Two broad classes of such functions of research may be
identified. First, the findings of research can provide the basis from
which role changes are *derived*. Second, research methods can provide
the procedures by which role changes are *evaluated*. In one case, the
research precedes the change; in the other, it follows.

THE DERIVATIONAL FUNCTION OF RESEARCH

The derivational function is served when research-based knowledge
of relationships between variables can be used to explain, predict, or
control teaching and learning. If the variables are related logically,
then the research finding has explanatory value. If the relationship is
merely a temporal and empirical one, without any necessary logical or
functional basis, then the research finding has predictive value. If the
relationship is a functional one, then the research has value for purposes of control, since manipulation of one variable causes the value
of the other to change.

Can knowledge issuing from educational research be used to illustrate these purposes? The *explanatory* value of research can be seen,
perhaps, in the realm of teacher-student relationships. We know from
Heider's analyses of the gestalt-like properties of interpersonal perception that one tends to like another person whom one perceives to
like oneself. From this tendency toward cognitive balance, or consistency, can be derived the research-supported hypothesis that pupils
tend to like one another better when they have a warm teacher, one
who likes and behaves approvingly toward her pupils.

The *predictive* value of research, where temporal but not necessarily
logical relationships between variables are known, can be seen in the
finding that the achievement of pupils is positively correlated with the
pupils' earlier scores on a vocabulary test. So the vocabulary test has
predictive value even though the correlation does not necessarily reflect logical or functional relationships.

The value of research findings for the *control* of variables can be

seen in the relationship between reinforcement and response probability. Experiments have shown that the probability of a given response
can be changed by manipulating reinforcement; the relationship here
is a functional one.

The point of these distinctions and illustrations is that research findings serving explanatory, predictive, or controlling functions can be
used in deriving, or laying the intellectual groundwork for, educational
innovations. Just as theoretical work in nuclear physics laid the basis
for medical uses of atomic energy, so the basic research of this century
on individual differences in intelligence and social-class differences in
acculturation has set the stage for such educational innovations as individualized instruction and culturally appropriate curricular materials.
The work on individual differences in readiness, including intelligence
and interest, led to the derivation of such further innovations as provisions for small-group, large-group, and independent study, which
were made possible through computerized solutions of the problems
of flexible scheduling. It was in part from research, such as that on
individual differences among teachers in competence and temperament,
that such innovations as team teaching and the differentiated teaching
staff, including the use of teacher assistants, were derived. It was in
part from research on operant conditioning that the innovation known
as programmed instruction was derived.

THE EVALUATIVE FUNCTION OF RESEARCH

In its evaluative function, research is used to determine whether
innovations deserve to be considered improvements. Again, such research consists in searching for relationships between variables. Here
the variables are discerned with relative ease. One variable, or set of
variables, is the innovation being evaluated, and the alternatives are
either the traditional procedure or other innovations against which it
is competing. The innovation may be any of those already mentioned—
team teaching, independent study, large-group instruction, small-group
instruction, programmed instruction—and any of the many possible
variables and specific forms of each of these.

The other variable, or set of variables, consists of the outcomes or
processes that the innovation is intended to improve. Measurements
of these outcomes or processes are made with tests, interviews, observations, ratings, and any of the other techniques in the behavioral
scientist's repertoire. Then, using either a correlational, an experimental, or a quasi-experimental design, the researcher determines the
relationship between the innovation and the outcome or process.

RESEARCH IN THE LIGHT OF INNOVATIONS

The two functions of research—derivation and evaluation—should help in the improvement of teaching as various educational innovations become more widely adopted. To indicate some of the needed research, we shall adopt an arbitrary classification of the kinds of teaching situation that will be found in the future.

Kinds of Teaching Situations

First, teaching will go on in the *conventional classroom* of 15-40 students for an entire school day (in the elementary school) or a 50-minute period (in the secondary school).

Second, teaching will take the form of *individualized instruction*, where the student works alone, for the most part, in a computer-assisted facility, or in a situation where programmed textbooks and individually prescribed work sheets and learning tasks are involved.

Third, teaching will occur in *small-group discussions*. Here the teaching situation typically permits far less control by the teacher of the details of content and method than is possible in the conventional classroom, the programmed individualized instruction situation, or as we shall note, the large-group situation.

Finally, teaching will consist of the *large-group lecture-demonstration* situation, where 50 or more students are brought together in the same place, at the same time, to experience the same set of instructional stimuli. Those stimuli can be presented by a live teacher, an audio tape, a sound film, or a television program, live or recorded.

New Teacher Roles

In each of these situations, the teacher's role takes different forms, and different teacher activities predominate. Since it is the oldest, the role in the conventional classroom has already received much attention from research workers, and need not receive further notice here. The role in the individualized instruction situation, however, is relatively new and has begun to engage research attention only recently. Briggs (1964) has presented some analyses, and Resnick (1967) has recently described a new research laboratory oriented toward this role, in which the teacher's diagnostic and adaptive functions in individualized instruction will be emphasized.

The teacher's role in small-group discussion situations is becoming increasingly important as programmed instruction promises to take over teaching toward various objectives of the type where knowledge and understanding can be clearly defined, with great specificity, in behavioral terms. The teacher is thus being freed to perform the uniquely

human functions of conducting and fostering a dialogue, which programmed instruction, even with computers, cannot be expected to
perform in the near future (Suppes, 1966). How to promote and guide
educational dialogues, or discussions, in ways that liberate the imagination and engage the intellect of all participants is a problem on which
socio-psychological research has not thus far been explicitly focused.
Small-group discussion classes are also being fostered by the availability of computer techniques for flexible scheduling (Bush & Allen,
1964). Such scheduling releases schools from their imprisonment in
a framework that provides only a fixed number of periods, each consisting of a fixed number of minutes, for all students and teachers in
all subjects every week.

Can teaching in the large-group situation survive the forces driving
instruction toward individualization? Yes, insofar as learners will always have enough characteristics in common, despite the facts about
individual differences, to be able to profit from lectures or other presentations aimed at all members of a large group. Concerts, plays,
movies, political speeches, and other "large-group occasions" have
continued despite the availability of more individualized opportunities
for such experiences and despite the wide individual differences among
members of their audiences. So it seems reasonable to expect schools
to find large-group presentations desirable and efficient for certain
kinds of teaching and learning. Unfortunately, although the lecture has
a long history, most research on lecturing has been aimed at comparing it with discussion classes or other alternatives. Relatively little
scientific work has been done to improve lecturing. Much can presumably be transferred for this purpose, however, from research on
training films and informative speech. And recently there has been
renewed scientific interest in the teacher's ability to explain (Gage,
et al., 1968) and in "learning from being told" (Carroll, 1968).

In short, the varieties of teaching that will emerge from educational
innovations are in one sense very few. To derive and evaluate the
details of desirable new roles for teachers within these new modes—
individualized instruction, small-group instruction, and large-group instruction—are major tasks of research on teaching in the years ahead.

TECHNIQUES FOR CHANGING ROLES

After new roles have been derived from and evaluated through research, how can they be widely disseminated and installed throughout
the educational system? That is, how can we best change the teacher's
behavior? A variety of approaches to this problem have been taken
and urged. The traditional approach has been to assume that, once the

researchers have done their work, the findings will be communicated to educational practitioners, who will then put them into practice. This approach seems to have worked in furthering broad doctrines and points of view. Thus, teachers can learn from books and articles about "individual differences," "the whole child," "social-class disadvantages," or "meaningfulness in the curriculum." But this method has not operated effectively in enabling educators to benefit from the detailed findings of research that may imply subtle and complex changes in teacher behavior. So, for example, it is ineffective to merely communicate verbally to teachers the ways in which they should reinforce student participation or ask higher-order questions.

Another approach attempts to arrange collaboration in school systems between practitioners and researchers. Such collaboration on joint enterprises aimed at solving educational problems will, it is hoped, lead to more realistic applications of behavioral science and their adoption by teachers—the only persons who can make them effective. But there are too few researchers with enough sophistication to fill the needs of all the school systems that need help of this kind.

Tool-Based Experimentation

A third approach is based on tools for teachers. Such tools would be based on a special kind of experimentation in which the independent variables, or treatments, would have certain advantageous characteristics: concreteness, psychological validity, relevance to the new roles of teachers, and differentiation by type of learning.

Concreteness. First, the treatments should be embodied in materials and equipment. Such treatments have great advantages in changing the instructional situation (Gagné, 1966). Textbooks, workbooks, instructional films, tests, audiotapes, videotapes, programmed textbooks, computer-assisted instructional materials, kits, manuals, models, games, simulators, and other devices for arranging instructional experiences in suitable sequences—these are the vehicles through which good influences on what actually happens in schools can be most dependably exerted. Without such material embodiment, attempts to improve teaching and learning run into all the forces that keep people from acting on good educational advice. The advice tends to be too theoretical, too vague as to its meaning for practice, and insufficiently coercive, in that it does not require the teacher to change his ways. Materials and equipment spell out the advice in practicable terms. If properly designed and accompanied by adequate instructions for use, they well-nigh "force" the teacher and student to do what is wanted of them by the experimenter.

Psychological Validity. Second, the new independent variables must possess psychological validity, i.e., reflect what we know about the factors and processes in learning. As indicated in Chapter 3, the most influential and perhaps most usable conceptions of learning are those embraced by operant conditioning theory. That theory specifies that the teacher should pay attention above all to the reinforcers in any learning situation. The teacher should provide reinforcers to strengthen desirable kinds of behavior and withhold them to weaken the undesirable. So the independent variables in experimental research in teaching should be developed with due regard to the central significance of reinforcement. They should embody attention to allied concepts, such as discriminative cues, preexisting operant levels, extinction, generalization, discrimination, reinforcement scheduling, and shaping.

Another kind of psychological validity can be derived from the structure of what is to be learned, remembered, or applied. Some arrangements of things to be learned are better than others. These arrangements may be called more "meaningful," better "structured," "mnemonically" aided, or "algorithmically" simplified. They take advantage of innate processes and previous learning so as to facilitate the work of the teacher and the student. The materials and equipment provided the teacher should embody what is known about these ways to improve the teacher's behavior and, through this, the student's learning.

Relevance to New Roles of Teachers. Third, the experimental variables should be relevant to the emergent roles of teachers. The technological revolution still underway in education—especially the salient called programmed instruction—is making some tasks of teachers less important, and heightening emphasis on others. Programmed instruction takes several forms: programmed textbooks, computer-assisted instruction, individually prescribed instruction (Lindvall & Bolvin, 1967), and the "program for learning according to needs" (Flanagan, 1967), among others. All these varieties diminish the teacher's role in communicating and inculcating knowledge—in the sense of increasing the student's ability to recall or recognize facts, definitions, rules, principles, formulas, and the like. They also take over much of the teacher's job of fostering other intellectual skills, such as ability to translate, analyze, synthesize, evaluate, interpret, extrapolate, and apply.

If programmed instruction can do all these things, and do them well, what is left for the human teacher to do? Hilgard (1968) offered a threefold answer: the teacher can (a) serve as a model to be imitated in improving the student's tendency to initiate inquiry on his own; (b) provide the kind of approval that only a human being can provide in helping the student develop a favorable view of himself, his learning ability, and his creativity; and (c) foster the student's effectiveness in dealing with other people, in cooperating, sharing, leading, following, resolving conflicts, and tolerating the frustrations of the social world.

Stukát (1970) made a survey of predictions and actual findings on changes in the teacher's role. He concluded that in the future teaching will entail increased emphasis on continuous diagnosis and evaluation of individual students, counseling and guiding students on short- and long-range plans, interacting with individual students and small groups, and team work and task differentiation among teachers.

Kersh (1965) held that certain objectives are most readily attained through human instruction, rather than automatic or self-instruction. Among these are patterns of behavior occurring at unpredictable intervals and reflecting "mediational" processes. Examples include problem formulation, or restructuring, and hypothesis formation, along with their component behaviors, such as shifting, being flexible, and searching for patterns.

None of this means that all older and well-established functions of teachers are altogether obsolete. In their work with individual students and small groups, in stimulating inquiry, and in serving as a model, teachers will still need to be skilled in listening to and understanding a student's question. They will still need to ask enlightening or provocative questions. They will still need to provide clear, extemporaneous, oral explanations of the processes operating in a phenomenon, so that the student need not always discover everything for himself. Accordingly, the experimental variables in tool-oriented research on teaching will still need to be aimed at improving the teacher's questioning, explaining, and listening skills.

Differentiation by Type of Learning. Fourth, the experimental manipulations of teacher behavior should be appropriate to different types of learning. As noted on pages 42-43, the categories of learning that should be distinguished have taken several different forms over the years. More recently, with greater attention to what goes on in schools, Gagné (1971) identified five "domains"—motor skills, verbal knowledge, intellectual skills, cognitive strategies, and attitudes—that require different kinds of learning and teaching.

These kinds of learning should be taken into account when designing tools for improving teacher behavior. If repetition is more important in learning motor skills than in acquiring verbal knowledge, teachers ought to behave accordingly. If, as Gagné indicated, having a meaningful context is more important in acquiring verbal knowledge than in intellectual skills, again teachers should be constrained to behave appropriately.

MAKING AVERAGE TEACHERS ABLE TO TEACH WELL

The new kind of experimental variable should also reduce the demands that teaching imposes upon practitioners of the art. Teaching is less effective than it ought to be because it requires skills, abilities, habits, and powers possessed by only a small proportion of the hundreds of thousands of adults needed as teachers. Teaching now requires levels of sensitivity, in listening to students, that only clinical psychologists and psychiatrists can routinely supply. It now requires adaptability and intellectual agility, in discussions with students, at levels that only professional debaters, trial lawyers, and parliamentarians can regularly attain. It requires the quick invention of definitions, explanations, and justifications, in classroom discourse, according to rules that only professors of logic can adhere to.

Other professions and crafts give their practitioners whole arrays of techniques, instruments, tools, devices, formulas, strategies, tactics, algorithms, and tricks of the trade. Engineering, medicine, law, and journalism, to name just a few, have all of these kinds of aids that make the job possible for ordinary mortals. The engineer has his slide rule, transit, and handbook of stress tables; the physician, his plethysmograph, sphygmomanometer, and pharmacopoeia; the lawyer, his codes, classified collections of precedents, and interrogation skills; the journalist, his formulas for writing leads and his standard rules of content and style.

But, in teaching, we find relatively few of these ways of making complex tasks more manageable. Teachers are expected to rediscover for themselves the formulas that experienced and ingenious teachers have acquired over the years. Each generation of teachers benefits too little from the inventions of its predecessors. Too little of the wisdom of the profession gets saved and passed along for the benefit of the novice. What teaching needs—if it is to be improved in the hands of ordinary persons, who are not geniuses or inspired artists, and if it is to be improved with resources at a level not inconceivably high—is a much more abundant and helpful supply of "tools of the trade."

The term "tools of the trade" has appropriately unpretentious connotations. It suggests not theoretical perspectives but quick and easy guides for asking questions and answering them; not conceptual frameworks, but easily applied rules of behavior and performance; not an emphasis on the complexities, subtleties, and profundities of the teacher's task in understanding and helping his students, but ways of making the task manageable. The tools must be usable by persons with the intellectual and emotional make-up that we can expect to find in two million teachers. What teachers need is a reduced demand for arcane insight and creativity and a greater supply of mundane tools.

PROGRAMMING: AN INFLEXIBLE APPROACH

During the last fifteen years, the programming approach has been offered to reduce the complexities and unmanageabilities of teaching in just the ways envisaged here. Programming helps the teacher cope with the problems of individualization and cognitive complexity (see pp. 54-55).

The programming approach has been extended into the realm of the human teacher's tasks. Lecturing, tutoring, and classroom teaching itself have been programmed. Let us look at some of these efforts. We consider them here as attempts to solve the problems of making teaching more manageable by ordinary persons. Before evaluating these approaches, we describe them.

Programmed Lecturing

Lecturing is hard to do well, and even when it is well done, everyone finds fault with it. It violates the assumptions that good instruction should provide feedback to the teacher and the student, should be adjusted to individual differences, and should entail activity on the part of the student.

The programmed lecture (McCarthy, 1970) was intended to remedy some of these defects. These medical school lectures were based on multiple-choice questions shown one at a time via 35mm. slides and also on sheets distributed to the students, one question to a page, with space for the student's notes. Ten or more questions were presented, in order of increasing difficulty. The earlier questions dealt with basic principles, and the later ones with applications. Pictorial material was presented as needed, with another slide projector.

The lecturer began by showing the first question and asking the students to answer it on their own sheets. Then he discussed the question fully. The students made notes on their sheets for that part of the lecture. Then the lecturer went on to a new projected question, discussing it fully, explaining the correct response, and discussing each possible incorrect response. The content was carefully arranged, moving toward increasing levels of achievement of the objectives. If the student made a correct response to the question, he received immediate confirmation; if he made an incorrect one, he quickly received corrective feedback and remedial instruction from the lecturer.

Such a programmed lecture does solve, in a sense, the problem of cognitive complexity that is so difficult to handle in the give and take of classroom discourse. But, as McCarthy recognized, the problem of individualization remains, since "remedial instruction is not provided for each individual, as the questions are discussed by the lecturer speaking to the whole audience." Further, the teacher receives no feedback inasmuch as he has no way of telling how well the students are grasping the ideas. According to McCarthy, the feedback to the student may mitigate this disadvantage. In any case, medical students have reacted favorably to the method. More important, this approach provides an example of a concrete tactic that can enable masses of teachers to lecture with greater effectiveness. The technique simplifies some otherwise awesomely complex aspects of lecturing.

Although McCarthy gave no evidence as to the advantage of the method over ordinary lecturing, some relevant findings have been provided by Berliner (1968). Of his three experimental groups, one received training questions approximately 2.5 minutes apart during the lecture; a second, at 5-minute intervals; and a third, at 15-minute intervals. The total number of questions was the same for all groups. A fourth group took notes during the lecture, and a fifth was merely instructed to pay attention. The lecture was presented by videotape to college freshmen in a psychology course. The results indicated that the use of the test-like events every 2.5 minutes of lecture produced substantial improvements in immediate test performance.

Programmed Tutoring

Tutoring is the teaching-learning situation in which each teacher has one student. It is frequently used to supplement the educational program of students from low-income areas. Students who are not doing as well as they ought to, in the opinion of their parents or their teachers, receive tutoring from their parents, from older students in their own schools, or from students in nearby colleges. Typically, the tutors are persons untrained in teaching except for the training they receive as part of the tutoring program.

Can professional and nonprofessional trainers, using prescribed training procedures, improve the performance of upper-grade elementary student tutors? Harrison (1969) had two professional educators and two non-professionals at each of five elementary schools train student tutors (fifth- and sixth-graders). The carefully prescribed training procedures were aimed at getting the tutor to put the learner at ease, clarify the prescribed task, teach the child how to verify his answer, have the learner read each problem aloud, have the learner mark his answer before receiving any feedback, have the learner verify his answer, avoid punishing behavior, provide the learner with verbal praise when appropriate, reward him when appropriate, and check for mastery on designated problems. The trained tutors worked with first-graders on "additive sentence equations." A test given during the week after the tutoring showed that the first-graders taught by the trained tutors had learned substantially more than similar children taught by untrained tutors. Thus, tutors equipped with explicit techniques were much more effective.

The most thoroughly programmed kind of tutoring has been developed by Ellson and his co-workers (1965, 1968). Their work is aimed at developing a technique useful in teaching elementary reading. Non-professional persons are trained to follow operational programs that specify in great detail how the teaching is done and content programs that specify what is taught and the order in which it is first presented. The tutors are "programmed" to emphasize success, reinforce correct responses with suggested appropriate words, ignore failures and go on without comment to the next procedure, all the while recording the child's responses. To observers, the program is hardly visible; the situation seems similar to that in traditional tutoring. Subsequently, the highly systematic character of the tutor's behavior becomes apparent. "An experimental psychologist might see it as a complex and flexibly modified form of the paired associates anticipation procedure, supplemented by verbal approval as a form of reinforcement" (Ellson, et al., 1968, p. 315). The program has loops, short steps, prompts, and branches. The discovery method is used: the first step presents the problem or task in its most difficult form with a minimum of context, and later steps progressively simplify and provide hints or additional information until the child discovers the solution for himself. Professional teachers, who attempted to learn about programmed tutoring through practicing it, felt that the program "did not allow them to teach." Apparently, these teachers wanted to give answers or help more rapidly than the program allowed and lacked the patience that the discovery method imposed on the non-professional programmed tutors.

Ellson and his co-workers have amassed impressive evidence that programmed tutoring permits persons with only a high school education and no other preparation as teachers to provide highly effective supplementation of traditional classroom experience in the first- and second-grade reading curricula. As contrasted with "direct tutoring," which is derived from current teaching practice, programmed tutoring produced significant improvement in reading achievement test scores when given twice daily (but not when given once daily).

The significant point in the present context is that programmed tutoring exemplifies the "tools of the trade" that can ease and improve the work of the teacher. The teacher of the future may serve as a tutor, working with one or two students at a time while the others are occupied elsewhere. This role, Stukát's study suggests, will be an increasingly important one. If so, highly structured, programmed tutoring could become more important.

Programmed Classroom Instruction

Classroom teaching is by far the most prevalent mode of teaching in American elementary and secondary schools. Accordingly, the attempt to provide classroom teachers with tools of their trade is extremely important.

Kersh (1965) has attempted to program classroom teaching. First, as already noted, he distinguished between objectives that could be attained by students working alone with programmed instructional materials and those that could be best achieved with the assistance of a teacher. He also referred to "compounded" objectives, those suitable for automatic or self-instructional techniques alongside others that call for human instruction. To attain such compounded objectives requires, in Kersh's opinion, the capabilities of an automated classroom. "Otherwise the teacher would be taxed beyond his ability in the attempt to control the experiences of the learners. To reduce the burden on the teacher and to allow him to concentrate on those activities which require human guidance, a systematically developed set of instructional materials and validated procedure also must be available" (Kersh, 1965, p. 346).

Accordingly, Kersh developed a notation and charting technique with which the programmer could prepare a detailed outline of the learning experience, specifying practice and reinforcement schedules, criteria for branching, and the like. The teacher was thus trained to work alongside the Teaching Research Automated Classroom (TRAC), which provided projectors housed in the students' desk units and a classroom communication system controlled automatically. Permanent records of each student's performance were made, and class summaries were immediately available to the teacher.

A flow chart, using a special notation developed to indicate specific teaching operations, provided detailed instructions and materials. One such flow chart specified the plan for teaching the idea that "A single quantity may be written in different ways."

The first box indicates to the programer that the instruction should start with an example concerning a boy with several names. The next box indicates that, by analogy, the rule is to be established that a quantity such as 10 may be referred to in a number of different ways including '5 + 5,' and '6 + 4.' At circle 10.1 (simply a location point or connecting link), the flow chart moves to a diamond-shaped frame which indicates that the program should follow with a test. The notation '3(1.0 +)' specifies that the learners should continue with the test until they achieve three examples in succession correctly. The notation '5 ±' specifies that should the learners fail to achieve the criterion after five examples, the program should return them to a new explanation of subfact 10 and then test them again. Circle 11 indicates that when the learners pass the test they are to go to subfact 11 (Kersh, 1965, pp. 355-356).

Kersh spelled out the approach in some detail; the present sample merely illustrates it. It represents an attempt to plan teaching carefully so as to reduce the need for creative improvisation.

NEEDED: AN ALTERNATIVE TO INFLEXIBILITY AND DISORDER

The great virtue of programmed learning, tutoring, and classroom instruction is specificity. These innovations reduce the amount of disorder in what the teacher does. But they go too far in a good direction. Because they spell out both the content and procedure of the teacher's work in great detail, they impose too much inflexibility on the teacher. Their procedures are topic-specific and must be changed whenever the topic is changed. What is needed are teaching procedures that are usable for many kinds of topics. Teachers cannot accept complete regimentation through programming of their behavior. What they teach requires more room for spontaneity, creativity, and artistry than such programming allows.

On the other hand, present-day classroom work with its "stray thoughts, sudden insights, meandering digressions, irrelevant asides, and other unpredicted events" (Jackson, 1968, p. 4) also makes life hard for teachers. The unpredictability and lack of order become intolerable and eventually lead to an inflexibility of a different kind. The teacher escapes from them to a monotonous acting out, and re-enacting, of the same unimaginative and sterile pattern. Thus the evidence, as marshalled by Hoetker and Ahlbrand (1969), indicates that there has been a "remarkable stability of classroom verbal behavior patterns over the last half century, despite the fact that each successive generation of educational thinkers, no matter how else they differed, has condemned the rapid-fire, question-answer pattern of instruction" (p. 163). As Bellack and his co-workers (1966) described it, "The core of the teaching sequence found in the classrooms studied is a teacher's question, a pupil's response and, more often than not, a teacher's reaction to that response" (p. 158). Teachers fall into this rut, and stay in it, despite our teacher education programs, and do what comes naturally, as if they had never been trained. For some writers (e.g., Stephens, 1967) this kind of teaching represents a spontaneous tendency on the part of humans in the role of teacher—a way of behaving that can probably be traced back to ancient times and can be found nowadays on the part of anyone, older child, parent, or professional teacher, who is placed in the role of teacher.

In short, the freedom of nonprogrammed teaching turns out to be spurious. Imprisoned by their technical poverty, teachers tend to do the same thing, no matter what or whom they are teaching, day after day and year after year.

We need a happy medium between the excessive systematization of topic-specific programmed lecturing, programmed tutoring, and programmed classroom teaching, on the one hand, and the spurious freedom of the opportunistic and unpredictable present-day classroom that Jackson describes.

TOOLS OF THE TRADE

If present-day classroom teaching is too planless and chaotic, and if programmed teaching is too inflexible, what is the alternative? The answer here is that research and development should be devoted to the invention, refinement, and widespread distribution of tools for teachers and trainers of teachers. Such tools would enhance the teacher's collection of things to do and the trainer's ways of training him to do them. Such tools would be applicable to many topics, contents, and subject matters.

The improvising musician can be creative and artistic only because he has great technical command of his instrument. He can play riffs and flourishes, crescendoes and diminuendoes, growls and whimpers, pure notes and chords, trills and sustained notes, fast and slow. These skills can be applied to almost any piece of written music and also to composing unwritten music on the run, or improvising. Such a musician is not forced—as is the untrained beginner—to pick out the same tune, haltingly and with error, again and again. To be comparable artists, teachers need comparable tools. Just as the musician's technical competence frees him for artistry, the teacher's competence in handling his own tools will free him to work artistically in the classroom. Teachers need tools with which to adapt their behavior extemporaneously to the minute-by-minute variations in classroom topics.

The necessary tools are of two kinds: those for the teacher himself, and those for the trainer of teachers. They can be embodied in materials and equipment. In some cases, the teacher will eventually abandon the concrete versions, just as the child learns to get along without the training wheels on his bicycle. Then the tools take the form of the skills, models, and rules that remain with the teacher after the materials have done their job.

Tools for Teachers and Trainers

Tools for teachers can take such forms as technical skills, decision-making skills, and various kinds of rules, models, and aids. A strong beginning has been made in developing such tools. Nearly a decade of work at Stanford University, initiated by Dwight Allen, Robert Bush, and Frederick McDonald, has resulted in the formulation and definition of an array of technical skills in teaching. Berliner (1969) has provided an account of much of this work. Some of these skills— higher-order questioning, reinforcement, probing, varying the stimulus situation, providing silence and non-verbal communication, and skills for controlling small-group discussions—have been fairly well defined in research on teacher training. In that research, different kinds of treatment for trainees have been evaluated through experiments, and their effects on subsequent performance in the laboratory and the classroom have been measured. Those experiments have given us assurance that technical skills can be defined and acquired by teachers. The evidence of their effect on students is still inadequate. But the lines of further work on these questions are clear. Work of that kind will give us a set of technical skills of teaching whose effects on students, when the skills are used judiciously, are known to be desirable.

The technical skills approach, combined with the microteaching technique, has served as the foundation for the Minicourse approach developed by Borg and his co-workers (1970) at the Far West Laboratory for Educational Research and Development. Each Minicourse is aimed at improving a specific skill on the part of a teacher. For example, Minicourse 1: Effective Questioning—Elementary Level, is aimed at 12 skills in using questions in a discussion. The trainee begins by seeing an introductory film describing the approach. Then he views an instructional practice lesson that describes two techniques for improving pupil readiness to respond to discussion questions; each technique is portrayed with examples from classroom discussions.

Then the trainee views the practice model lesson in which a model teacher demonstrates each technique several times, the trainee being given cues as to what he should be noticing. On the first day the trainee also reads part of the teacher's handbook for the course and prepares a ten-minute discussion lesson. On the second day, the trainee conducts the microteaching lesson he has planned, while it is recorded on videotape. Then the tape is played back while the trainee studies his performance and notes what could be improved. Then he again plays back the lesson, using a checklist of specific behaviors to be evaluated. Then he reads the third chapter of the handbook and takes a short test on it. On the third day, the trainee again teaches the microteaching lesson with different pupils from his class, again watches the playback of the videotape recording of this lesson, first for general characteristics and then for specific evaluations, and perhaps for a third time with another trainee, the two of them viewing one another's videotapes and exchanging feedback and suggestions.

In addition to skills, the teacher needs aids, models, and rules. In diagnosing and evaluating the work of individual students, he can use aids in the form of tests and other diagnostic tools that are easily administered yet usefully valid. In prescribing the student's next steps, he can use charts, tables, guides, and checklists that embody what has been learned from research about the level of difficulty, variety, precision, or discovery that the student's next steps should incorporate. Enormously complex procedures have been made manageable for aircraft pilots and surgeons by means of checklists of all kinds. In the same way, the intricacies of making decisions about what should be prescribed for students can be simplified for ordinary teachers through the use of such devices.

The teacher whose class is engaged in small-group discussions can be guided by flow charts that portray the typical or ideal flow of an argument or discussion on a given topic. He can be aided by forms that help him keep track of the frequency of participation by students. He can be assisted by post-meeting reaction sheets on which students can communicate their evaluations of the discussion in which they have just participated. His work can be made more manageable by the use of algorithms (Lewis, et al., 1967) that facilitate his own or his students' analysis of the logic or thoroughness of a group's problem-solving effort.

In teaching by telling, as in lecturing or explaining, the teacher can be helped by checklists that will remind him of research-based rules (such as a rule-example-rule pattern of discourse). He can use simple devices for obtaining instantaneous feedback that reflects his audience's comprehension, such as cards to be used by students for indicating answers to questions posed by the lecturer or for indicating a need for repetition or further elucidation. The teacher can also be helped with outlines that remind him to organize his presentation along sufficiently redundant and logical lines.

An Example of Tool-Oriented Research

Tools of the trade should have value not merely as the outcomes of research and development. Rather, they should be the entry-point for such work. The independent variables in the experimental work on improving the effects of teachers on their students are themselves the tools—technical skills, decision-making skills, diagnostic devices, behavior guides, checklists, rules for guiding behavior, and devices of all sorts—that will emerge from such work.

An example of such work will clarify what is being advocated. After several investigations in which my co-workers and I sought behavioral correlates of effectiveness in lecturing or explaining, we turned to an experimental study. In this experiment, we sought a method for improving explanations rather than merely knowledge of the correlates of their effectiveness. So, after having read some treatments of the logic of explanation, Robert Miltz (1971) and I developed a manual, "How to Explain." The manual and instructions for its use in self-training were given to an experimental group of 30 teacher trainees and were withheld from a control group, who engaged in some other useful activity. The manual presented some relatively simple rules for explaining. First, the trainees were given some simple rules for improving their ability to listen to a student's request for an explanation. Second, the trainees were told, they should look for the "things," or elements, involved in the process or phenomenon to be explained. Third, they should identify the relationship between those things. Fourth, they should show how that relationship was an instance of a more general relationship. Finally, they were given some simple rules for the pattern of their discourse, such as the rule-example-rule pattern that seemed in one previous study to be a correlate of effectiveness in explaining.

The manual was used by two-man teams of teacher trainees. Each team had a tape recorder, and after one member of the team had practiced a given step, the other criticized and discussed his performance. Then they exchanged roles. They worked through the manual in five one-hour sessions on each of five school days. The evidence from ratings (e.g., see Table 13-1) and content analyses (including some made by Jack Hiller with a computer) of the trainees' pretest

TABLE 13-1. MEAN RATINGS ON PRETEST AND POSTTEST
EXPLANATIONS BY EXPERIMENTAL AND CONTROL GROUPS[a]

	EXPERIMENTAL GROUP (N = 30)		CONTROL GROUP (N = 30)	
	Pretest	Posttest	Pretest	Posttest
Organization	2.92	3.62	3.29	3.33
Clarity	2.79	3.59	3.23	3.26
Quality	2.84	3.68	3.31	3.34

[a] Based on Miltz, 1971. Ratings of explanations by 10 judges were made on a
5-point scale (5 = excellent, 4 = good, 3 = average, 2 = poor, 1 = very poor).
Differences between experimental and control group posttest means, both unadjusted and adjusted by analysis of covariance, were significant at the .01 level.

and posttest explanations indicated that the manual and its accompanying instructions brought about a substantial improvement in the explanations of the experimental group. It also revealed some shortcomings in the manual that can be remedied in its revision.

This experiment yielded more than theory-relevant findings to be reported in a scientific journal. In addition, it led to a tool usable in improving teacher behavior. Whether that improvement will last, whether it will show up in actual classrooms, whether it would produce improved student achievement—these are questions for the future. But they can be answered readily by the same experimental approach as that already used. And the outcome will be a set of tools, i.e., validated manuals, procedures, and rules for teachers engaged in giving explanations, that can be widely transported and installed in dependable ways.

IN CONCLUSION

The foregoing single example is, of course, not the only one that could be cited. As already indicated, much tool-oriented research has already been done elsewhere, especially in research and development centers and regional laboratories. It seems fair to say even now, in the early years of this approach, that a research and development program of this kind will produce tools that will significantly enhance the quality and amount of the difference that teachers are able to make.

Research on teaching has come a long way. From the naive effort of the 1920's and 1930's to the more sophisticated work of the 1970's, we can see genuine progress. Where the earlier effort sought well-nigh miraculous predictions of overall teacher effectiveness on the basis of a few test scores, the later work aims to improve such effectiveness in specific skills on the basis of intensive and validated training procedures. Where the earlier effort made much use of global ratings, the present-day work relies much more on reliable counts of specific behaviors. Where the earlier effort focused on overall comparisons of extremely complex and vaguely defined "teaching methods," the more recent work focuses on evaluations of much more modest but also more thoroughly controlled and described sequences of instructional acts evaluated on the basis of specific and reliably measured effects on students. Where the earlier work was hard to apply because the independent and dependent variables could seldom be pinned down or transported from one situation to another, the more recent work uses packages and products that can have the same form and meaning regardless of the situation or the user. Where the earlier work failed to differentiate among teacher roles, types of students, and varieties of educational objectives, the more recent work is much more modest and recognizes the need for specificity in these respects.

In short, the question with which we began—Can science contribute to the art of teaching?—is more and more being answered positively. The search for a scientific basis for teacher education and the improvement of teacher effectiveness is reaching solid ground. With increased support and improved intellectual tools, that search seems destined in the years just ahead to bring about teaching that makes for more effective and happier learning on the part of students throughout the world.

References and
Author Index

*(Numbers in parentheses at the end of each reference
indicate the pages on which the reference is cited.)*

Ackerman, W. I. (1954) Teacher competence and pupil change. *Harvard Educational Review*, 24, 273–289. (87)

Allen, D. W., & Ryan, K. (1969) *Microteaching*. Reading, Mass.: Addison-Wesley. (116)

Allen, D. W. See also Bush & Allen (1964).

Allen, R. (1965) Creativity. Unpublished manuscript, Stanford University, c/o N. L. Gage. (51)

American Educational Research Association, Committee on the Criteria of Teacher Effectiveness. (1952) Report of the .... *Review of Educational Research*, 22, 238–263. (89)

American Educational Research Association, Committee on the Criteria of Teacher Effectiveness. (1953) Second report of the .... *Journal of Educational Research*, 46, 641–658. (29, 82, 90, 91)

American Psychological Association, Education and Training Board. (1959) Education for research in psychology. *American Psychologist*, 14, 167–179. (79, 80)

Anderson, H. H., Brewer, J. E., & Reed, M. F. (1946) Studies of teachers' classroom personalities. III. Follow-up studies of the effects of dominative and integrative contacts on children's behavior. *Applied Psychology Monographs*, No. 11. (174)

Atkinson, R. C., & Wilson, H. A. (Eds.) (1969) *Computer-assisted instruction: A book of readings.* New York: Academic Press. (133)

Ausubel, D. P. (1963) *The psychology of meaningful verbal learning: An introduction to school learning.* New York: Grune & Stratton. (37)

Ausubel, D. P. (1968) *Educational psychology: A cognitive view.* New York: Holt, Rinehart & Winston. (49, 60, 155)

Ballachey, E. L. See Krech, Crutchfield, & Ballachey (1962).

Bandura, A. (1962) Social learning through imitation. In M. R. Jones (Ed.), *Nebraska Symposium on Motivation.* Lincoln: University of Nebraska Press. Pp. 211–269. (64)

Bandura, A. (1969) Social-learning theory of identificatory processes. In D. A. Goslin (Ed.), *Handbook of socialization theory and research.* Chicago: Rand McNally. Pp. 213–262. (46)

Bandura, A., & Walters, R. H. (1963) *Social learning and personality development.* New York: Holt, Rinehart & Winston. (46)

Barr, A. S. (1948) The measurement and prediction of teaching efficiency: A summary of investigations. *Journal of Experimental Education,* 16, 203–283. (84)

Barr, A. S., et al. (1961) Wisconsin studies of the measurement and prediction of teacher effectiveness: A summary of investigations. *Journal of Experimental Education,* 30, 1–155. (84, 86)

Beecher, C. (1961) Data-gathering devices employed in the Wisconsin studies. *Journal of Experimental Education,* 30, 30–47. (86)

Belgard, M. See Gage, Belgard, Dell, Hiller, Rosenshine, & Unruh (1968).

Bellack, A. A., and others. (1966) *The language of the classroom.* New York: Teachers College Press. (54, 129, 174, 201)

Berelson, B., & Steiner, G. (1964) *Human behavior: An inventory of scientific findings.* New York: Harcourt, Brace, & World. (115)

Berliner, D. C. (1968) The effects of test-like events and note-taking on learning from lecture instruction. Unpublished doctoral dissertation, Stanford University. (197)

Berliner, D. C. (1969) *Microteaching and the technical skills approach to teacher training.* Technical Report No. 8. Stanford Center for Research and Development in Teaching. (202)

Biddle, B. J. (1964) The integration of teacher effectiveness research. In B. J. Biddle & W. J. Ellena (Eds.), *Contemporary research on teacher effectiveness.* New York: Holt, Rinehart and Winston. Pp. 1–40. (92)

Biddle, B. J. (1967) Methods and concepts in classroom research. *Review of Educational Research,* 37, 337–357. (148)

Bigge, M. L., & Hunt, M. P. (1968) *Psychological foundations of education.* (2nd ed.) New York: Harper & Row. (155)

Blair, G. M., Jones, R. S., & Simpson, R. H. (1968) *Educational psychology.* (3rd ed.) New York: Macmillan. (159, 162)

Bloom, B. S. (1954) The thought processes of students in discussion. In S. French (Ed.), *Accent on teaching.* New York: Harper. Pp. 23–46. (174)

Bloom, B. S. See also Krathwohl, Bloom, & Masia (1964).

Bolvin, J. O. See Lindvall & Bolvin (1967).

Borg, W. R., Kelley, M. L., Langer, P., & Gall, M. (1970) *The minicourse: A microteaching approach to teacher education.* Beverly Hills, Calif.: Macmillan Educational Services. (202)

Bower, G. H. See Hilgard & Bower (1966).

Bowles, S., & Levin, Henry M. (1968a) The determinants of scholastic achievement—An appraisal of some recent evidence. *Journal of Human Resources,* 3, 3–24. (32)

Bowles, S., & Levin, Henry M. (1968b) More on multicollinearity and the effectiveness of schools. *Journal of Human Resources,* 3, 393–400. (33)

Brewer, J. E. See Anderson, Brewer, & Reed (1946).

Briggs, L. J. (1964) The teacher and programed instruction: Roles and role potentials. *Audio-Visual Instruction,* 9, 273–276. (137, 190)

Brim, O. G., Jr. (1958) *Sociology and the field of education.* New York: Russell Sage Foundation. (29)

Broudy, H. S. (1962) Teaching machines: Threats and promises. *Educational Theory*, 12, 151–156. (55)

Broudy, H. S. (1963) Can we save teacher education from its enemies and friends? (16th Yearbook of the American Association of Colleges for Teacher Education). Washington, D.C.: The Association. Pp. 85–91. (147)

Broudy, H. S., Smith, B. O., & Burnett, J. R. (1964) *Democracy and excellence in American secondary education.* Chicago: Rand McNally. (153)

Brown, G. I. (1965) A second study in the teaching of creativity. *Harvard Educational Review*, 35, 39–54. (51)

Bruner, J. S. (1966a) *Toward a theory of instruction.* Cambridge: Harvard University Press. (37, 60)

Bruner, J. S. (Ed.) (1966b) *Learning about learning: A conference report.* Washington, D.C.: U.S. Government Printing Office. U.S. Dept. of Health, Education, and Welfare, Office of Education, Cooperative Research Monograph No. 15. (60)

Bryan, R. C. (1963) *Reactions to teachers by students, parents and administrators.* Kalamazoo, Mich.: Western Michigan University.

Burnett, J. R. See Broudy, Smith, & Burnett (1964).

Burns, M. B. (1969) The effects of feedback and commitment to change on the behavior of elementary school principals. Unpublished doctoral dissertation, Stanford University. (186)

Bush, R. N., & Allen, D. W. (1964) *A new design for high school education assuming a flexible schedule.* New York: McGraw-Hill. (191)

Callis, R. See Cook, Leeds, & Callis (1951).

Campbell, D. T. (1967) Administrative experimentation, institutional records, and non-reactive measures. In J. C. Stanley (Ed.), *Improving experimental design and statistical analysis.* Chicago: Rand McNally. Pp. 257–291. (148, 149)

Carroll, J. B. (1961) Neglected areas in educational research. *Phi Delta Kappan*, 42, 339–343. (141)

Carroll, J. B. (1965) School learning over the long haul. In J. D. Krumboltz (Ed.), *Learning and the educational process.* Chicago: Rand McNally. Pp. 249–269. (95)

Carroll, J. B. (1968) On learning from being told. *Educational Psychologist*, 5 (2), 1, 6–10. (191)

Castetter, D. D., Standlee, L. S., & Fattu, N. A. (1954) *Teacher effectiveness: An annotated bibliography.* Bloomington: Institute of Educational Research, School of Education, Indiana University. (84)

Charters, W. W., Jr. (1963) Social class and intelligence tests. In W. W. Charters, Jr., and N. L. Gage (Eds.), *Readings in the social psychology of education.* Boston: Allyn & Bacon. Pp. 12–21. (164)

Chatterjee, B. B. See Gage, Runkel, & Chatterjee (1960, 1963).

Clarke, C. M. See Stinnett & Clarke (1960).

Coale, J. M. See Sheldon, Coale, & Copple (1959).

Coats, W. D., & Smidchens, U. (1966) Audience recall as a function of speaker dynamism. *Journal of Educational Psychology*, 57, 189–191. (38)

Cogan, M. L. (1958) The behavior of teachers and the productive behavior of their pupils: I. "Perception" analysis. II. "Trait" analysis. *Journal of Experimental Education*, 27, 89–105, 107–124. (35)

Cogan, M. L. (1963) Research on the behavior of teachers: A new phase. *Journal of Teacher Education*, 14, 238–243. (148)

Coleman, J. S., and others. (1966) *Equality of educational opportunity*. Washington, D.C.: U. S. Government Printing Office. (31, 32)

Conant, J. B. (1963) *The education of American teachers*. New York: McGraw-Hill. (141, 142, 157)

Cook, W. W., Leeds, C. H., & Callis, R. (1951) *The Minnesota Teacher Attitude Inventory*. New York: Psychological Corp. (34)

Coombs, J. See Smith & Meux, in collaboration with Coombs, Eierdam, & Szoke (1962).

Copple, R. See Sheldon, Coale, & Copple (1959).

Coulson, J. E., & Silberman, H. F. (1960) Effects of three variables in a teaching machine. *Journal of Educational Psychology*, 51, 135–144. (113)

Cronbach, L. J. (1949) *Essentials of psychological testing*. New York: Harper. (86)

Cronbach, L. J. (1958) Proposals leading to analytic treatment of social perception scores. In R. Tagiuri & L. Petrullo (Eds.), *Person perception and interpersonal behavior*. Stanford, Calif.: Stanford University Press. Pp. 353–379. (101)

Cronbach, L. J. (1963) *Educational psychology*. (2nd ed.) New York: Harcourt, Brace & World. (162)

Cronbach, L. J. (1967) How can instruction be adapted to individual differences? In R. M. Gagné (Ed.), *Learning and individual differences*. Columbus, Ohio: Charles E. Merrill Books. Pp. 23–39. (97, 136)

Crutchfield, R. S. See Krech, Crutchfield, & Ballachey (1962).

Dachler, H. P. See Humphreys & Dachler (1969a; 1969b).

Daw, R. W., & Gage, N. L. (1967) Effect of feedback from teachers to principals. *Journal of Educational Psychology*, 58, 181–188. (186)

DeCecco, J. P. (1968) *The psychology of learning and instruction: Educational psychology*. Englewood Cliffs, N.J.: Prentice-Hall. (155)

Dell, D. See Gage, Belgard, Dell, Hiller, Rosenshine, & Unruh (1968).

Della Piana, G. M., & Gage, N. L. (1955) Pupils' values and the validity of the Minnesota Teacher Attitude Inventory. *Journal of Educational Psychology*, 46, 167–178. (168)

Dollard, J. See Miller & Dollard (1941).

Domas, S. J., & Tiedeman, D. V. (1950) Teacher competence: An annotated bibliography. *Journal of Experimental Education*, 19, 101–218. (84, 88)

Dubin, R., & Taveggia, T. C. (1968) *The teaching-learning paradox: A comparative analysis of college teaching methods*. Eugene, Ore.: Center for the Advanced Study of Educational Administration, University of Oregon. (29)

Eierdam, D. See Smith & Meux, in collaboration with Coombs, Eierdam, & Szoke (1962).

Elkins, D. See Taba & Elkins (1966).

Ellson, D. G., Barber, L., Engle, T. L., & Kampwerth, L. (1965) Programed tutoring: A teaching aid and a research tool. *Reading Research Quarterly*, 1, 77–127. (198)

Ellson, D. G., Harris, P., & Barber, L. (1968) A field test of programed and directed tutoring. *Reading Research Quarterly*, 3, 307–367. (198)

English, A. C. See English & English (1958).

English, H. B., & English, A. C. (1958) *A comprehensive dictionary of psychological and psychoanalytical terms*. New York: Longmans Green. (57)

Ericksen, S. C. (1967) The zigzag curve of learning. In L. Siegel (Ed.), *Instruction: Some contemporary viewpoints*. San Francisco: Chandler Publishing Co. Pp. 141–179. (134)

Estes, W. K. (1960) Learning. In C. W. Harris (Ed.), *Encyclopedia of educational research*. (3rd ed.) New York: Macmillan. Pp. 752–768. (56)

Fattu, N. A. See Castetter, Standlee, & Fattu (1954).

Fisher, G. See Hiller, Fisher, & Kaess (1969).

Fitzgerald, D. See Ausubel & Fitzgerald (1961).

Flanagan, J. C. (1967) Functional education for the Seventies. *Phi Delta Kappan*, 49, 27–32. (135, 193)

Flanders, N. A. (1965) *Teacher influence, pupil attitudes, and achievement*. U.S. Department of Health, Education, and Welfare, Office of Education, Cooperative Research Monograph No. 12 (OE-25040). Washington, D.C.: U.S. Government Printing Office. (127)

Flanders, N. A., & Simon, A. (1969) Teacher effectiveness. In R. L. Ebel (Ed.), *Encyclopedia of educational research*. (4th ed.) New York: Macmillan. Pp. 1423–1436. (36)

Flexner, A. (1910) *Medical education in the United States and Canada*. Bulletin No. 4. New York: Carnegie Foundation for the Advancement of Teaching. (142)

Fortune, J. C., Gage, N. L., & Shutes, R. E. (1966) Generality of the ability to explain. Paper presented at the meeting of the American Educational Research Association, Chicago. (118)

Gage, N. L. (1958) Explorations in teachers' perceptions of pupils. *Journal of Teacher Education*, 9, 97–101. (178)

Gage, N. L. (Ed.) (1963) *Handbook of research on teaching.* Chicago: Rand McNally. (84)

Gage, N. L., Belgard, M., Dell, D., Hiller, J. E., Rosenshine, B., & Unruh, W. R. (1968) Explorations of the teacher's effectiveness in explaining. Stanford, Calif.: Stanford Center for Research and Development in Teaching. Technical Report No. 4 (Multilith) (118–122, 191)

Gage, N. L., Leavitt, G. S., & Stone, G. C. (1957) The psychological meaning of acquiescence set for authoritarianism. *Journal of Abnormal and Social Psychology,* 55, 98–103. (34)

Gage, N. L., Runkel, P. J., & Chatterjee, B. B. (1960) Equilibrium theory and behavior change: An experiment in feedback from pupils to teachers. Urbana: Bureau of Educational Research, University of Illinois. (Mimeographed). (179)

Gage, N. L., Runkel, P. J., & Chatterjee, B. B. (1963) Changing teacher behavior through feedback from pupils: An application of equilibrium theory. In W. W. Charters, Jr., & N. L. Gage (Eds.), *Readings in the social psychology of education.* Boston: Allyn & Bacon. Pp. 173–181. (179)

Gage, N. L. See also Daw & Gage (1967).

Gage, N. L. See also Della Piana & Gage (1955).

Gage, N. L. See also Fortune, Gage, & Shutes (1966).

Gagné, R. M. (1965) *The conditions of learning.* New York: Holt, Rinehart & Winston. (37, 43, 49, 53, 55, 135)

Gagné, R. M. (1966) How can centers for educational research influence school practices. In *Organizations for research and development in education.* Bloomington, Ind.: Phi Delta Kappa. Pp. 21–31. (192)

Gagné, R. M. (1970) Policy implications and future research: A response. In *Do teachers make a difference? A report on recent research on pupil achievement.* Washington, D.C.: Bureau of Educational Personnel Development, Office of Education. Pp. 169–173. (34)

Gagné, R. M. (1971) Domains of learning. Presidential address, American Educational Research Association, New York. (194–195)

Getzels, J. W., & Jackson, P. W. (1963) The teacher's personality and characteristics. In N. L. Gage (Ed.), *Handbook of research on teaching.* Chicago: Rand McNally. Pp. 506–582. (29, 127)

Getzels, J. W. See also Guba & Getzels (1955).

Glaser, R. (1969) Learning. In R. L. Ebel (Ed.), *Encyclopedia of educational research.* (4th ed.) New York: Macmillan. Pp. 706–733. (56)

Glaser, R., & Reynolds, H. H. (1964) Instructional objectives and programmed instruction: A case study. In C. M. Lindvall (Ed.), *Defining educational objectives.* Pittsburgh: University of Pittsburgh Press. Pp. 47–76. (37)

Glaser, R. See also Taber, Glaser, & Schaefer (1965).

Great Cities Program for School Improvement, Research Council. (1963) Teacher Education Project: Follow-up of selected practices. Chicago: The author. (Mimeographed). (163, 168)

Gronlund, N. E. (1959) *Sociometry in the classroom.* New York: Harper. (165)

Gross, C. F. See Mitzel & Gross (1956).

Gross, N. (1959) The sociology of education. In R. Merton, et al. (Eds.), *Sociology today.* New York: Basic Books. Pp. 128–142. (141)

Guba, E., & Getzels, J. W. (1955) Personality and teacher effectiveness: A problem in theoretical research. *Journal of Educational Psychology,* 46, 330–344. (78)

Harrison, G. V. (1969) The effects of professional and non-professional trainers using prescribed training procedures on the performance of upper-grade elementary school tutors. Unpublished doctoral dissertation, University of California at Los Angeles. (197)

Hayes, R. B., Keim, F. N., & Neiman, A. M. (1967) The effect of student reactions to teaching methods. Harrisburg, Pa.: Bureau of Research, Administration, and Coordination, Department of Public Instruction. (184, 185)

Heider, F. (1958) *The psychology of interpersonal relationships.* New York: Holt, Rinehart & Winston. (52, 179, 183)

Henry, J. (1957) Working paper on creativity. *Harvard Educational Review,* 27, 148–152. (51)

Hickey, A. E., & Newton, J. M. (1964) The logical basis of teaching: I. The effect of sub-concept sequence on learning. Final Report to Office of Naval Research, Personnel and Training Branch, Contract Nonr-4215(00). (37)

Highet, G. (1955) *The art of teaching.* New York: Vintage Books. (57)

Hilgard, E. R. (1956) *Theories of learning.* (2nd ed.) New York: Appleton-Century-Crofts. (56, 59)

Hilgard, E. R. (1968) Psychological heuristics of teaching. Paper for symposium of the National Academy of Sciences, California Institute of Technology, October 28, 1968 (Mimeographed). (193)

Hilgard, E. R., & Bower, G. H. (1966) *Theories of learning.* (3rd ed.) New York: Appleton-Century-Crofts. (56, 155)

Hilgard, E. R. See also Sears & Hilgard (1964)

Hiller, J. E. (1968) An experimental investigation of the effects of conceptual vagueness on speaking behavior. Unpublished doctoral dissertation, University of Connecticut. (122)

Hiller, J. E., Fisher, G., & Kaess, W. (1969) A computer investigation of verbal characteristics of effective classroom lecturing. *American Educational Research Journal,* 6, 661–675. (123)

Hiller, J. E. See also Gage, Belgard, Dell, Hiller, Rosenshine, & Unruh (1968).

Hoetker, J., & Ahlbrand, W. P., Jr. (1969) The persistence of the recitation. *American Educational Research Journal,* 6, 145–167. (200)

Hovenier, P. J. (1966) Changing the behavior of social studies department heads through the use of feedback. Unpublished doctoral dissertation, Stanford University. (187)

Humphreys, L. G., & Dachler, H. P. (1969a) Jensen's theory of intelligence. *Journal of Educational Psychology*, 60, 419–426. (165)

Humphreys, L. G., & Dachler, H. P. (1969b) Jensen's theory of intelligence: A rebuttal. *Journal of Educational Psychology*, 60, 432–433. (165)

Hunt, M. P. See Bigge & Hunt (1968).

Husek, T. R. See Sorenson & Husek (1963).

Jackson, P. W. (1966) The way teaching is. In *The way teaching is: Report of the seminar on teaching*. Washington, D.C.: National Education Association, Association for Supervision and Curriculum Development and the Center for the Study of Instruction. Pp. 7–27. (97)

Jackson, P. W. (1968) *The teacher and the machine*. Pittsburgh: University of Pittsburgh Press. (200)

Jackson, P. W. See also Getzels & Jackson (1963).

Jensen, A. R. (1969a) How much can we boost IQ and scholastic achievement? *Harvard Educational Review*, 39, 1–123. (156)

Jensen, A. R. (1969b) Jensen's theory of intelligence: A reply. *Journal of Educational Psychology*, 60, 427–431. (165)

Jones, R. S. See Blair, Jones, & Simpson (1968).

Kaess, W. See Hiller, Fisher, & Kaess (1969).

Kearney, N. C. See Rocchio & Kearney (1956).

Keislar, E. See Shulman & Keislar (1966).

Keppel, F. (1962) The education of teachers. In H. Chauncey (Ed.), *Talks on American education: A series of broadcasts to foreign audiences by American scholars*. New York: Columbia University, Teachers College, Bureau of Publications. Pp. 83–94. (142)

Kersh, B. Y. (1965) Programming classroom instruction. In R. Glaser (Ed.), *Teaching machines and programed learning, II*. Washington, D.C.: Department of Audiovisual Instruction, National Education Association. Pp. 321–368. (194, 199, 200)

Klapper, P. (1949) The professional preparation of the college teacher. *Journal of General Education*, 3, 228–244. (176)

Krathwohl, D. R. (1969) *Educational research: Perspective, prognosis, and proposal*. Presidential address, American Educational Research Association, Los Angeles. (150)

Krathwohl, D. R., Bloom, B. S., & Masia, B. B. (1964) *Taxonomy of educational objectives: The classification of educational goals. Handbook II: Affective domain*. New York: David McKay Co. (126)

Krech, D., Crutchfield, R. S., and Ballachey, E. L. (1962) *Individual in society*. New York: McGraw-Hill. (67)

Kuhn, T. S. (1962) *The structure of scientific revolutions*. Chicago: University of Chicago Press. (75, 114)

Lane, R. E. (1961) *The liberties of wit: Humanism, criticism, and the civic mind*. New Haven, Conn.: Yale University Press. (72)

Lazarsfeld, P. F. (1949) The American soldier—An expository review. *Public Opinion Quarterly*, 13, 377–404. (145)

Leavitt, G. S. See Gage, Leavitt, & Stone (1957).

Leeds, C. H. See Cook, Leeds, & Callis (1951).

Levin, Henry M. See Bowles & Levin (1968a; 1968b).

Lewin, K. (1942) Field theory of learning. In T. R. McConnell (Ed.), *Psychology of learning*. (41st Yearbook of the National Society for the Study of Education, Part II) Chicago: University of Chicago Press. Pp. 215–237. (42)

Lewin, K. (1946) Behavior and development as a function of the total situation. In L. Carmichael (Ed.), *Manual of child psychology*. New York: Wiley. Pp. 791–844. (99)

Lewis, B. N., Horabin, I. S., & Gane, C. P. (1967) *Flow charts, logical trees, and algorithms for rules and regulations*. London: Her Majesty's Stationery Office. CAS Occasional Paper No. 2. (203)

Lewis, W. W. See Withall & Lewis (1963).

Lindvall, C. M., & Bolvin, J. O. (1967) Programed instruction in the schools: An application of programing principles in "Individually Prescribed Instruction." In P. C. Lange (Ed.), *Programed instruction*. (66th Yearbook of the National Society for the Study of Education, Part II) Chicago: University of Chicago Press. Pp. 217–254. (135, 193)

Luchins, A. S. (1961) Implications of Gestalt psychology for AV learning. *AV Communications Review*, 9 (5), 7–31. (65)

MacLeod, R. (1962) Retrospect and prospect. In H. Gruber, T. Glenn, and M. Wertheimer (Eds.), *Contemporary approaches to creative thinking*. New York: Atherton Press. Pp. 175–212. (51)

Masia, B. B. See Krathwohl, Bloom, & Masia (1964).

Mastin, V. E. (1963) Teacher enthusiasm. *Journal of Educational Research*, 56, 385–386. (38)

McCarthy, W. H. (1970) Improving large audience teaching: The 'programmed' lecture. *British Journal of Medical Education*, 4, 29–31. (196–197)

McGee, H. M. (1955) Measurement of authoritarianism and its relation to teachers' classroom behavior. *Genetic Psychology Monographs*, 52, 89–146. (34, 35, 174)

McIntyre, D. See Morrison & McIntyre (1969).

Medley, D. M., & Mitzel, H. E. (1959) Some behavioral correlates of teacher effectiveness. *Journal of Educational Psychology*, 50, 239–246. (92)

Melton, A. W. (Ed.) (1964) *Categories of human learning*. New York: Academic Press. (42)

Meux, M. O., & Smith, B. O. (1961) Logical dimensions of teaching behavior. Urbana: University of Illinois, Bureau of Educational Research. (Mimeographed). (37, 99)

Meux, M. O. See also Smith & Meux, in collaboration with Coombs, Eierdam, & Szoke (1962)

Miller, G. E. (1962) Medicine. In G. L. Anderson (Ed.), *Education for the professions.* (61st Yearbook of the National Society for the Study of Education, Part II) Chicago: University of Chicago Press. Pp. 103–119. (142)

Miller, N. E., & Dollard, J. (1941) *Social learning and imitation.* New Haven: Yale University Press. (64, 155)

Miltz, R. J. (1971) Development and evaluation of a manual for improving teachers' explanations. Unpublished doctoral dissertation, Stanford University. (204–205)

Mitzel, H. E. (1957) A behavioral approach to the assessment of teacher effectiveness. New York: Division of Teacher Education, College of the City of New York. (Mimeographed). (91–94)

Mitzel, H. E. (1960) Teacher effectiveness. In C. W. Harris (Ed.), *Encyclopedia of educational research.* (3rd ed.) New York: Macmillan. Pp. 1481–1486. (84, 85, 89, 96)

Mitzel, H. E., & Gross, C. F. (1956) A critical review of the development of pupil growth criteria in studies of teacher effectiveness. New York: Board of Higher Education of the City of New York, Division of Teacher Education, Office of Research and Evaluation. (Research Series 31). (87)

Mitzel, H. E. See also Medley & Mitzel (1959).

Mood, A. (1970) Do teachers make a difference? In *Do teachers make a difference? A report on recent research on pupil achievement.* Washington, D.C.: Bureau of Educational Personnel Development, Office of Education. Pp. 1–24. (33–34)

Morrison, A., & McIntyre, D. (1969) *Teachers and teaching.* Baltimore: Penguin Books. (185)

Morsh, J. E., & Wilder, E. W. (1954) *Identifying the effective instructor: A review of the quantitative studies 1900–1952.* USAF Personnel Training Research Center. (Research Bulletin No. AFPTRC-TR-54-44). (84)

Mouly, G. J. (1960) *Psychology for effective teaching.* New York: Holt, Rinehart & Winston. (51)

Mowrer, O. H. (1960) *Learning theory and behavior.* New York: John Wiley. (64)

Murphy, G. (1961) *Freeing intelligence through teaching.* New York: Harper. (126)

Newcomb, T. M. (1959) Individual systems of orientation. In S. Koch (Ed.), *Psychology: A study of a science.* Vol. 3. New York: McGraw-Hill. Pp. 384–422. (179)

Newton, J. M. See Hickey & Newton (1964).

Oliver, W. S. See Tuckman & Oliver (1968).

Orleans, J. S. (1952) *The understanding of arithmetic processes and concepts possessed by teachers of arithmetic.* New York: Board of Education of the City of New York, Division of Teacher Education, Office of Research and Evaluation. (37)

Peterson, O. L., et al. (1956) An analytical study of North Carolina general practice: 1953–1954. *Journal of Medical Education,* 31 (12), Part 2, 1–165. (174)

Phi Delta Kappa. (1964) *Education and the structure of knowledge.* Chicago: Rand McNally. (76)

Reed, M. F. See Anderson, Brewer, & Reed (1946).

Resnick, L. (1967) Developing new teaching skills for new educational programs. *Newsletter of the Learning Research and Development Center, University of Pittsburgh,* 4, 1–2. (190)

Reynard, H. E. (1963) Pre-service and in-service education of teachers. *Review of Educational Research,* 33, 369–380. (141)

Reynolds, H. H. See Glaser & Reynolds (1964).

Riessman, F. (1962) *The culturally deprived child.* New York: Harper & Row. (164–168)

Rivlin, H. N. (1962) Teachers for the schools in our big cities. New York: City University of New York, Division of Teacher Education. (Mimeographed). (149, 168)

Rocchio, P. D., & Kearney, N. C. (1956) Teacher-pupil attitudes as related to non-promotion of secondary school pupils. *Educational and Psychological Measurement,* 16, 244–252. (75)

Rosenshine, B. (1968) Objectively measured behavioral predictors of effectiveness in explaining. Unpublished doctoral dissertation, Stanford University. (121)

Rosenshine, B. (1970) Enthusiastic teaching: A research review. *School Review,* 78, 499–514. (38)

Rosenshine, B. See also Gage, Belgard, Dell, Hiller, Rosenshine, & Unruh (1968).

Runkel, P. J. See Gage, Runkel, & Chatterjee (1960, 1963).

Ryan, K. See Allen & Ryan (1969).

Ryans, D. G. (1960a) *Characteristics of teachers.* Washington, D.C.: American Council on Education. (35, 89, 96, 99, 100, 101, 127, 147)

Ryans, D. G. (1960b) Prediction of teacher effectiveness. In C. W. Harris (Ed.), *Encyclopedia of educational research.* (3rd ed.) New York: Macmillan. Pp. 1486–1491. (84, 85)

Ryans, D. G. (1963) Teacher behavior theory and research: Implications for teacher education. *Journal of Teacher Education,* 14, 274–293. (97)

Sarason, S. B., et al. (1962) *The preparation of teachers.* New York: Wiley. (141)

Scandura, J. M. (1966) Teaching—Technology or theory. *American Educational Research Journal,* 3, 139–146. (59)

Schaefer, H. H. See Taber, Glaser, & Schaefer (1965).

Schmid, J. (1961) Factor analysis of the teaching complex. *Journal of Experimental Education*, 30, 58–69. (85)

Sears, P. S., & Hilgard, E. R. (1964) The teacher's role in the motivation of the learner. In E. R. Hilgard (Ed.), *Theories of learning and instruction*. (63rd Yearbook of the National Society for the Study of Education, Part I) Chicago: University of Chicago Press. Pp. 182–209. (52)

Sears, R. R. (1951) A theoretical framework for personality and social behavior. *American Psychologist*, 6, 476–483. (99, 101)

Sheldon, M. S., Coale, J. M., & Copple, R. (1959) Concurrent validity of the "warm teacher scales." *Journal of Educational Psychology*, 50, 37–40. (34)

Shulman, L., & Keislar, E. (Eds.) (1966) *Learning by discovery: A critical appraisal*. Chicago: Rand McNally. (36)

Shutes, R. E. See Fortune, Gage, & Shutes (1966).

Siegel, L., & Siegel, Lila C. (1967) A multivariate paradigm for educational research. *Psychological Bulletin*, 68, 306–326. (95, 136)

Siegel, Lila C. See Siegel & Siegel (1967).

Silberman, H. F. See Coulson & Silberman (1960).

Simon, A. See Flanders & Simon (1969).

Simpson, R. H. See Blair, Jones, & Simpson (1968).

Skinner, B. F. (1950) Are theories of learning necessary? *Psychological Review*, 57, 193–216. (81)

Skinner, B. F. (1953). *Science and human behavior*. New York: Free Press. (48)

Skinner, B. F. (1959) A case history in scientific method. *Cumulative Record*. New York: Appleton-Century-Crofts. Pp. 76–100. (80, 81)

Skinner, B. F. (1968) *The technology of teaching*. New York: Appleton-Century-Crofts. (135, 160, 162)

Smidchens, U. See Coats & Smidchens (1966).

Smith, B. O. (1960) A concept of teaching. *Teachers College Record*, 61, 229–241. (60, 98, 99)

Smith, B. O. (1964) The need for logic in methods courses. *Theory into Practice*, 3, 5–8. (53)

Smith, B. O., & Meux, M. O., in collaboration with Coombs, J., Eierdam, D., & Szoke, R. (1962) A study of the logic of teaching. Urbana: Bureau of Educational Research, College of Education, University of Illinois. (Mimeographed). (129)

Smith, B. O., & others. (1964) A tentative report on the strategies of teaching. Urbana: Bureau of Educational Research, College of Education, University of Illinois. (Mimeographed). (129, 174)

Smith, B. O. See also Broudy, Smith, & Burnett (1964).

Smith, B. O. See also Meux & Smith (1961).

Sorenson, G., & Husek, T. (1963) Development of a measure of teacher role expectations. *American Psychologist*, 18, 389 (Abstract). (63)

Spence, K. W. (1959) The relation of learning theory to the technology of education. *Harvard Educational Review*, 29, 84–95. (56)

Standlee, L. S. See Castetter, Standlee, & Fattu (1954)

Steiner, G. See Berelson & Steiner (1964).

Stephens, J. M. (1967) *The process of schooling.* New York: Holt, Rinehart & Winston. (30, 31, 201)

Stinnett, T. M., & Clarke, C. M. (1960) Teacher education programs. In C. W. Harris (Ed.), *Encyclopedia of educational research.* (3rd ed.) New York: Macmillan. Pp. 1461–1473. (141)

Stolurow, L. M. (1961) *Teaching by machine.* Washington, D.C.: U.S. Government Printing Office. (U.S. Office of Education, Cooperative Research Monograph No. 6 OE-34010). (109, 110, 112)

Stolurow, L. M. (1965) Model the master teacher or master the teaching model. In J. D. Krumboltz (Ed.), *Learning and the educational process.* Chicago: Rand McNally. Pp. 223–247. (132)

Stone, G. C. See Gage, Leavitt, & Stone (1957).

Stukát, K-G. (1970) *Teacher role in change.* Gothenburg, Sweden: Department of Educational Research, Gothenburg School of Education, Research Bulletin No. 4. (194, 199)

Suppes, P. (1966) The uses of computers in education. *Scientific American*, 215, No. 3, 206–220. (191)

Szoke, R. See Smith & Meux, in collaboration with Coombs, Eierdam, & Szoke (1962).

Taba, H. (1963) Teaching strategy and learning. *California Journal for Instructional Improvement*, 6, 3–11. (133)

Taba, H. (1964) Teaching strategies and thought processes. *Teachers College Record*, 65, 524–534. (53)

Taba, H., & Elkins, D. (1966) *Teaching strategies for the culturally disadvantaged.* Chicago: Rand McNally. (168)

Taber, J. I., Glaser, R., & Schaefer, H. H. (1965) *Learning and programmed instruction.* Reading, Mass.: Addison-Wesley. (50, 68)

Taveggia, T. C. See Dubin & Taveggia (1968).

Thomas, R. M., & Thomas, S. M. (1965) *Individual differences in the classroom.* New York: David McKay Co. (134)

Thomas, S. M. See Thomas & Thomas (1965).

Tiedeman, D. V. See Domas & Tiedeman (1950).

Tolman, E. C. (1949) There is more than one kind of learning. *Psychological Review*, 56, 144–155. (42)

Tomlinson, L. R. (1955a) Pioneer studies in the evaluation of teaching. *Educational Research Bulletin*, 34, 63–71. (84)

Tomlinson, L. R. (1955b) Recent studies in the evaluation of teaching. *Educational Research Bulletin*, 34, 172–186. (84)

Travers, R. M. W. (1958) *An introduction to educational research.* New York: Macmillan. (79)

Travers, R. M. W. (1966) Towards taking the fun out of building a theory of instruction. *Teachers College Record,* 68, 49–60. (61)

Travers, R. M. W. See also Wallen & Travers (1963).

Tuckman, B. W., & Oliver, W. S. (1968) Effectiveness of feedback to teachers as a function of source. *Journal of Educational Psychology,* 59, 297–301. (184)

Unruh, W. R. (1967) The modality and validity of cues to lecture effectiveness. Unpublished doctoral dissertation, Stanford University. (120)

Unruh, W. R. See also Gage, Belgard, Dell, Hiller, Rosenshine, & Unruh (1968).

Walker, H. M. (1935) Preface. In W. H. Lancelot, et al., *The measurement of teaching efficiency.* New York: Macmillan. Pp. ix–xiv. (114)

Wallen, N. E., & Travers, R. M. W. (1963) Analysis and investigation of teaching methods. In N. L. Gage (Ed.), *Handbook of research on teaching.* Chicago: Rand McNally. Pp. 448–505. (29)

Walters, R. H. See Bandura & Walters (1963).

Washburne, C. W. (1952) Design for long-range research in teacher education. *Journal of Educational Research,* 46, 711–715. (141)

Wattenberg, W. (1963) Evidence and the problems of teacher education. *Teachers College Record,* 64, 374–380. (141)

Watters, W. A. (1954) Annotated bibliography of publications related to teacher evaluation. *Journal of Experimental Education,* 22, 351–367. (84)

Wilder, E. W. See Morsh & Wilder (1954).

Wingo, G. M. See Morse & Wingo (1962).

Withall, J. (1956) An objective measurement of a teacher's classroom interactions. *Journal of Educational Psychology,* 47, 203–212. (174)

Withall, J., & Lewis, W. W. (1963) Social interaction in the classroom. In N. L. Gage (Ed.), *Handbook of research on teaching.* Chicago: Rand McNally. Pp. 683–714. (29)

Yee, A. H. (1968) Is the Minnesota Teacher Attitude Inventory valid and homogeneous? *Journal of Educational Measurement,* 4, 151–161. (35)

Yeshiva University, Graduate School of Education. (1963) Training programs in Project Beacon. New York: The author. (Mimeographed). (168)

Subject Index